AF583343

IT'S IN THE POST!

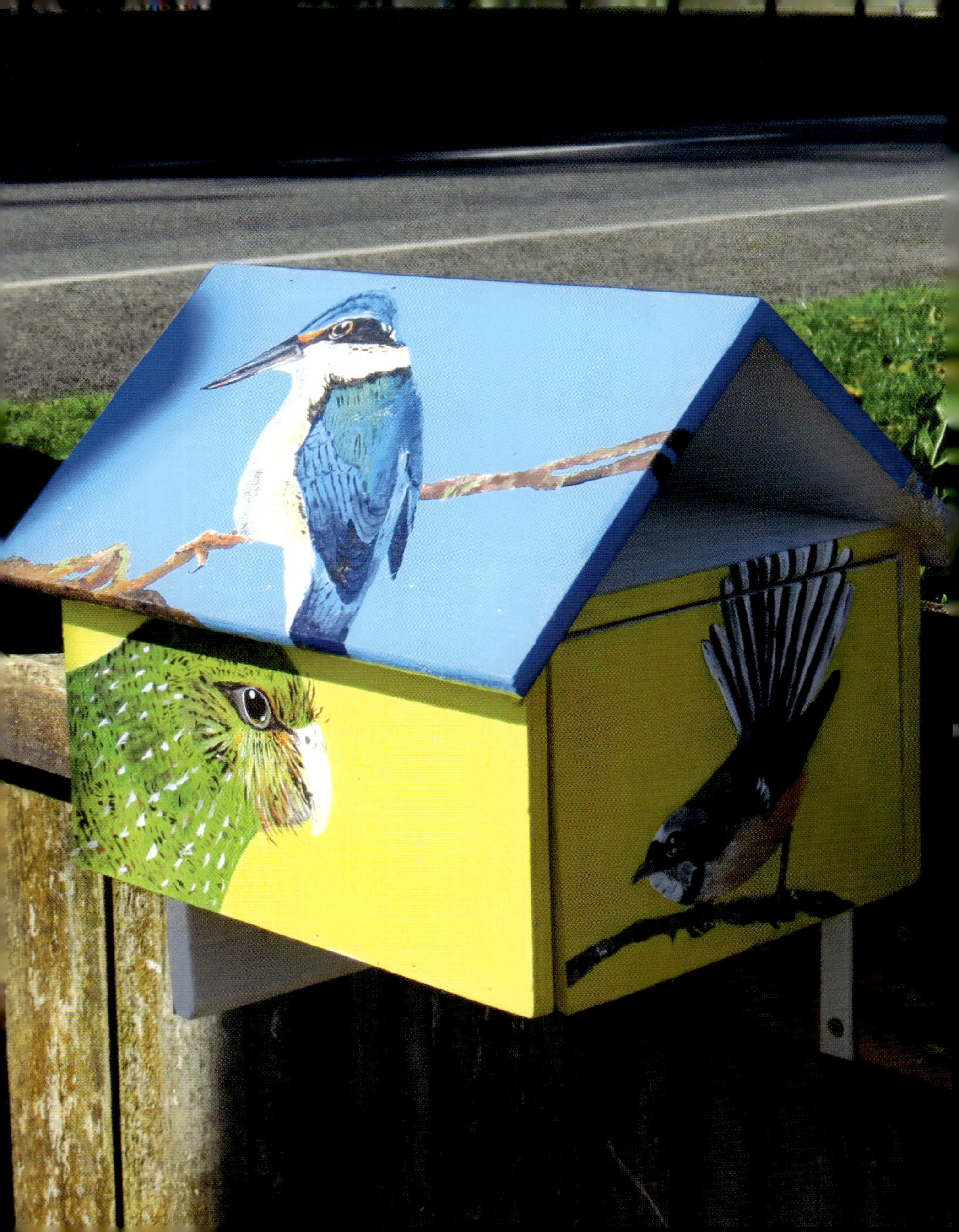

IT'S IN THE POST!

AWESOME LETTERBOXES FROM AROUND NEW ZEALAND

RACHAEL REID

BATEMAN BOOKS

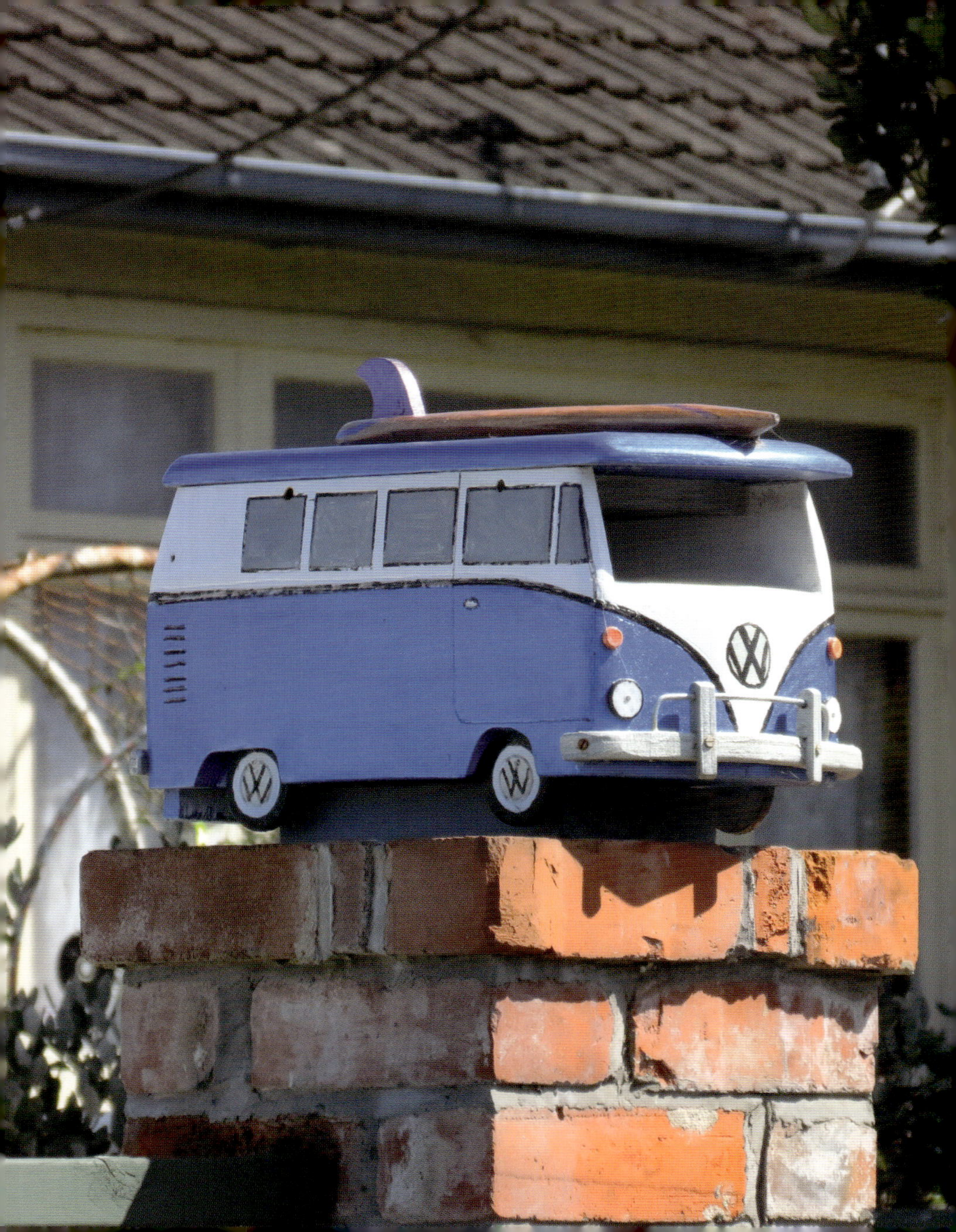

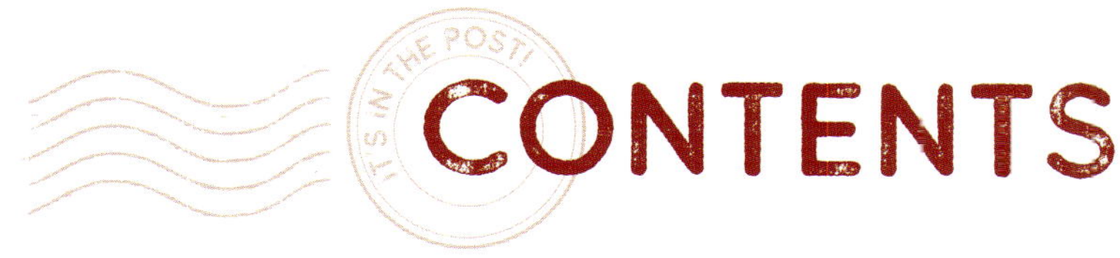

CONTENTS

Text and photography © Rachael Reid

Typographical design © David Bateman Ltd, 2020

Published in 2020 by David Bateman Ltd

Unit 2/5 Workspace Drive, Hobsonville, Auckland 0618, New Zealand

www.batemanbooks.co.nz

ISBN: 978-1-98-853842-6

This book is copyright. Except for the purposes of fair review, no part may be stored or transmitted in any form or by any means, electronic or mechanical, including recording or storage in any information retrieval systems, without permission in writing from the publisher. No reproduction may be made, whether by photocopying or any other means, unless a licence has been obtained from the publisher or its agent.

A catalogue record for this book is available from the National Library of New Zealand.

The moral rights of the author have been asserted.

Book design: Nick Turzynski, redinc. Book Design, www.redinc.co.nz

Printed in China by Toppan Leefung Printing Ltd

INTRODUCTION

It's in the Post! Awesome Letterboxes from Around New Zealand has been 20 years in the making. I didn't know it at the time but the journey to complete this book started on Sumner Road in Lyttelton sometime in the 1990s.

Walking around Lyttelton streets looking at cute cottages I came across a letterbox hand painted with yellow and white daisies and red script. The letterbox was next to a cornflower blue iron gate and the harbour gleamed in the background. Thinking it would make a pretty photo I pressed the button on my old film camera. A pretty photo did develop, and it got me wondering how many other unusual letterboxes could be found.

Travelling around New Zealand over the following years I have been thrilled to find plenty of colourful and creative letterboxes on our streets and country roads. Finding two house letterboxes on the same street in Waihi was a bit like Christmas morning, and as a VW fan my stomach flipped when I found a Kombi van mailbox in Taupo.

Almost all of the letterboxes were found at random and as the number of photos grew, I started to see themes develop. The result is a collection of 140 photos divided into 13 themes.

Kiwi ingenuity and a Do It Yourself (DIY) vibe run through the collection and, as you'll see, anything from a coffee machine to a dive tank can be used to collect the mail.

Given agriculture is a key industry in New Zealand it's not uncommon to see letterboxes in the shape of animals sitting at farm gates. The most popular animal letterbox found on my travels was the cow, especially the black-patched Friesian.

Corrugated iron is a popular material for making mailboxes, which also reflects our rural heritage. You will find a number of corrugated iron letterboxes within these pages including a rooster, a whale and a toothy donkey.

Lots of letterboxes made me laugh, including an eye-catching collection built by John Armstrong in Auckland. The square wooden letterboxes all depict men, or as I cheekily call them: 'Kiwi Blokes' (p.32). John did a letter drop offering to make letterboxes for the neighbours in his leafy Orakei street. Several neighbours took him up on the offer and I can't help wondering if there is a distinguished gentleman living at number 10 (p.36), and a bad boy with a scar on his face behind the blue door at number 43 (p.37).

Some creative Kiwis have modelled their mailboxes on cartoon characters. In Hokitika, SpongeBob SquarePants waits for the post, and a one-eyed Minion with spiky hair has his arm out for the paper in Rotorua.

Before door-to-door mail delivery began, people needed to collect their mail from the local post office. By the end of the 1860s private boxes at post offices had been introduced and mail was also being delivered to the door in urban areas.

Door-to-door mail delivery was time consuming, and a labour shortage during the First World War meant that it became compulsory to have a letterbox at the front gate from 1 April 1917. The labour shortage also meant women were employed to deliver the mail, although it wasn't common to see women posties cycling the streets until around the 1960s.

In her book *Whistles for the Postie*, published in 1972, author Freda Bream wrote about the variety of letterboxes she saw on her postie run. Little houses, empty biscuit tins, apple cases, and old oil drums were all used as letterboxes, proving that the reuse and do-it-yourself approach to mailboxes has been around for some time.

In 1996 New Zealand Post ran a competition to find the wackiest letterboxes in the country. Over 300 entries were received and 10 were chosen for the Wackiest Letterboxes collection of stamps to be released in March 1997. Among the 10 chosen for stamps were two houses and a large castle. House letterboxes have always been popular and the Location, Location, Location section (p.44), features houses of all shapes and styles.

One of the requirements for the competition was that the letterboxes needed to be 'postie friendly'. For those thinking about creating their own awesome letterbox, New Zealand Post has mailbox specifications on their website. Creative letterboxes are allowed (encouraged by the author), and as long as they meet size requirements and are located appropriately, they'll get the unofficial stamp of approval.

Today letterboxes compete with email and social media as a means of communication. There could be a time in the future when both novel and standard letterboxes end up as relics from our past. This possibility is reflected in New Zealand Post's 2018 annual results. The results showed that typically 1.2 million fewer letters were delivered every week in the financial year ending June 2018 compared to the previous year.

Ironically, though, the letterbox may be saved from extinction due to the continual rise in online shopping. New Zealand Post now makes more revenue from courier delivery than mail delivery so the letterbox of today may become the courier box of tomorrow. Some DIYers (Do It Yourselfers) are already using fridges and microwaves to collect the mail. These savvy folks may have foreseen the day when the delivery of larger packages will be more likely than the delivery of envelopes and small parcels.

Here's to all the colourful and quirky letterboxes to be found at the front gates of New Zealand properties, and to the inspired people that create them. I hope you enjoy the 140 letterbox photos within these pages as much as I have enjoyed finding them. Happy trails and may you be pleasantly surprised where the journey takes you.

RURAL DELIVERY

The rural mail delivery service started in New Zealand in 1905. A variety of transport options including horse-drawn coach, motorcycle and sawmill locomotive delivered mail to rural communities.

These days if they're not travelling by boat, the rural postie drives through small townships and into the countryside where they may find all sorts of unusual letterboxes at the farm gate. Cows, especially the black-patched Friesian, are a popular choice.

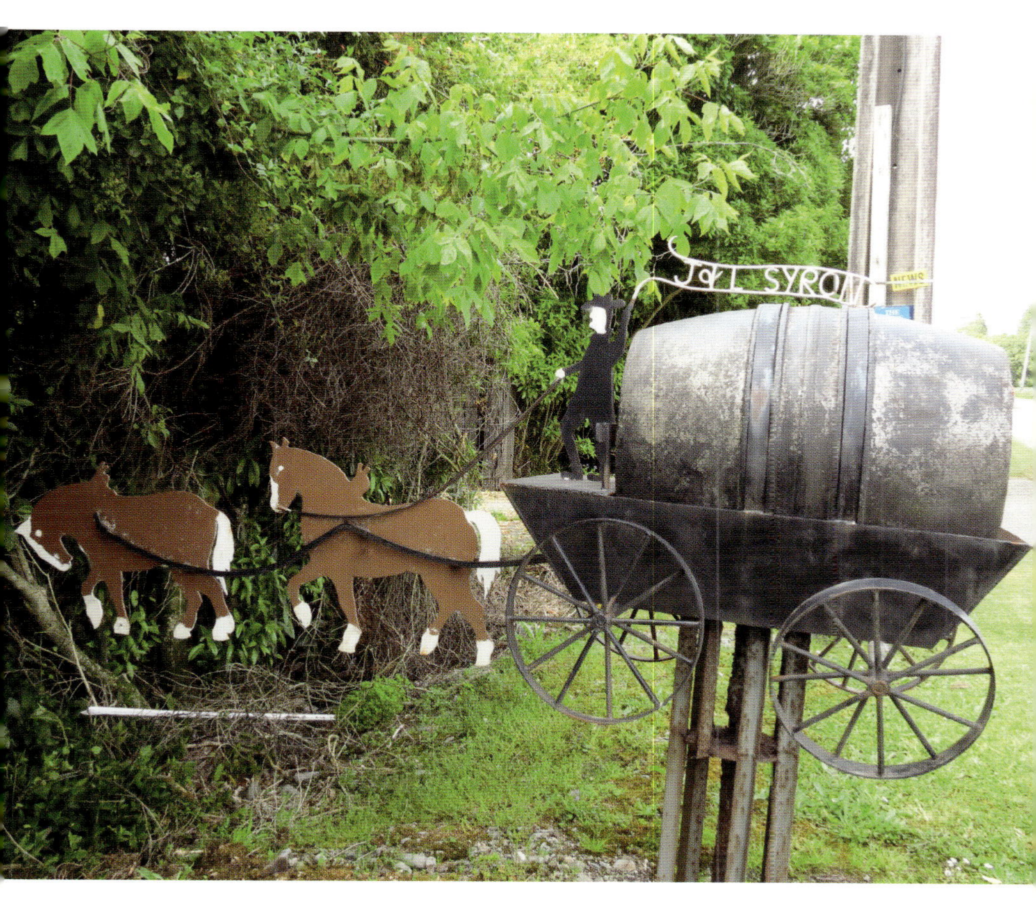

Horses once powered rural mail delivery.

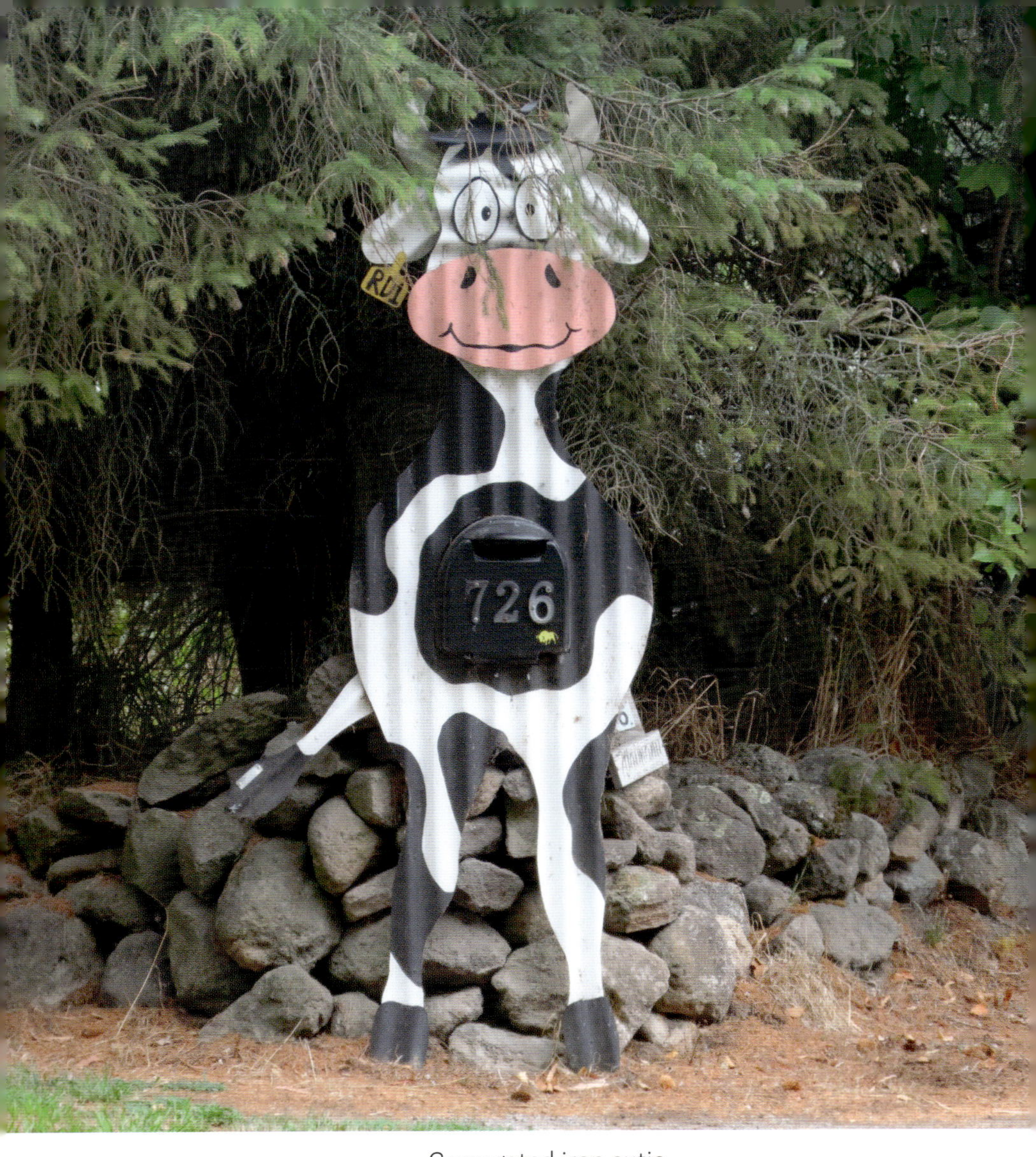

Corrugated iron cutie.

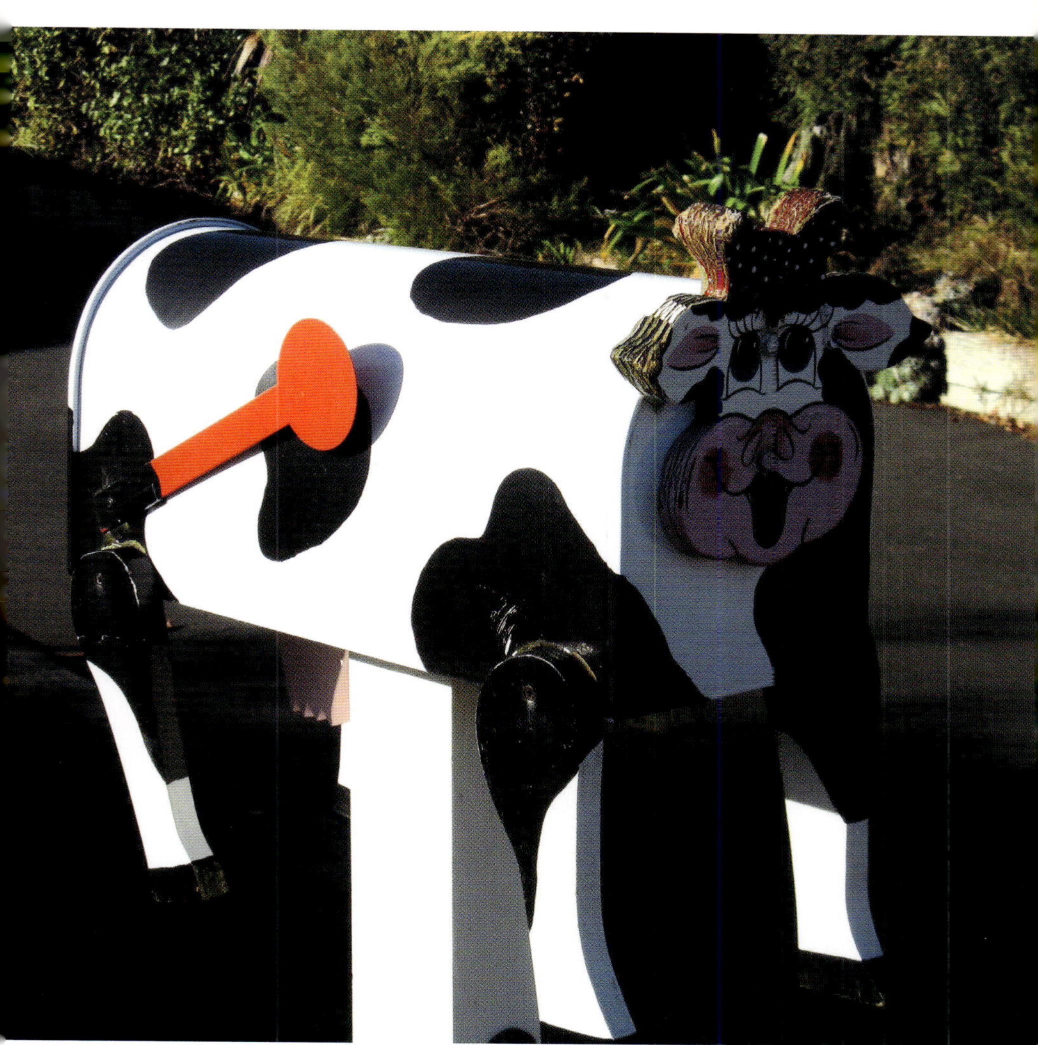

Cowabunga, she's a real lady!

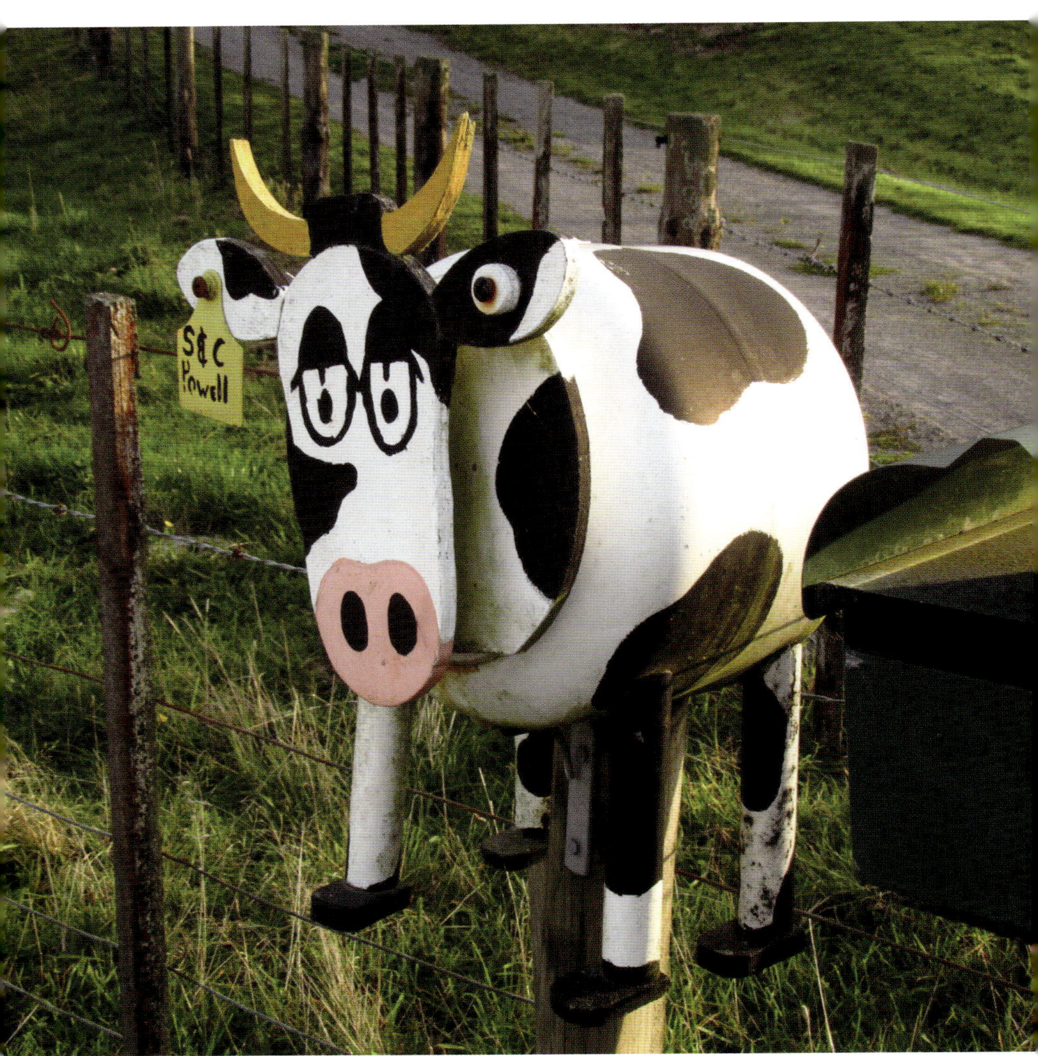

Deja-moo.

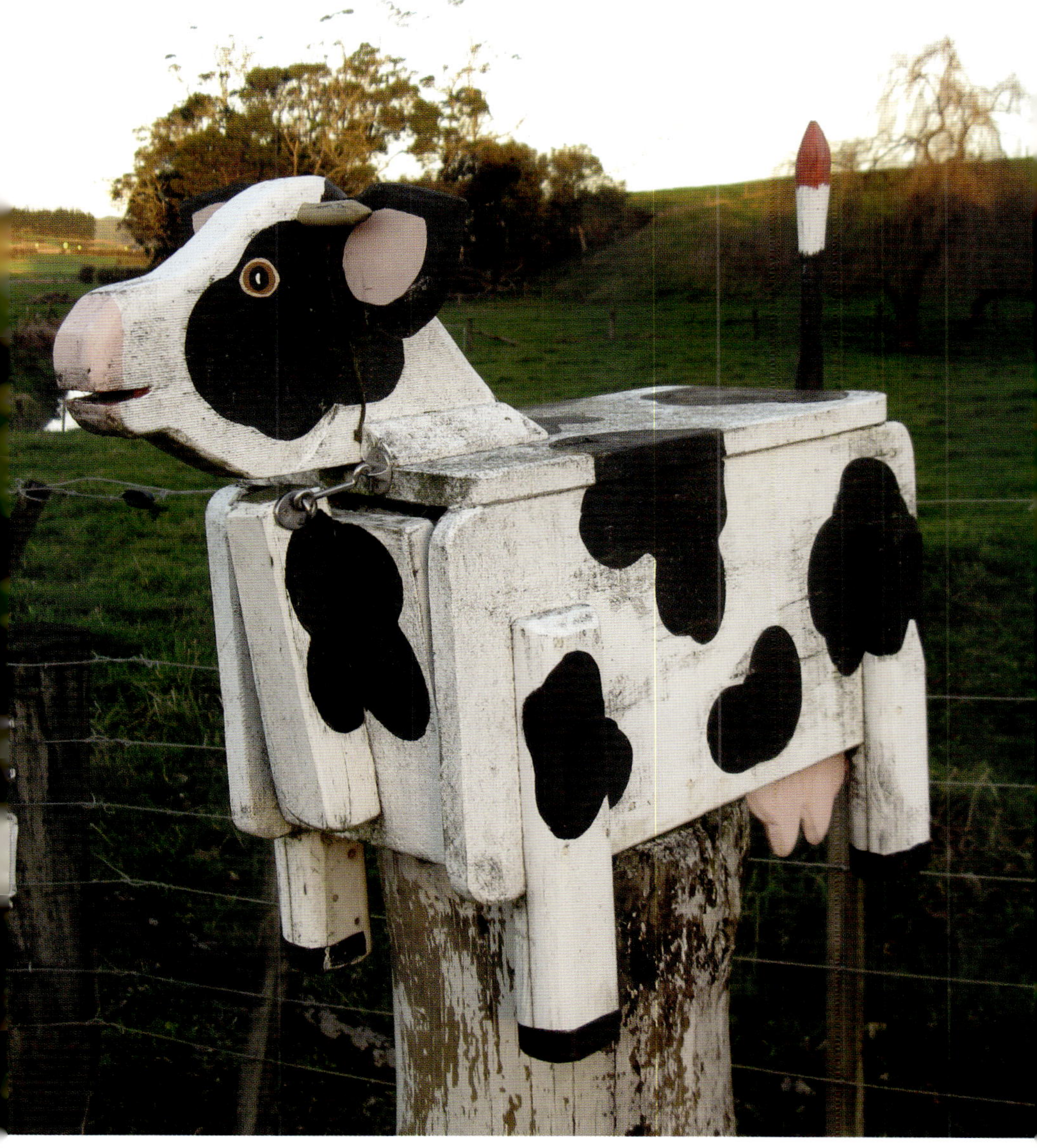

A letterbox like no udder.

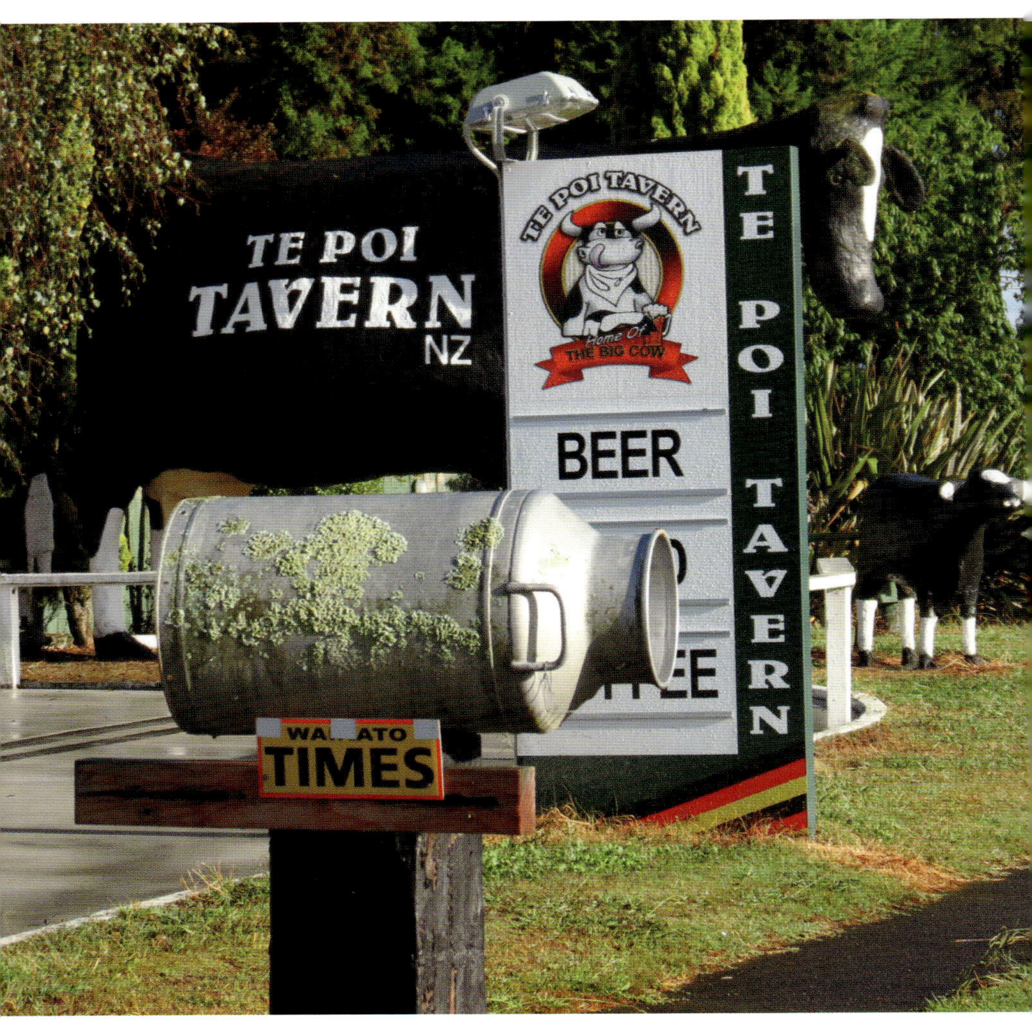

When you've already got a giant cow and a life-sized calf,
a milk can mailbox it is.

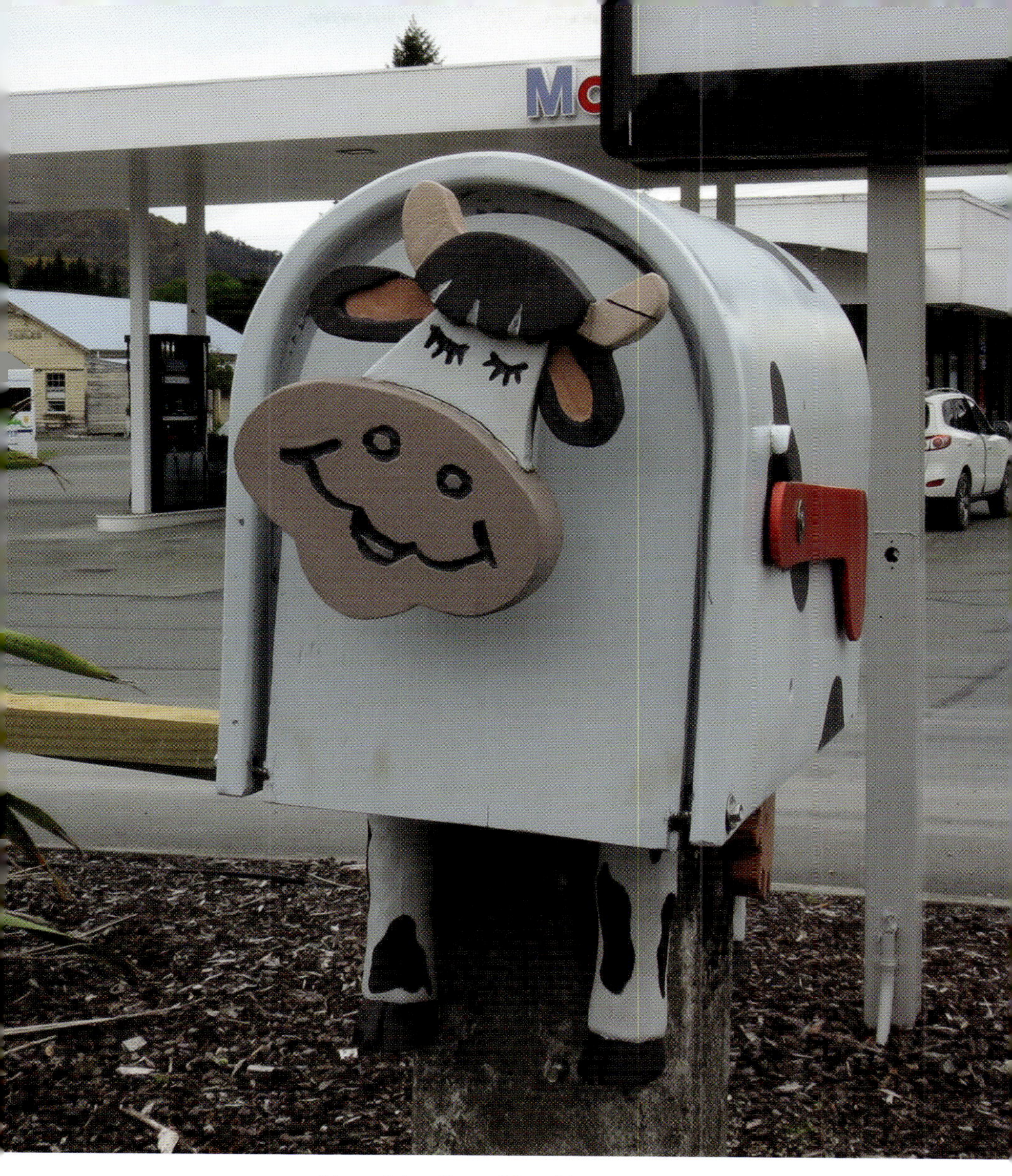

Mary-Moo from Murchison.

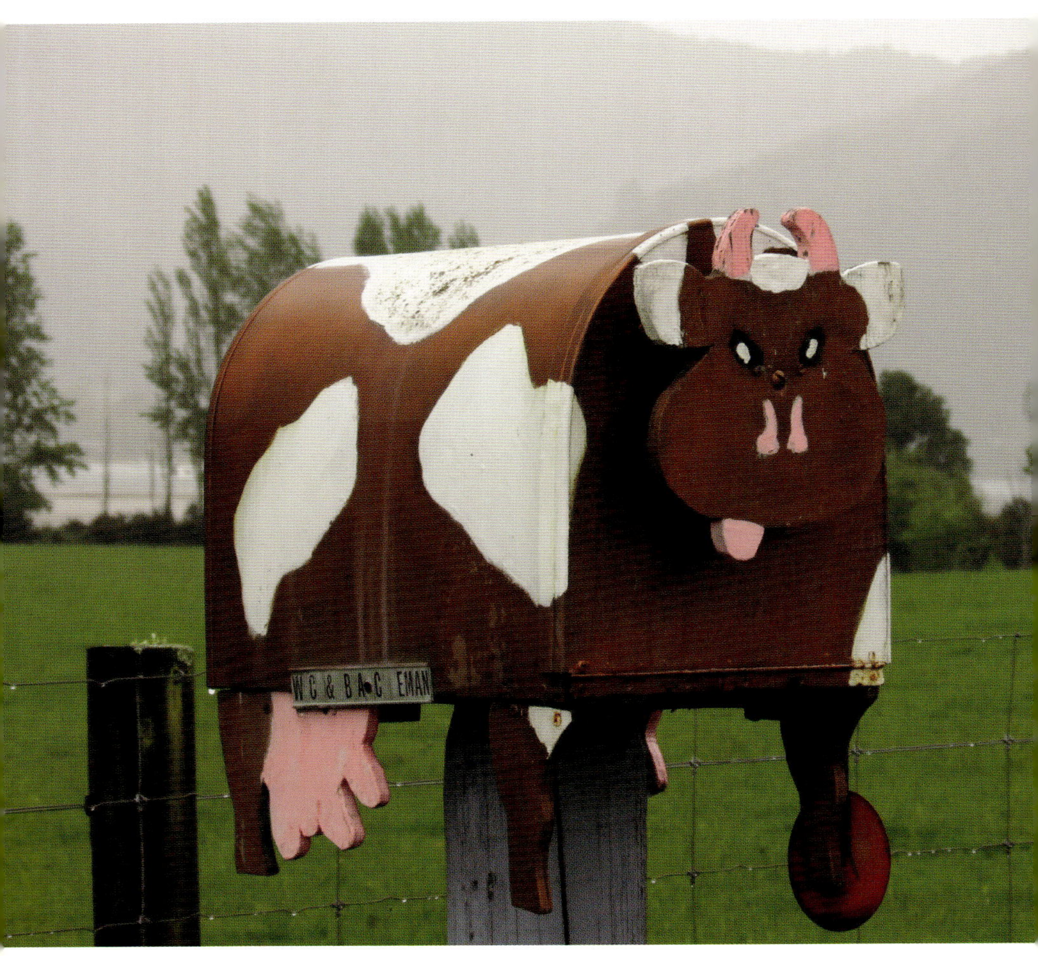

Moo-licious — A US Dairy survey found 7% of Americans think chocolate milk comes from brown cows!

ON THE FARM

It's not just a 'moo moo here' and a 'moo moo there' for the rural postie, they may find an 'Old McDonald's Farm' of letterboxes on their mail run.

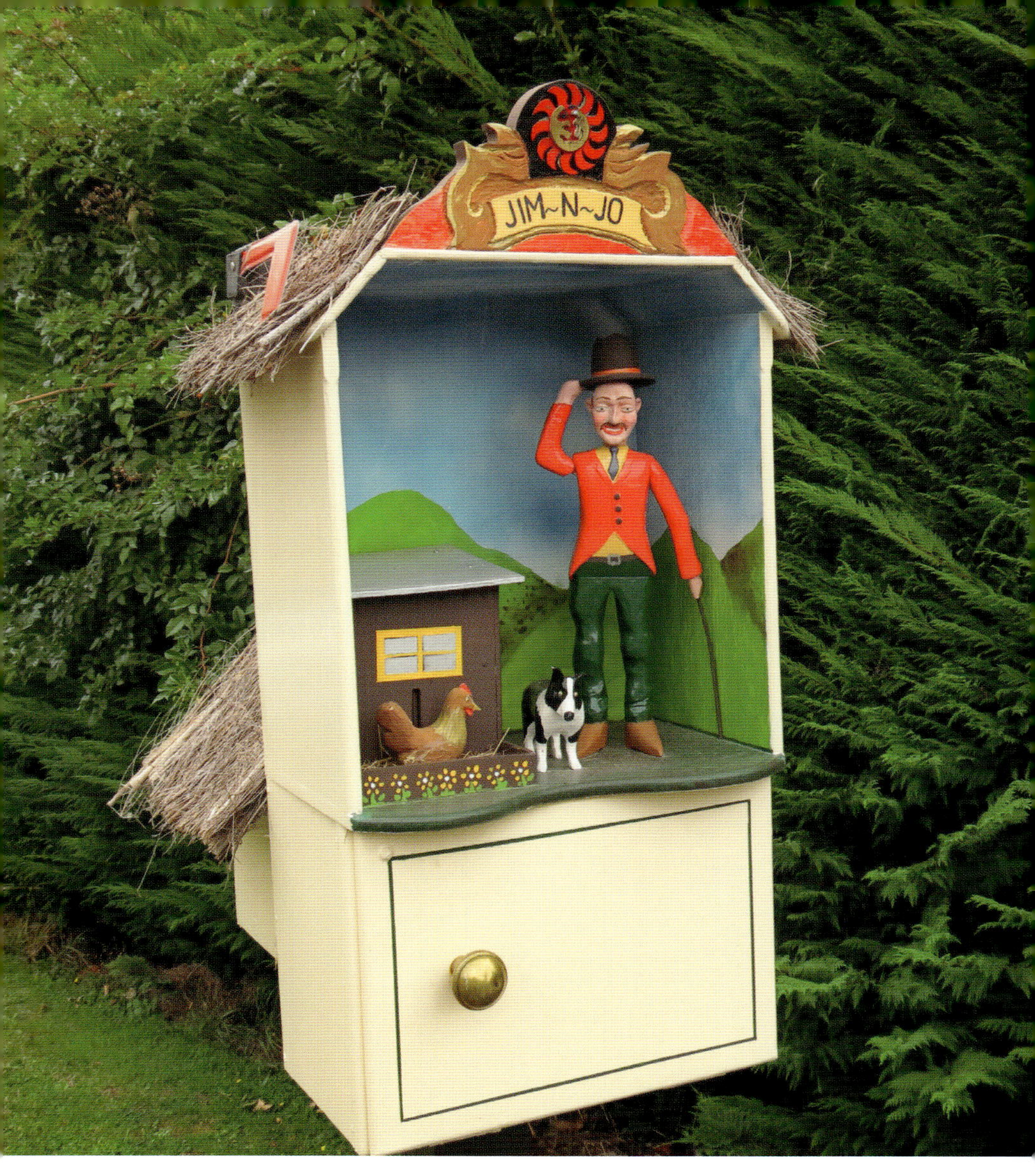

Gentleman Farmer Jim surveying his patch of paradise.

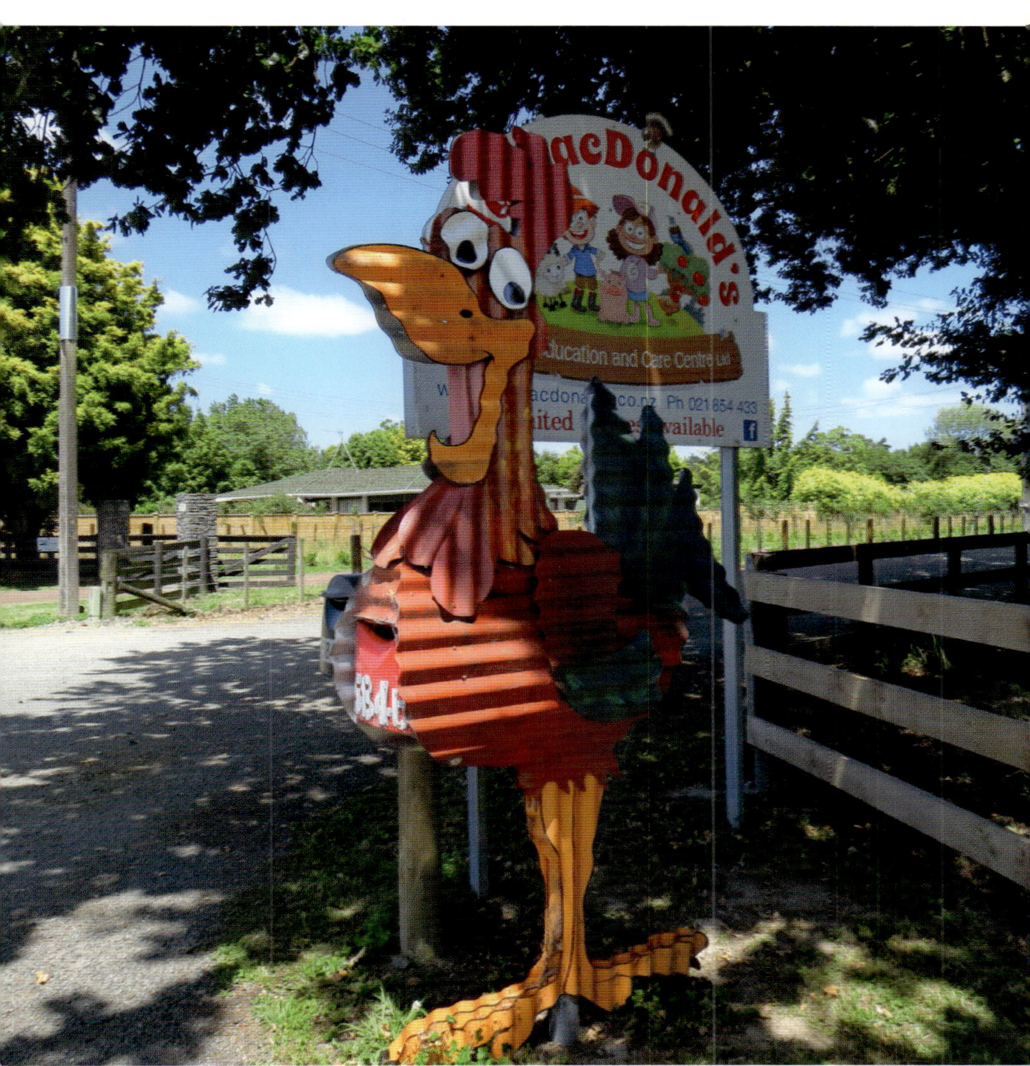

Red rooster, also known as the farm alarm.

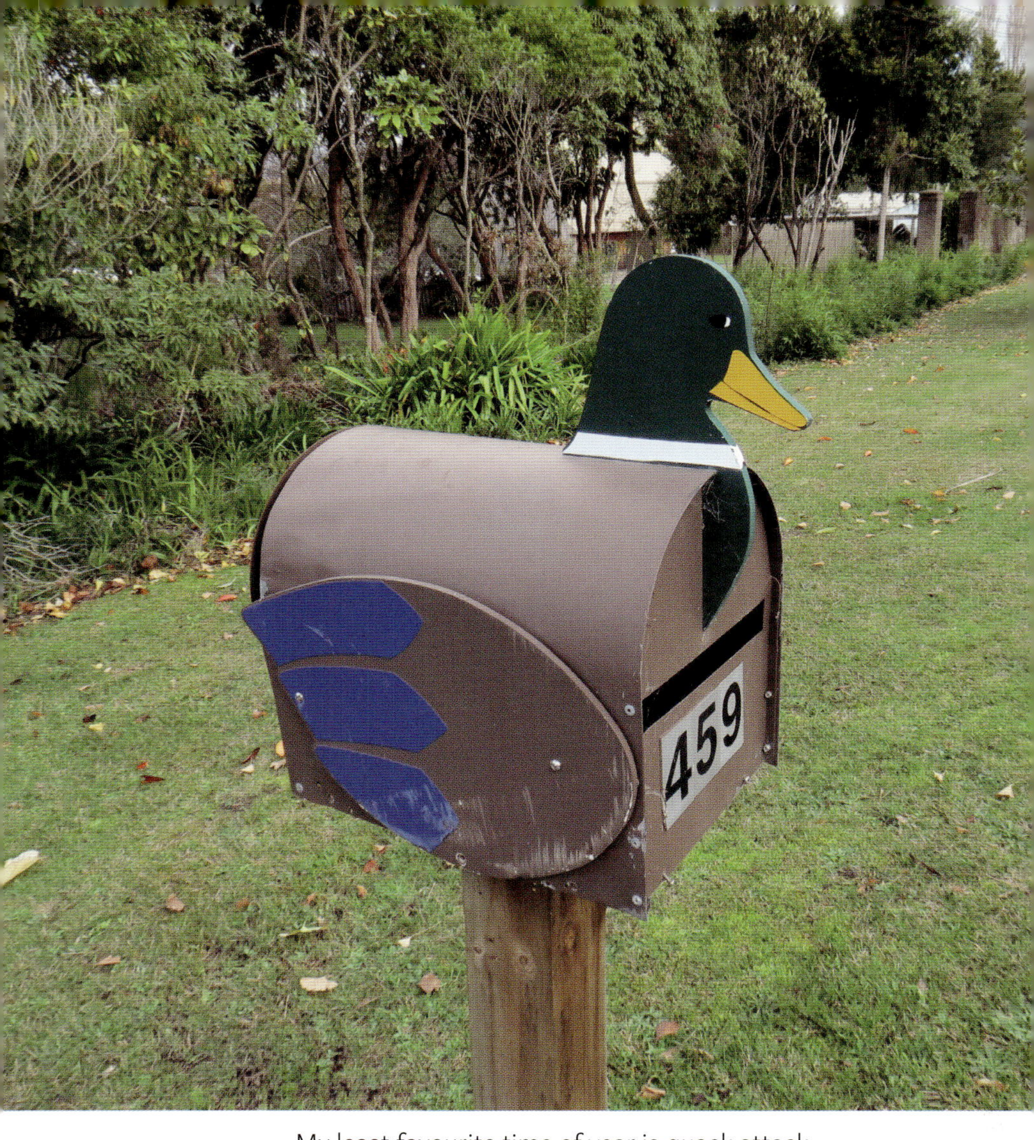

My least favourite time of year is quack attack,
or as you Kiwis call it: Duck Shooting Season.

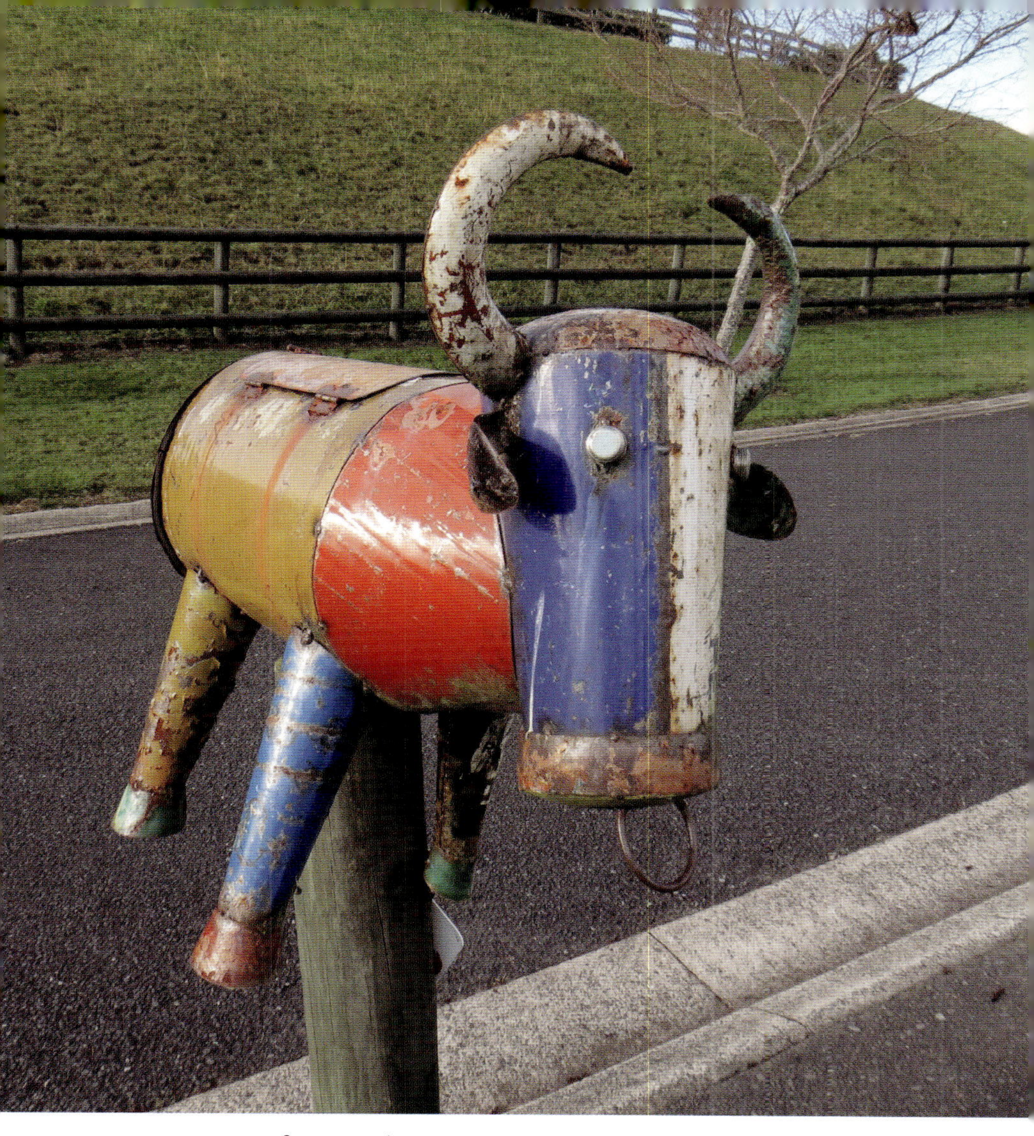

Increase farm productivity — take the bull by the ho-ns.

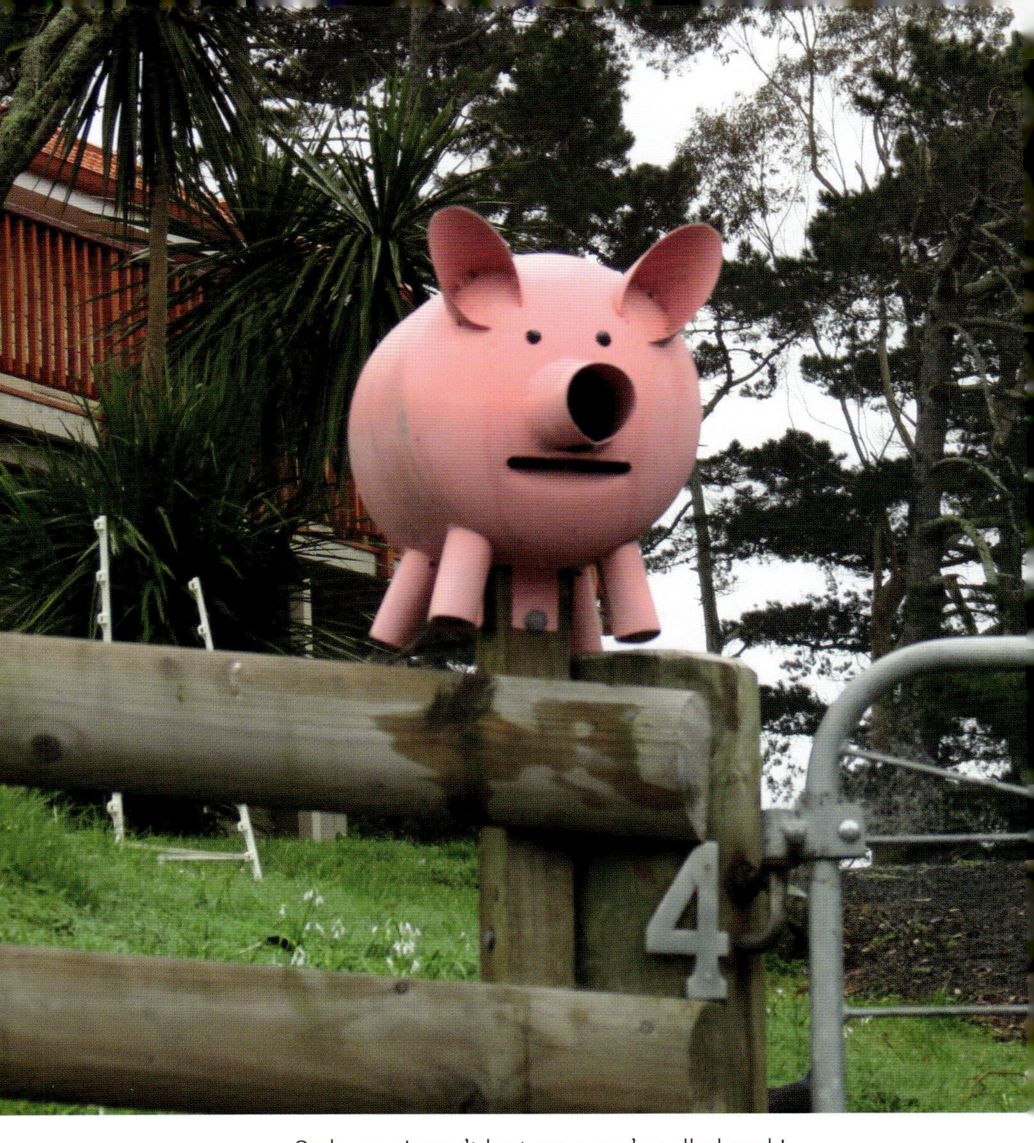

So happy I won't be tomorrow's pulled pork!

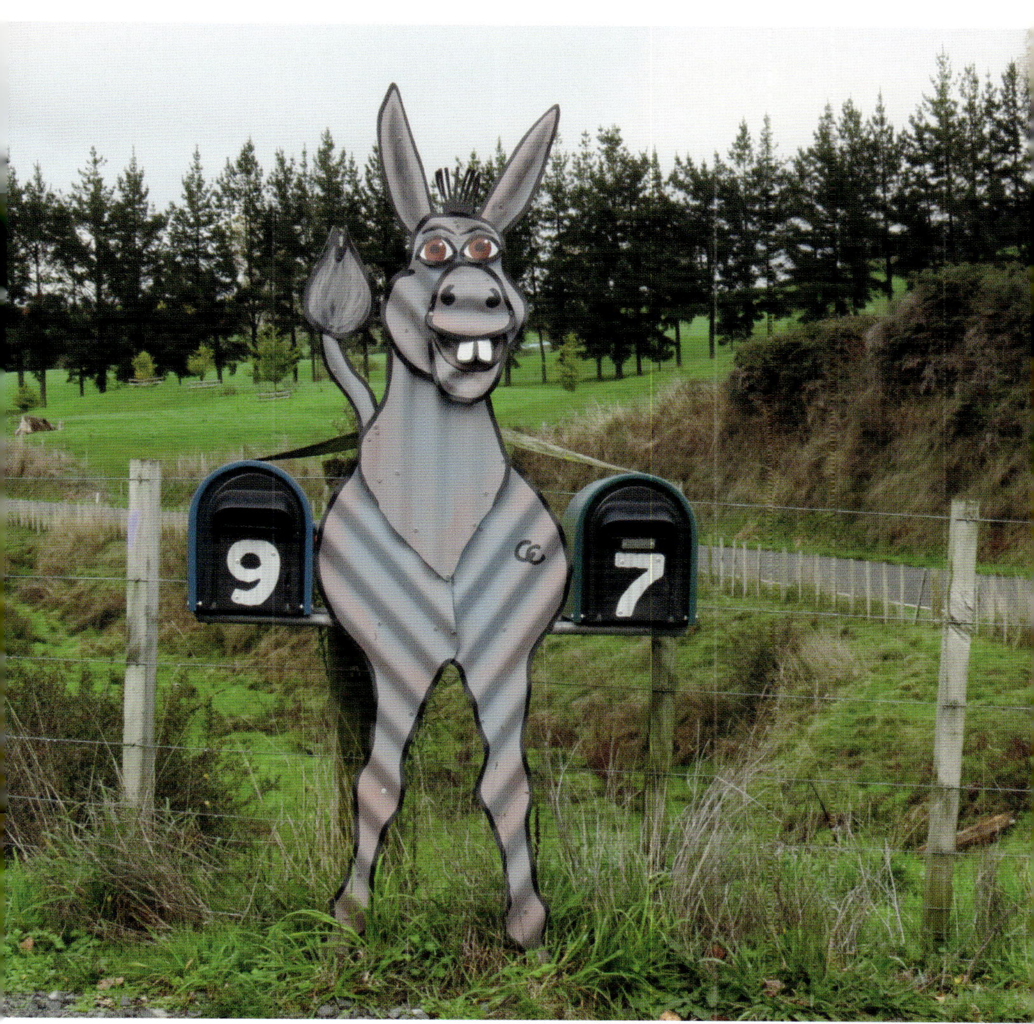

Donkey eagerly awaiting letters from Far Far Away.

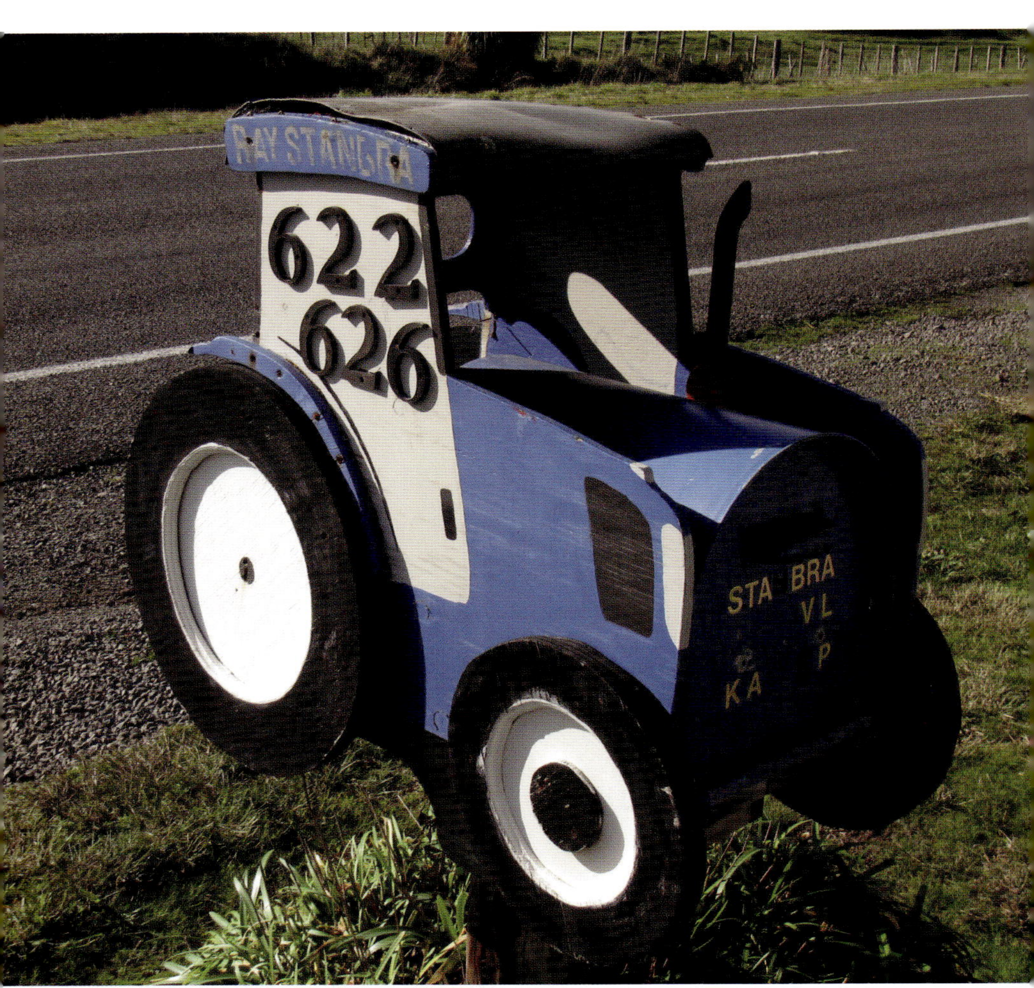

Big dairy pay out this year equals flash new tractor next year.

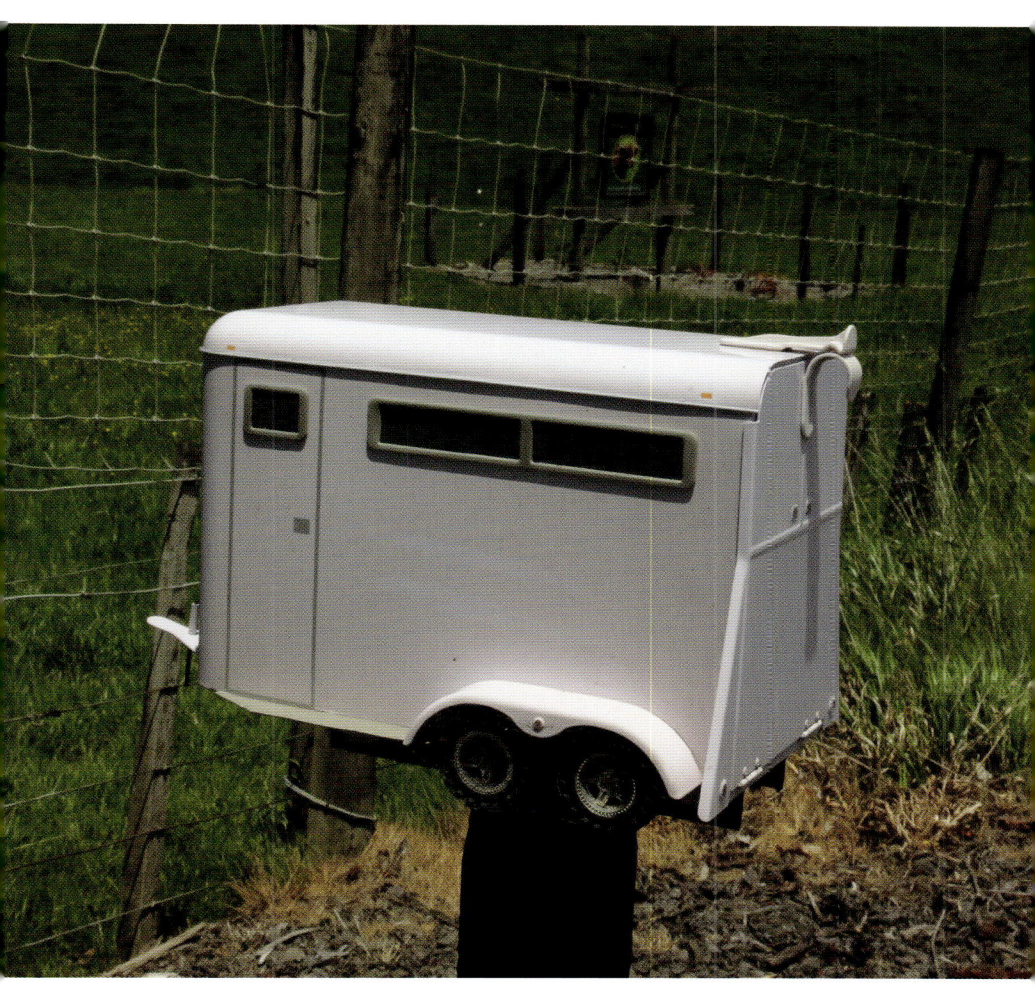

No horsing around — just deliver the mail and hoof it!

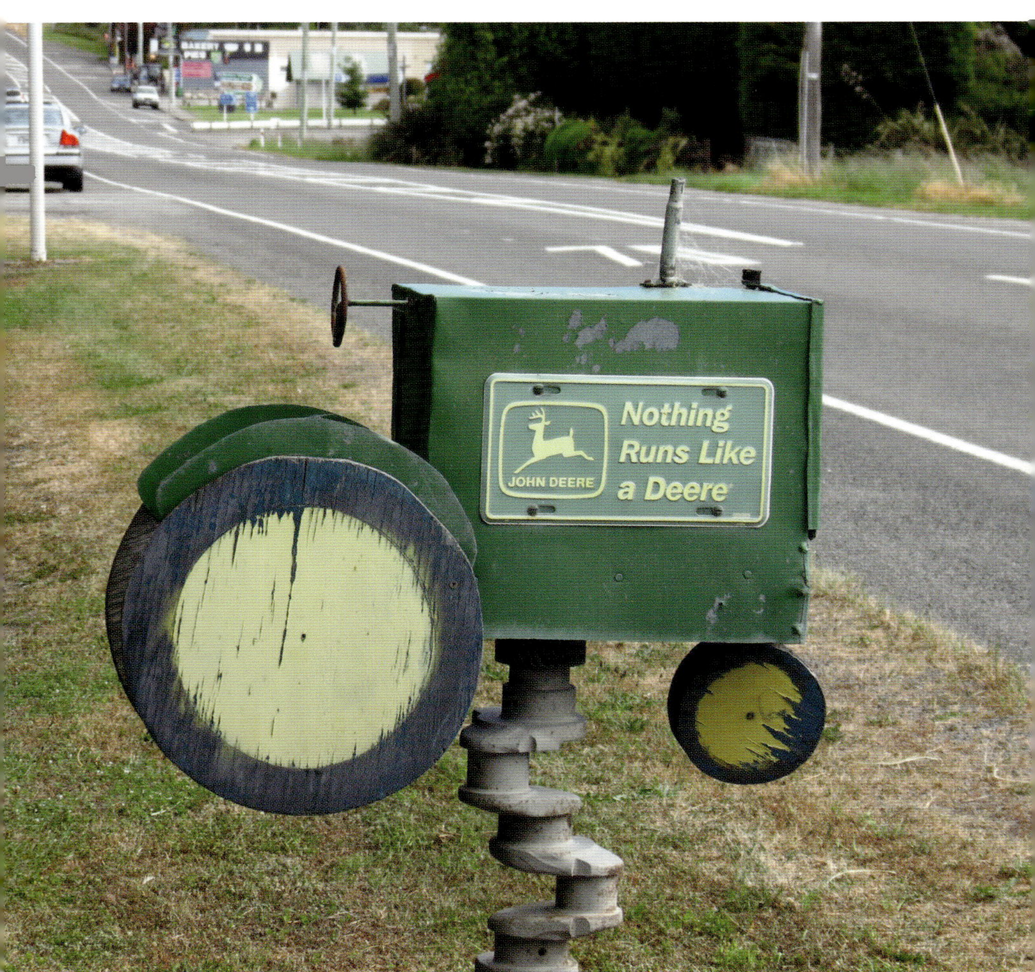

Driving a John Deere is the way to travel 'round here.

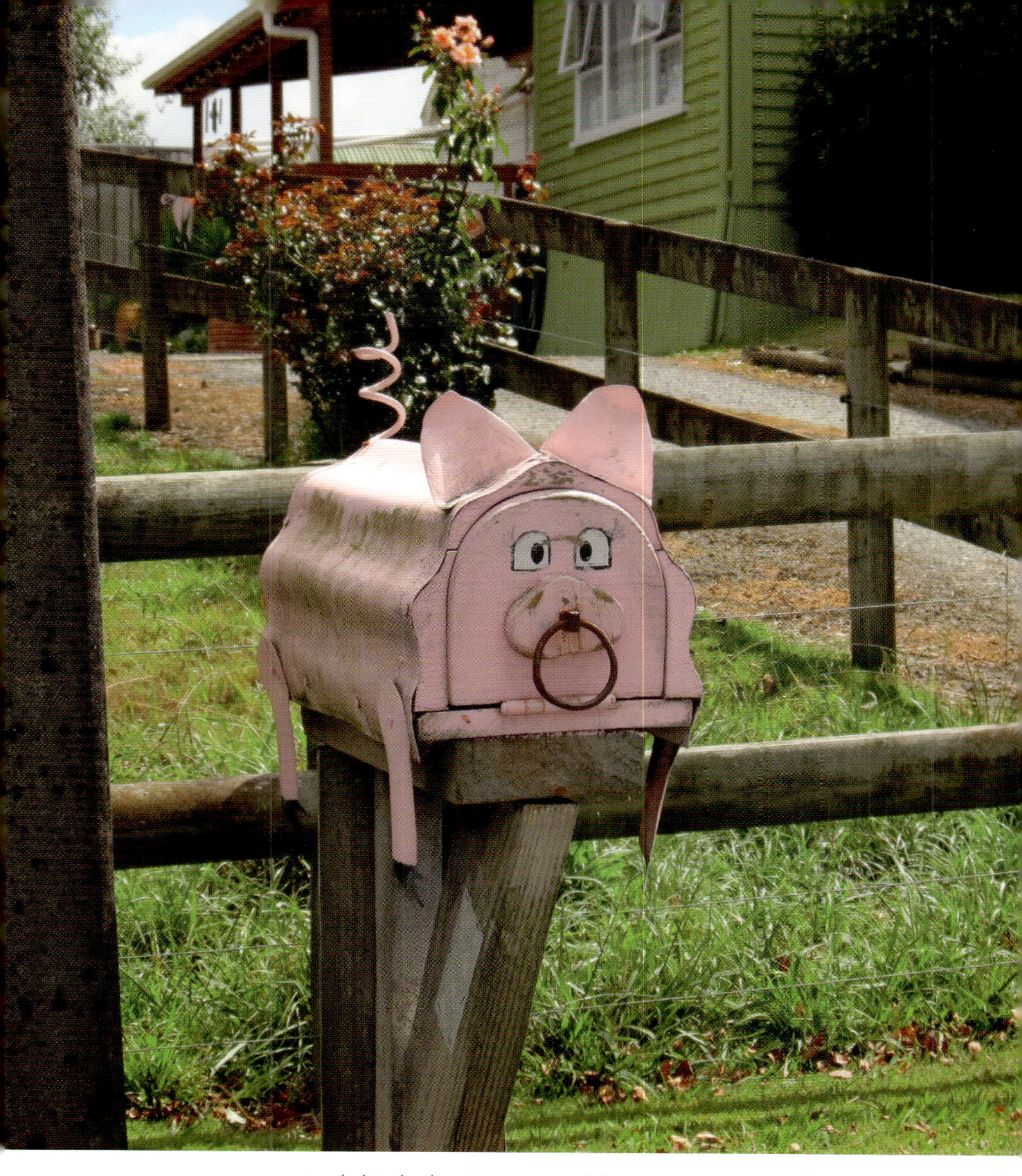

And this little piggy stayed home.

KIWI BLOKES

'Bloke' is an informal name for a man in New Zealand and it's not uncommon to hear an honest man referred to as a 'good bloke'.

Like men all over the world, Kiwi blokes can express their personalities by the way they dress and through the hobbies and interests they pursue. This collection of letterboxes is a cheeky nod to the Kiwi bloke in all his guises.

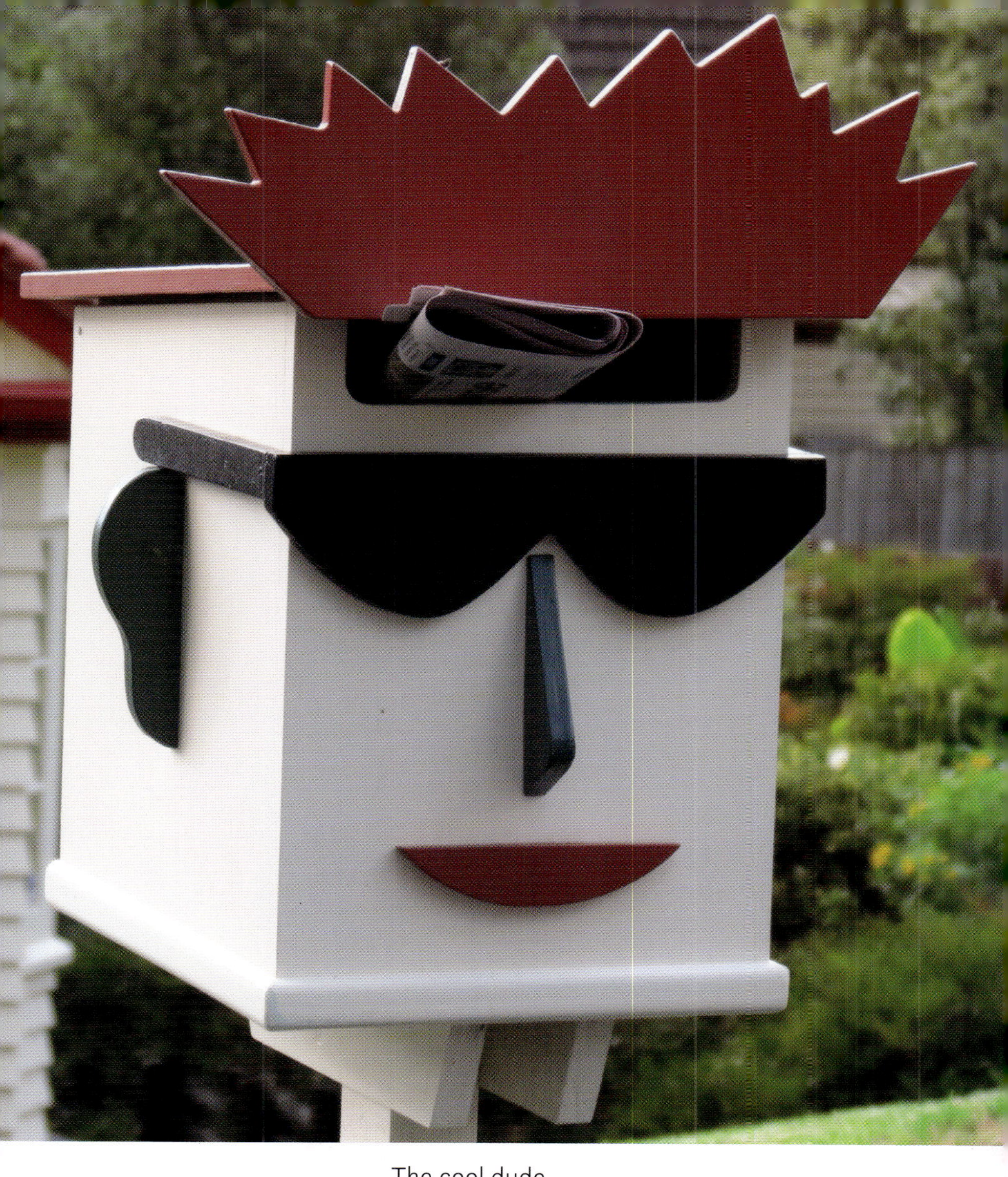

The cool dude.

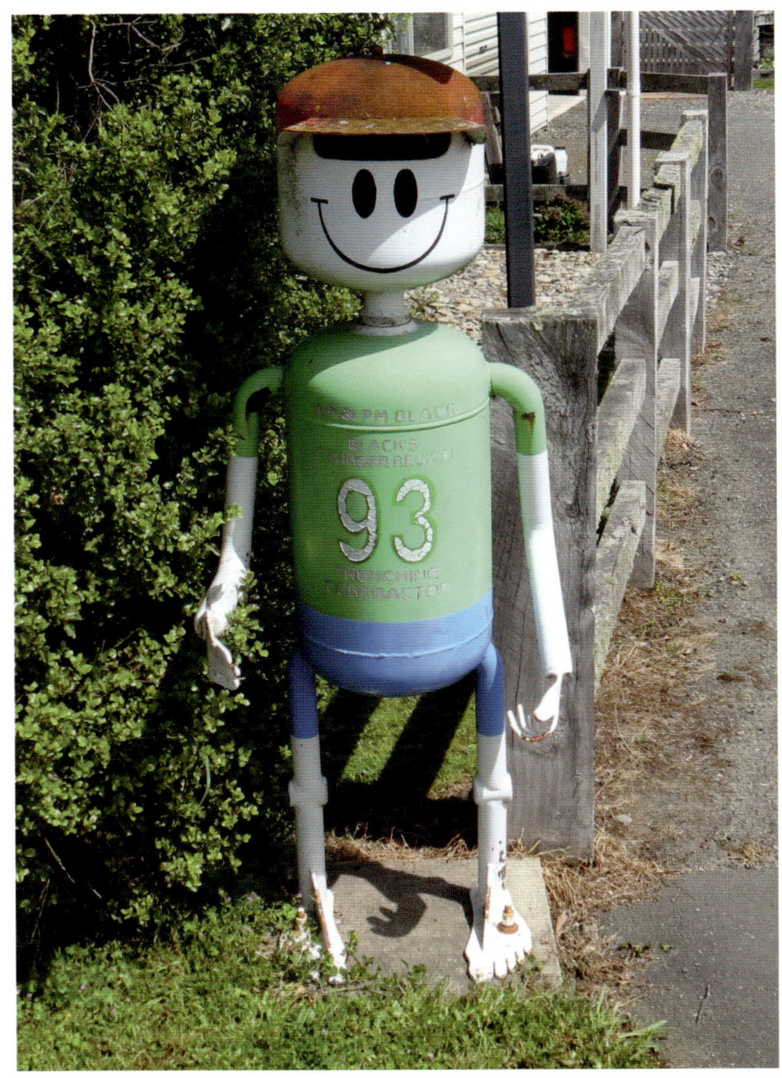

The cheerful chap.

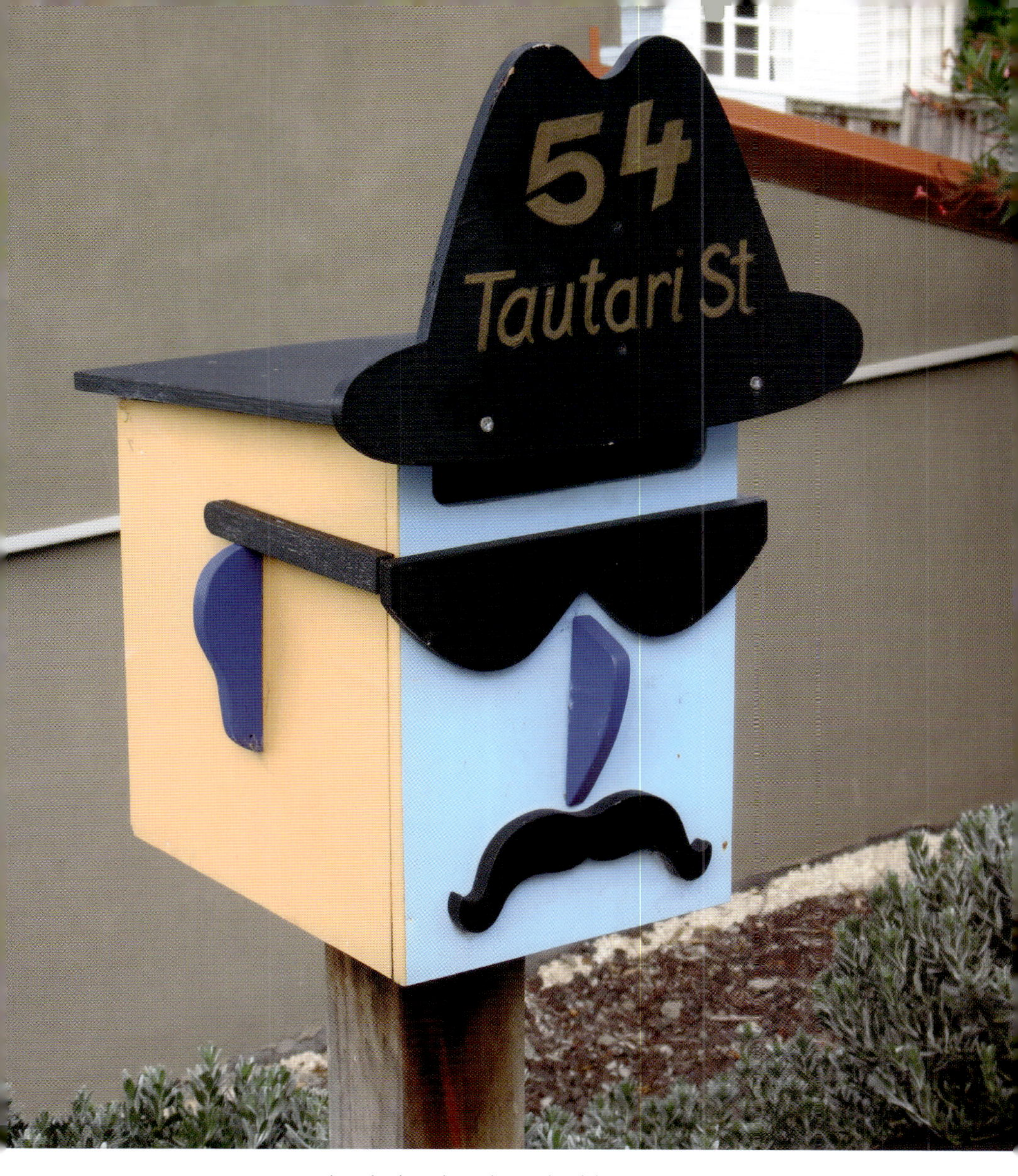

The dude who plays the blues.

The distinguished gentleman.

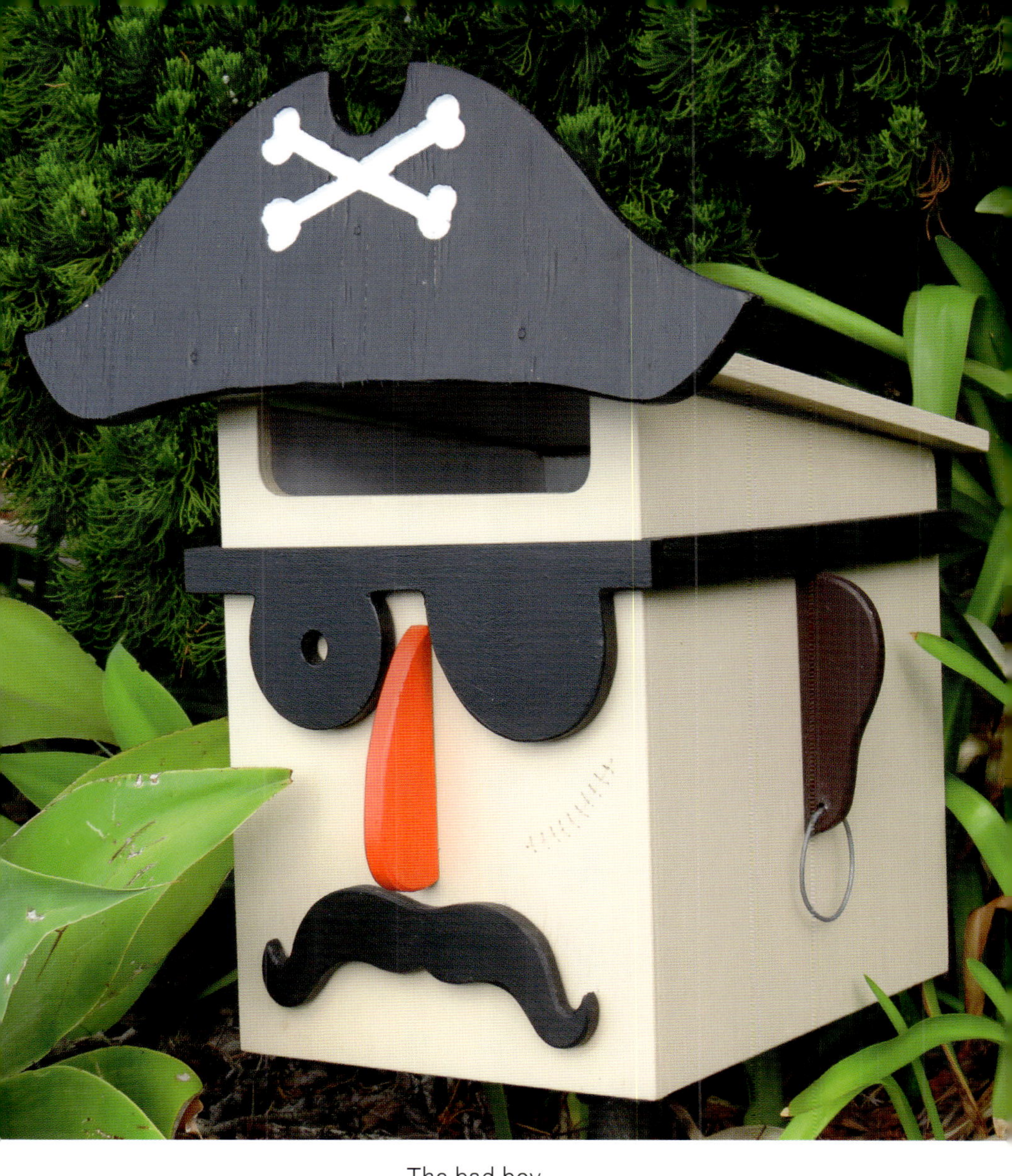

The bad boy.

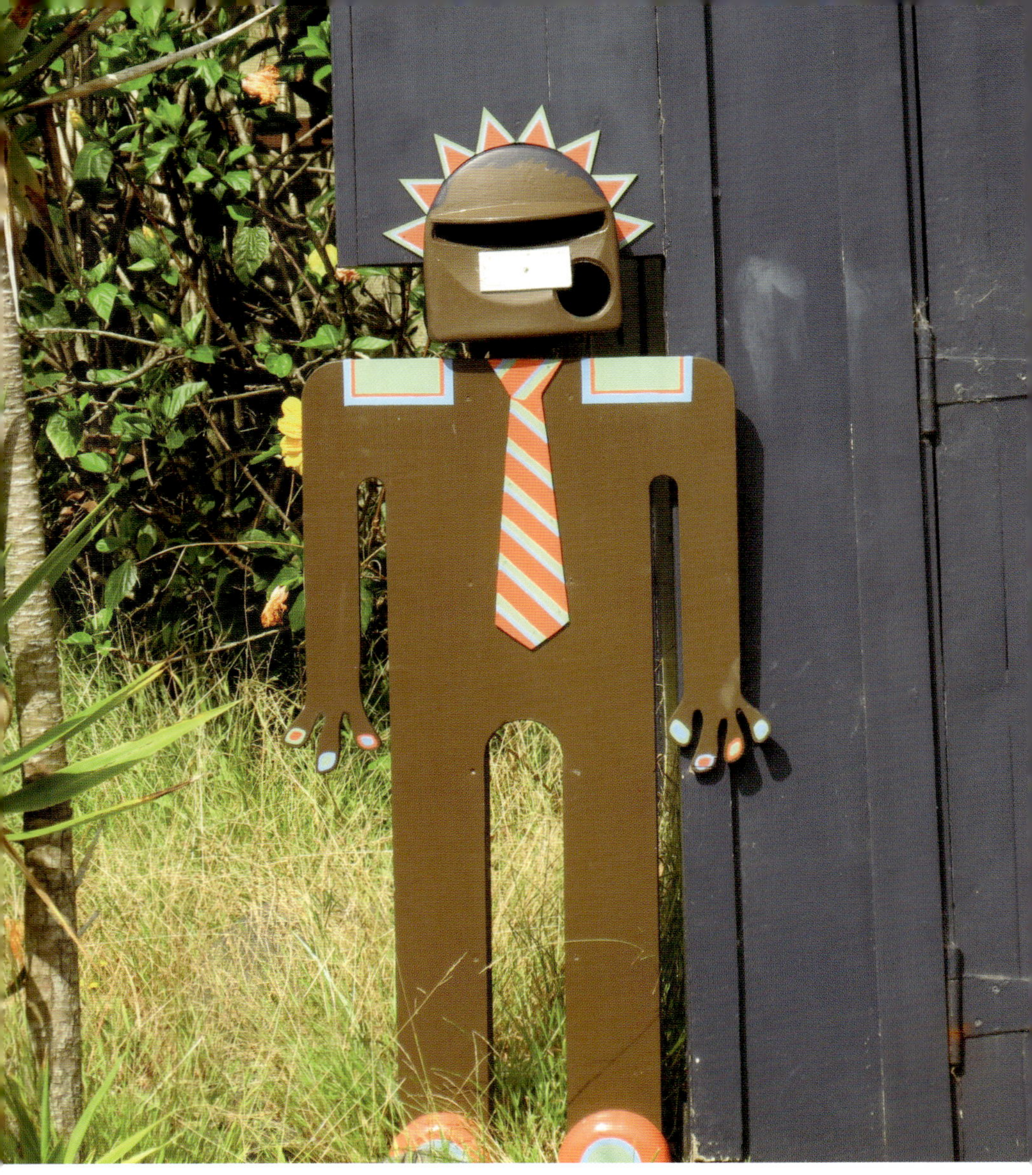

The businessman.

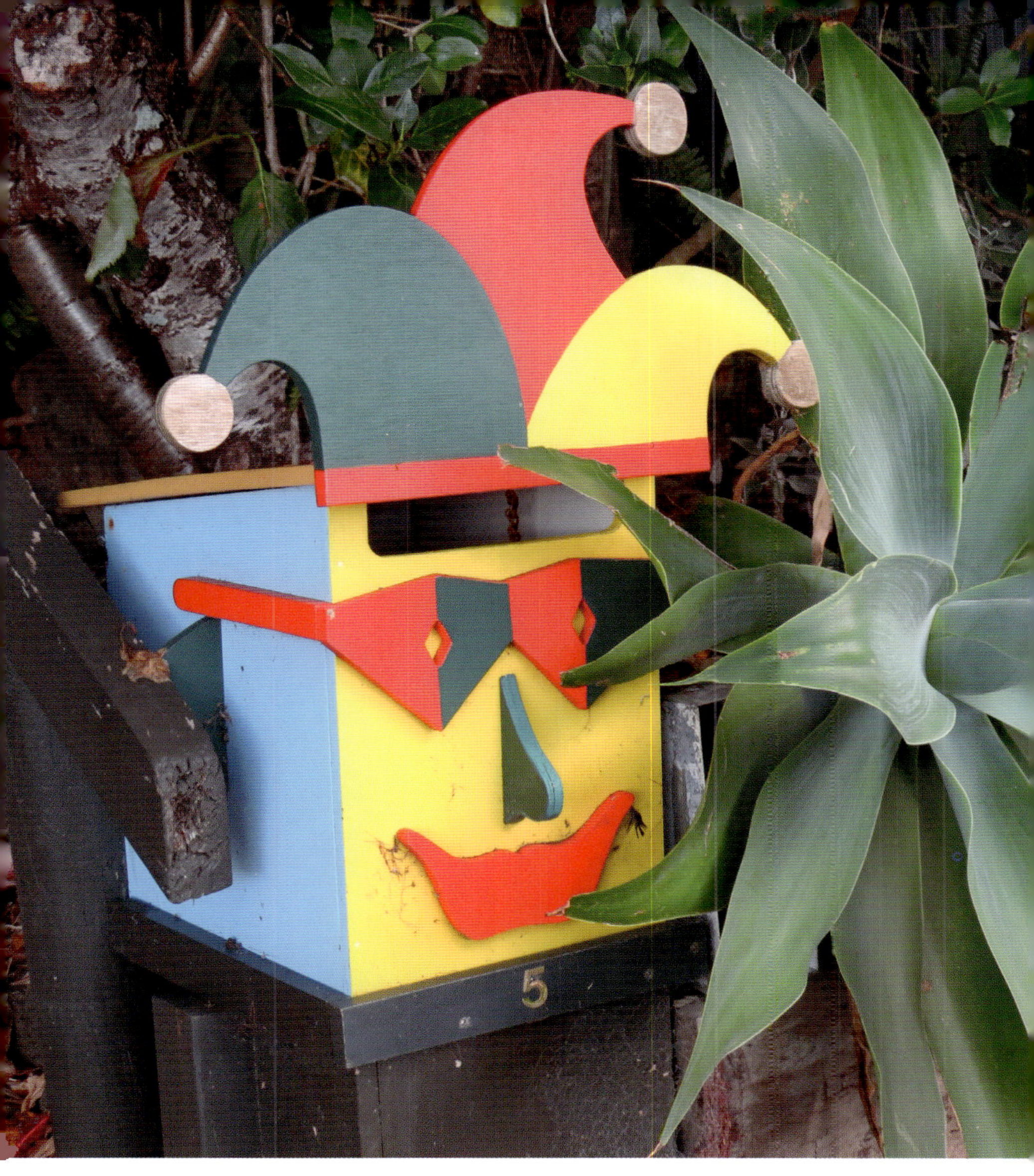

The funny fella.

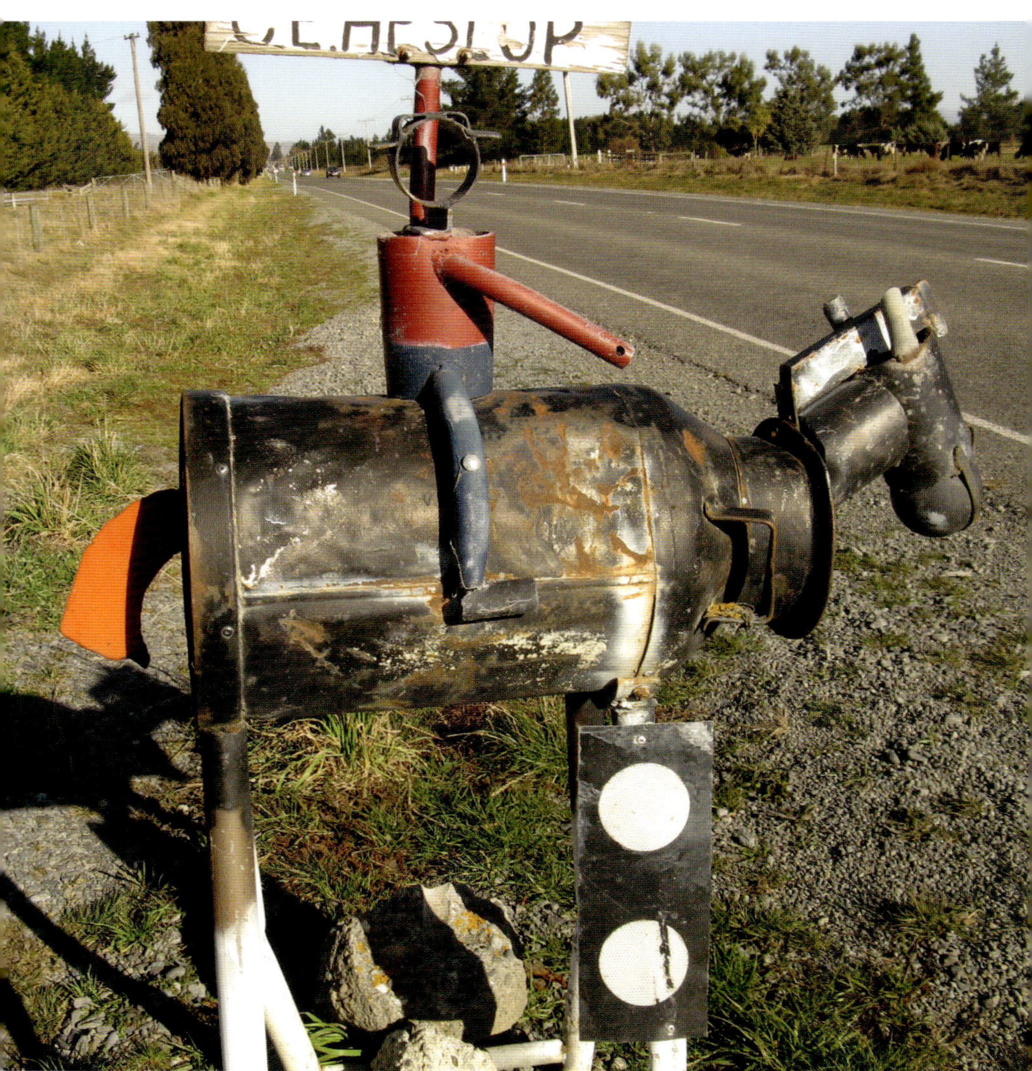

The stockman.

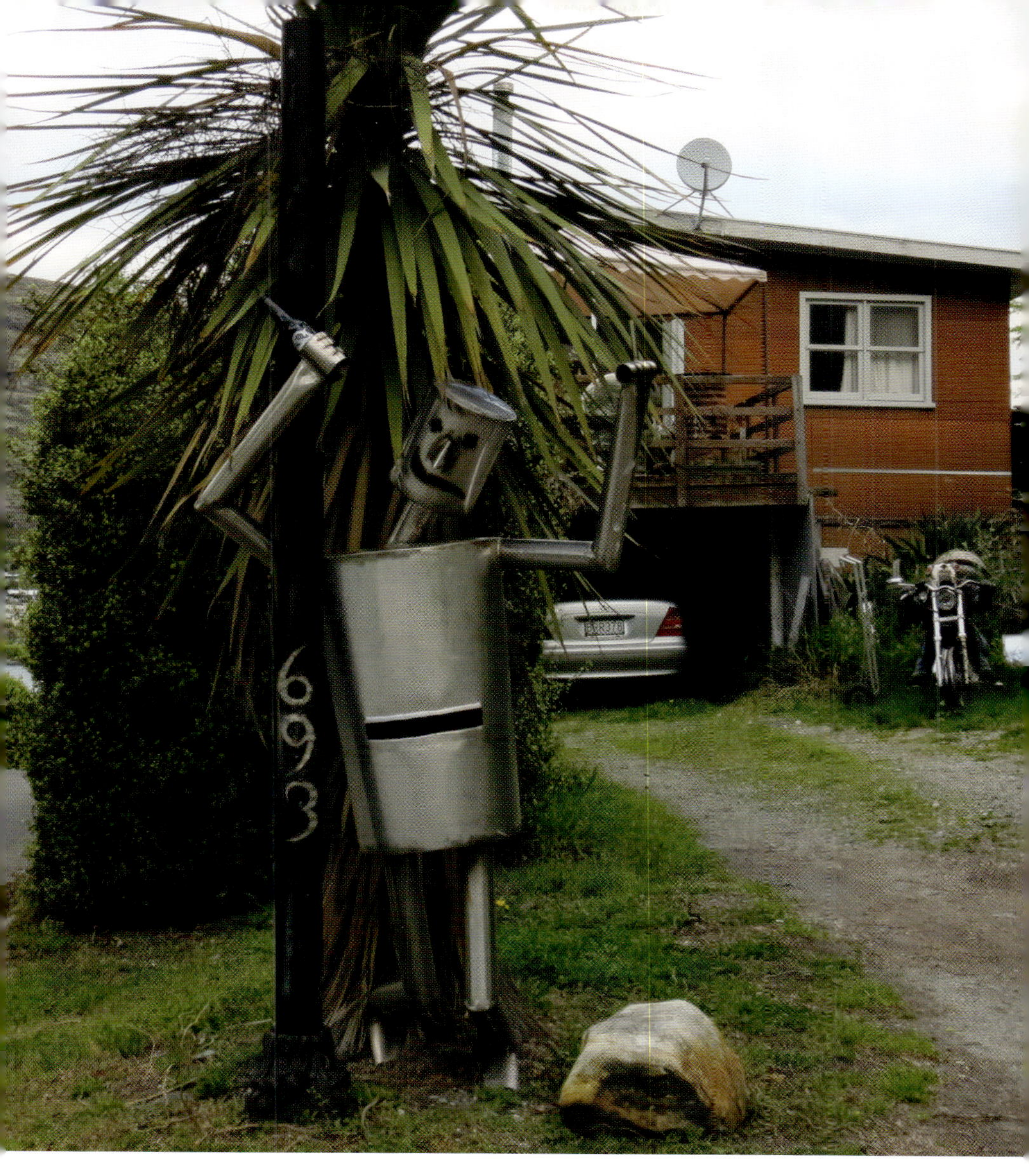

The party boy.

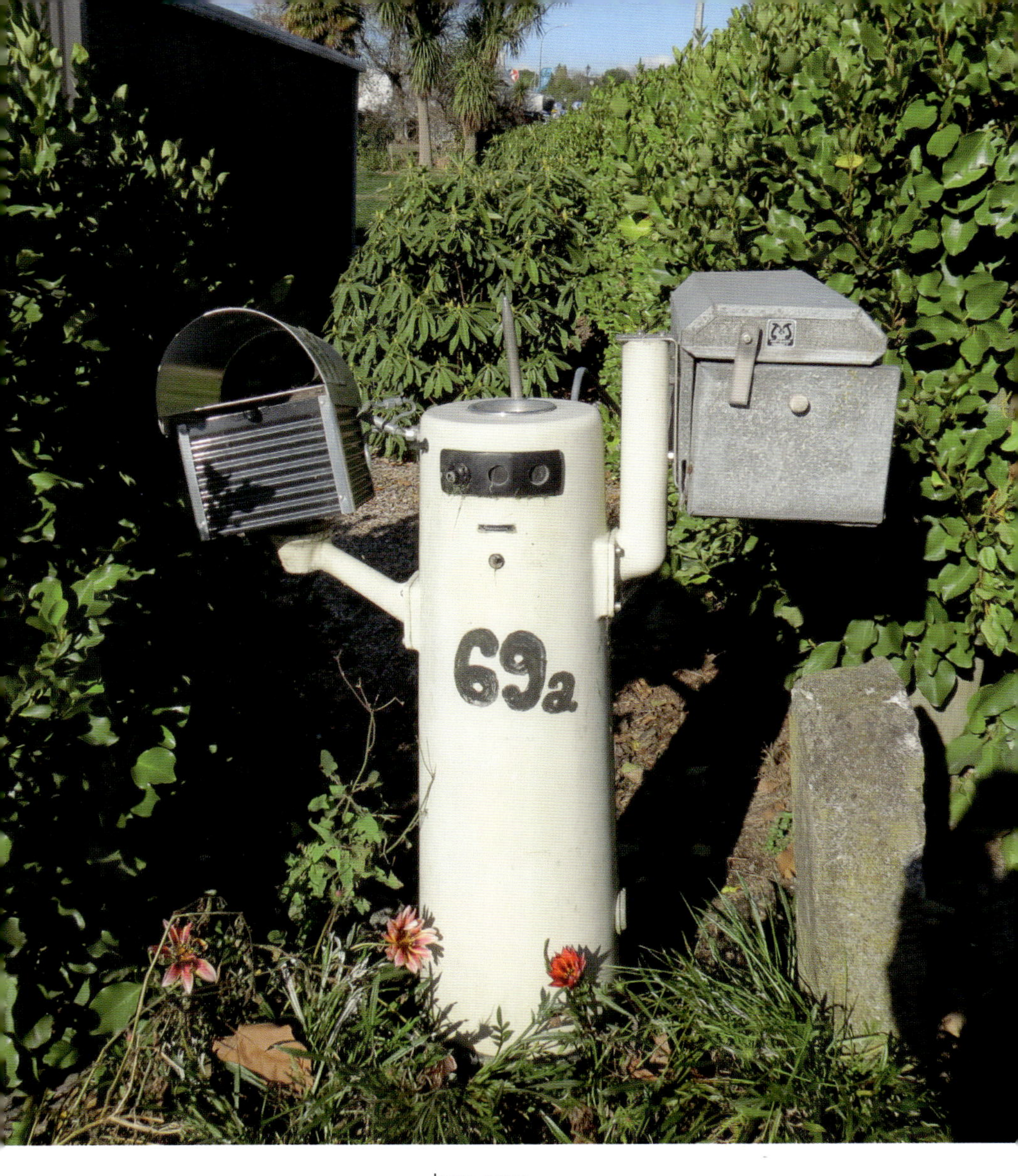

Iron man.

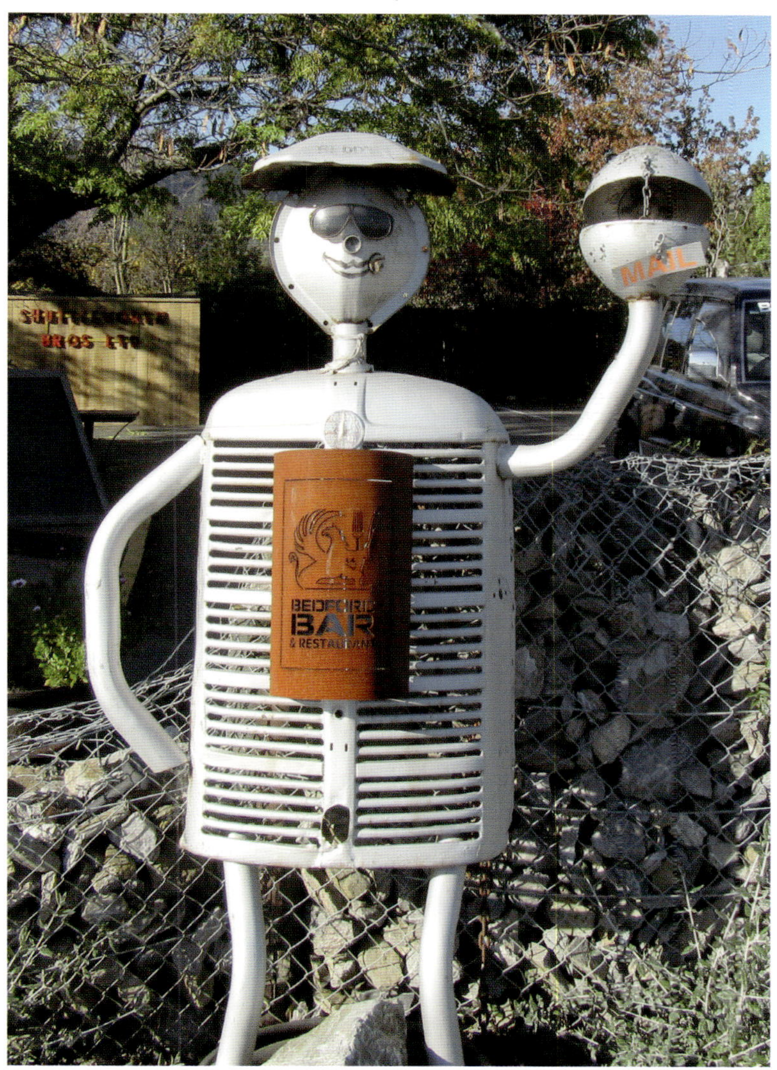

Heavy metal fan.

LOCATION, LOCATION, LOCATION

If you're looking to buy a new home there are plenty of catchy slogans real estate agents use to advertise properties for sale. The catchy slogans can be open to interpretation — does 'handyman's dream' really mean 'should be demolished'? Does 'charming character cottage' mean 'very old and very small'?

The letterbox houses in the following pages might not be quite big enough to fulfill most househunters' requirements, but they're pretty cute to look at.

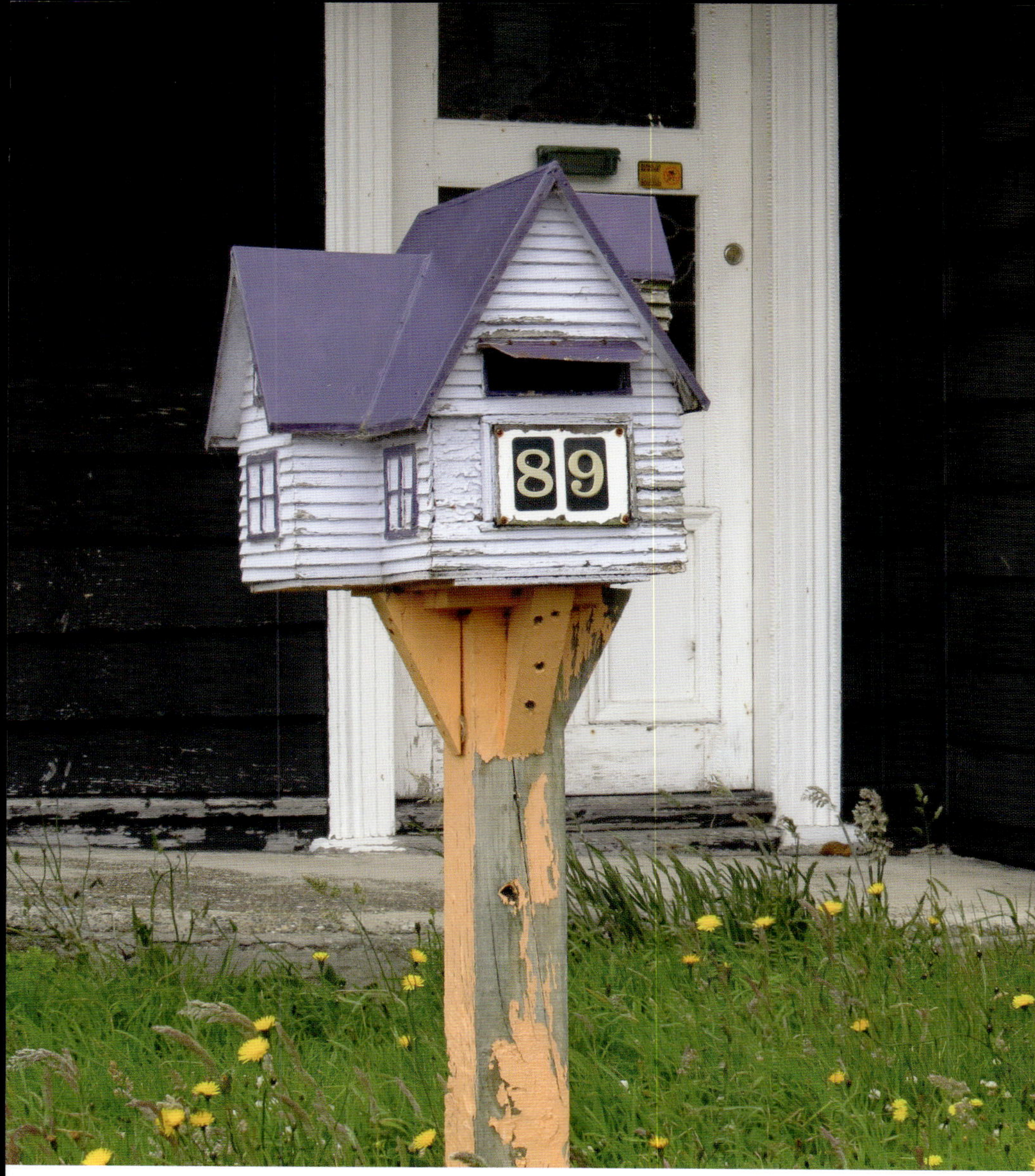

Handyman's delight.

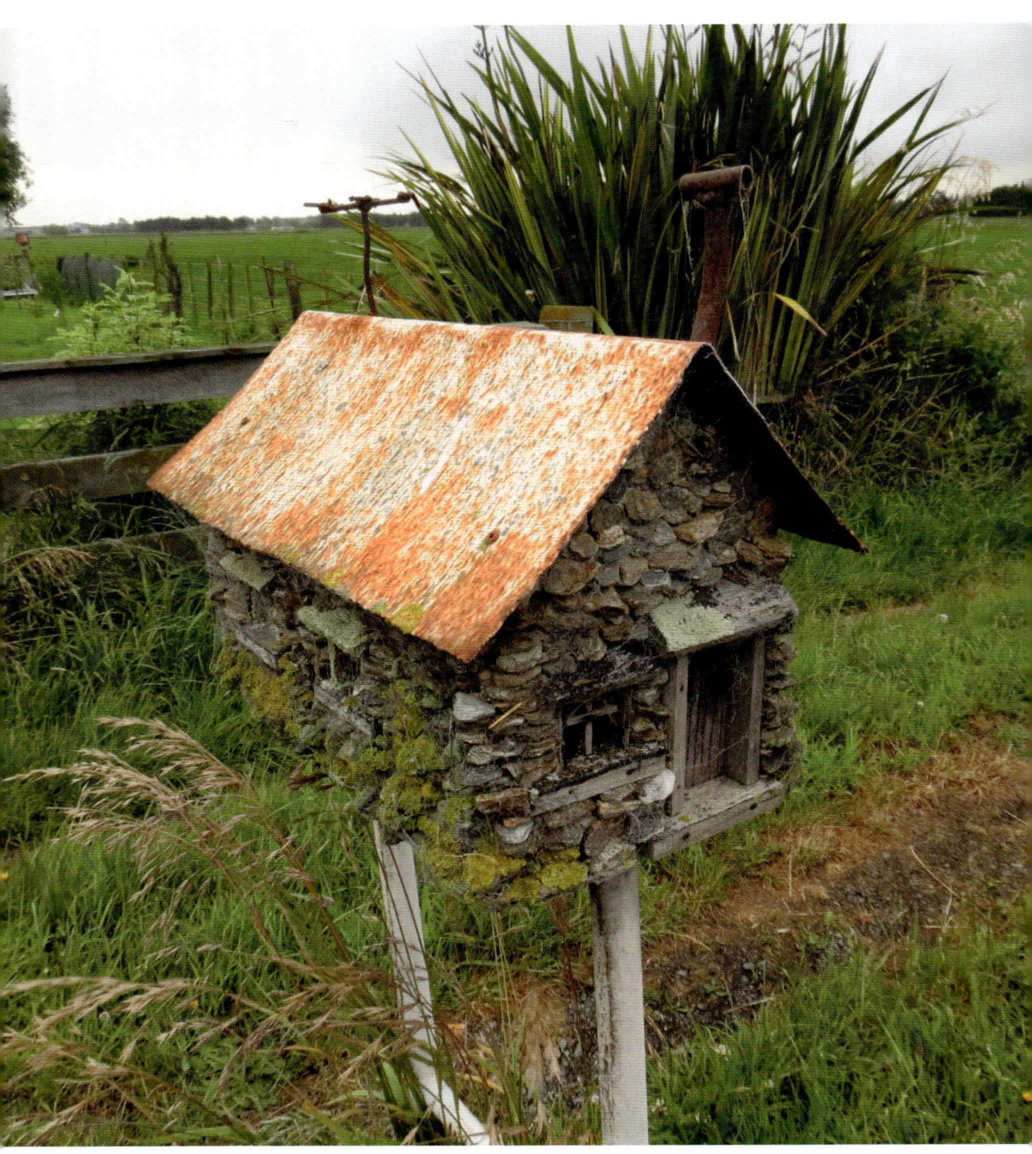

Rustic cottage charm.

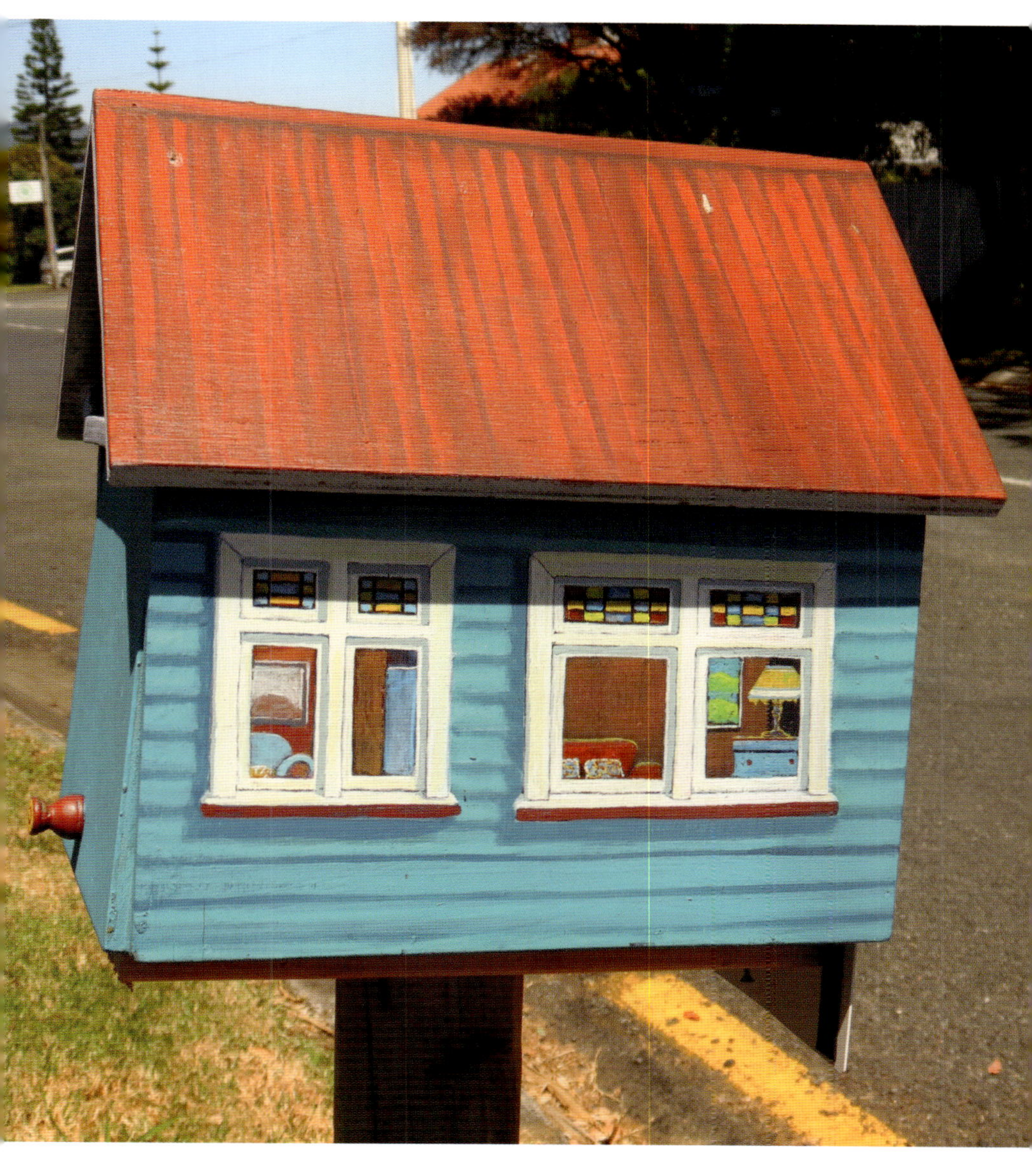

A window into their world.

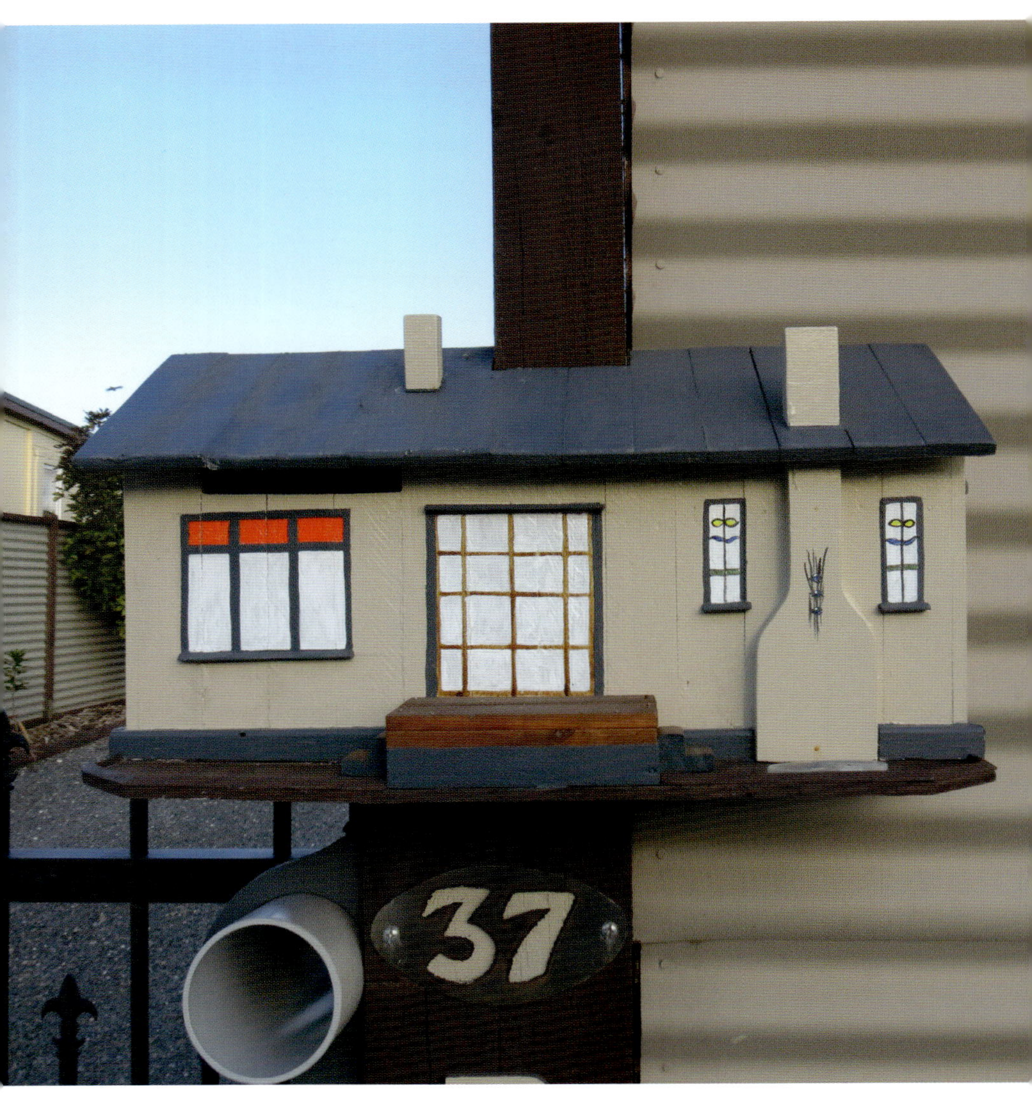

Ain’t no place like it.

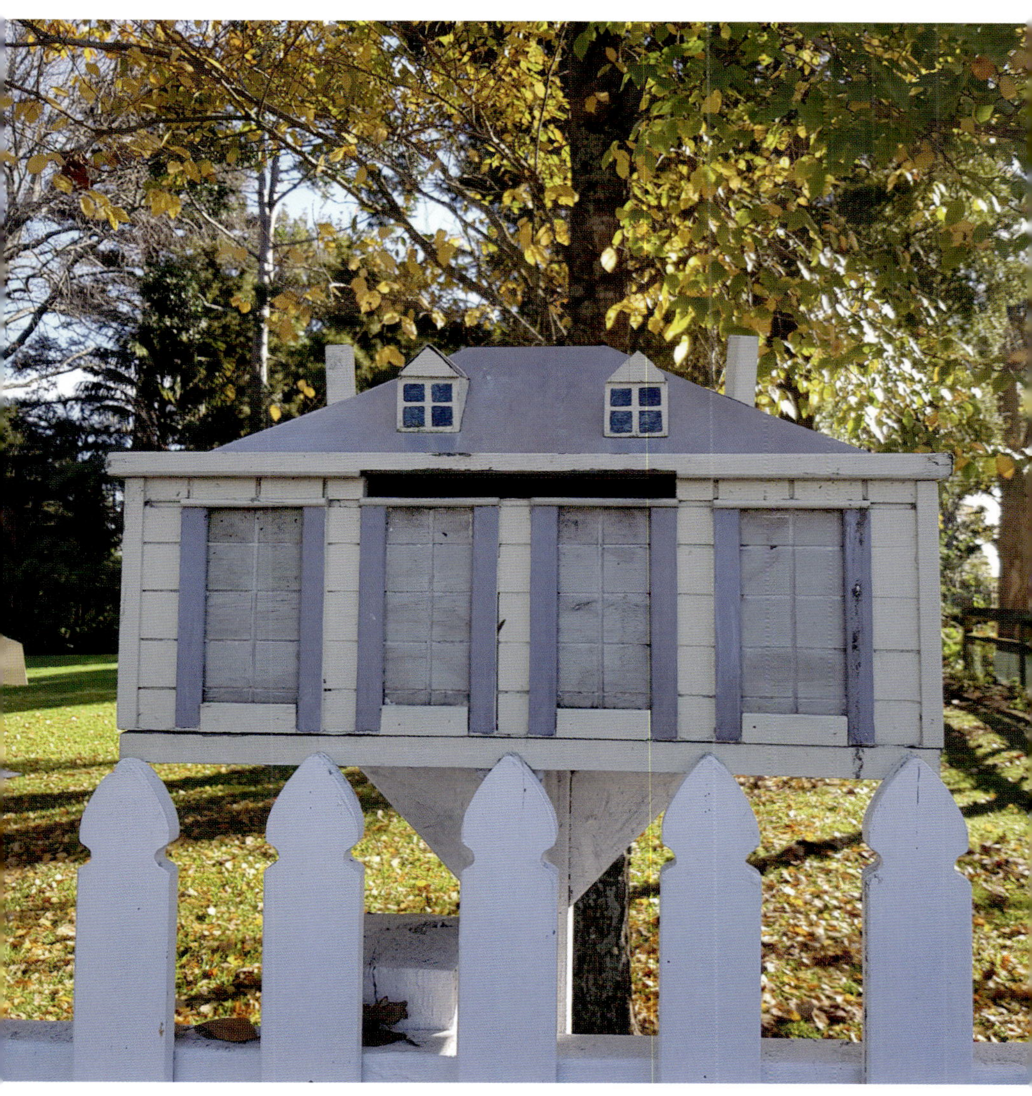

Opportunity knocks — presuming you can find the door.

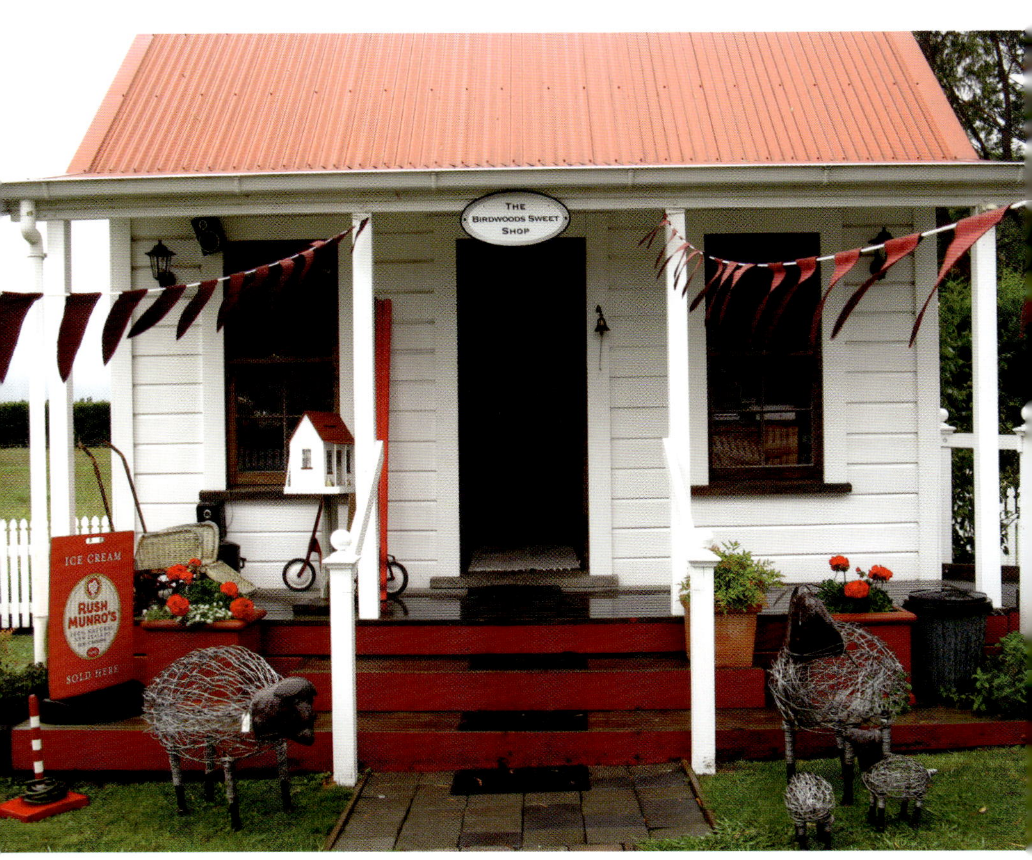

Downsizer's dream.

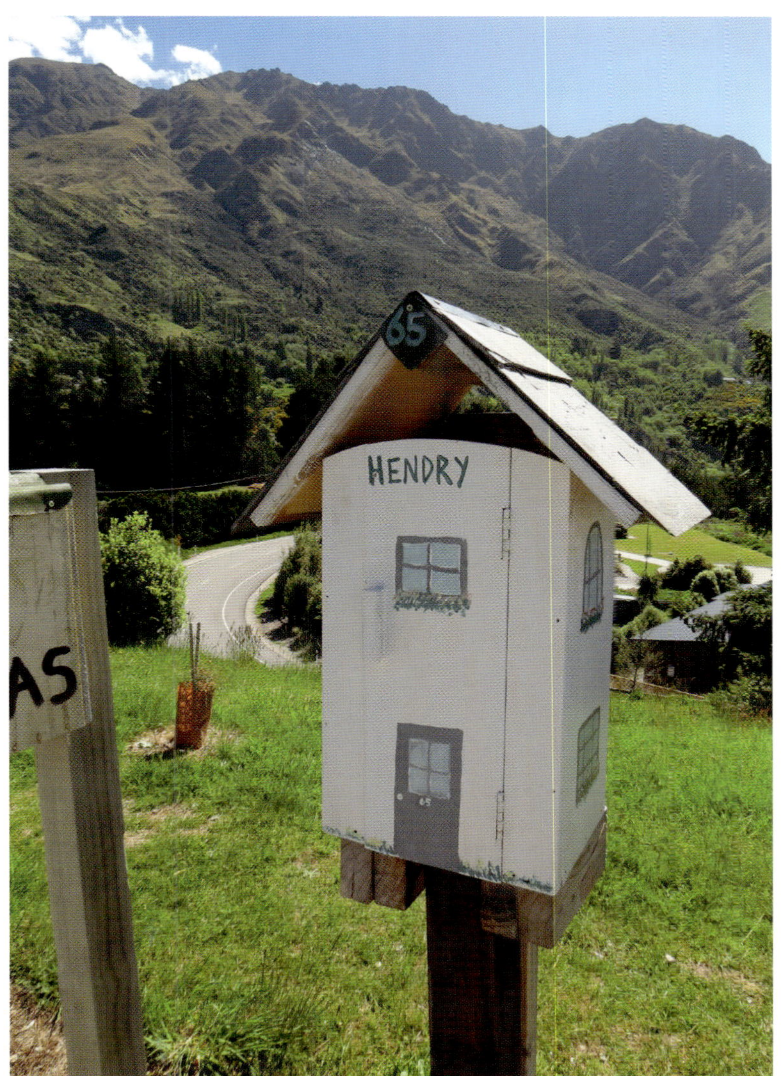

Room with a view.

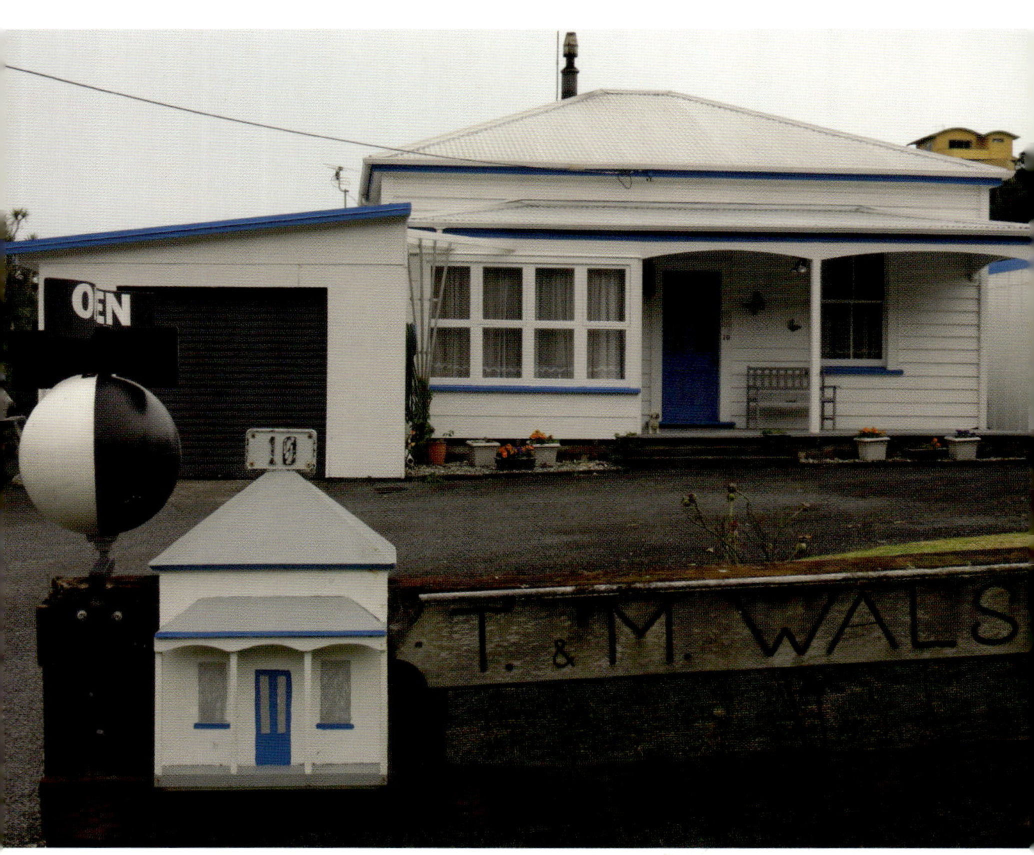

Viva la Villa.

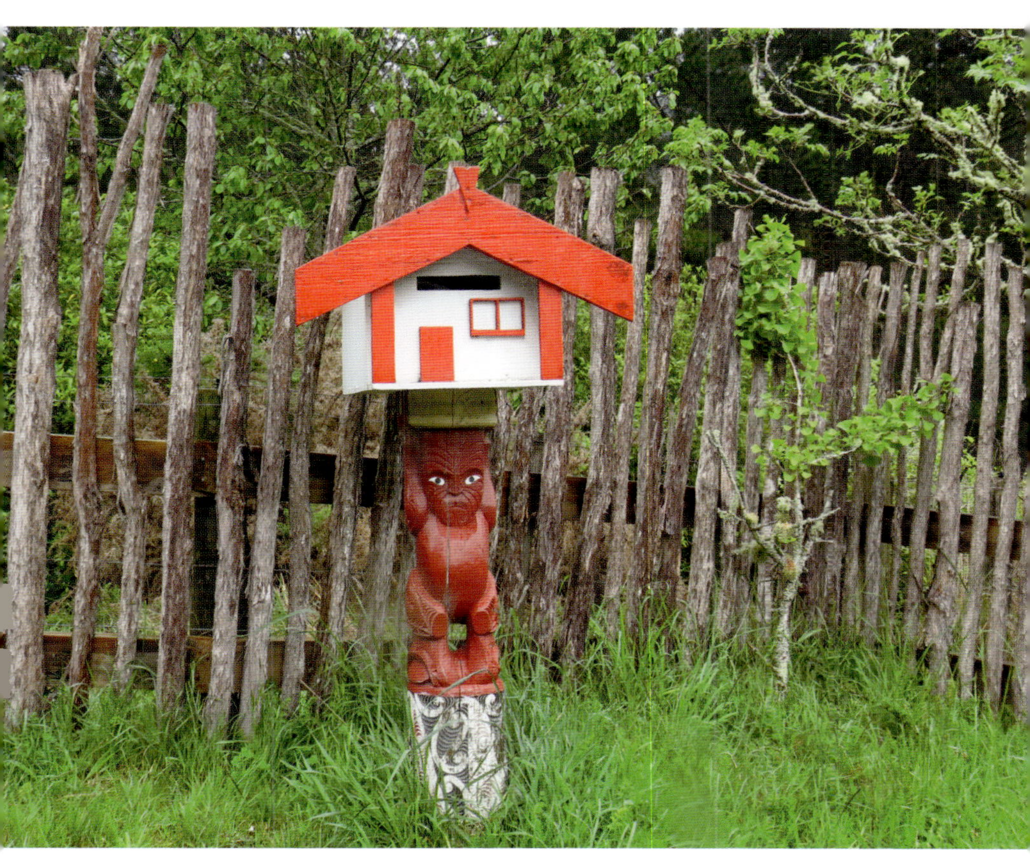

Whare Sweet Whare.

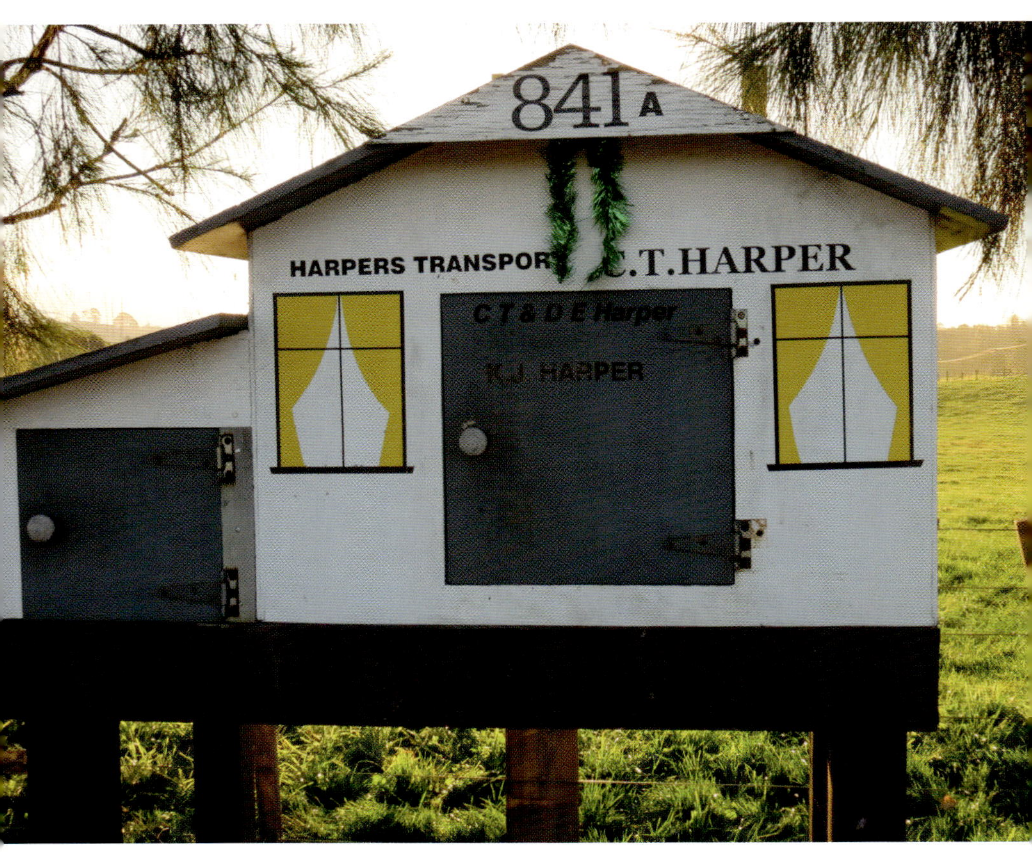

House and land package.

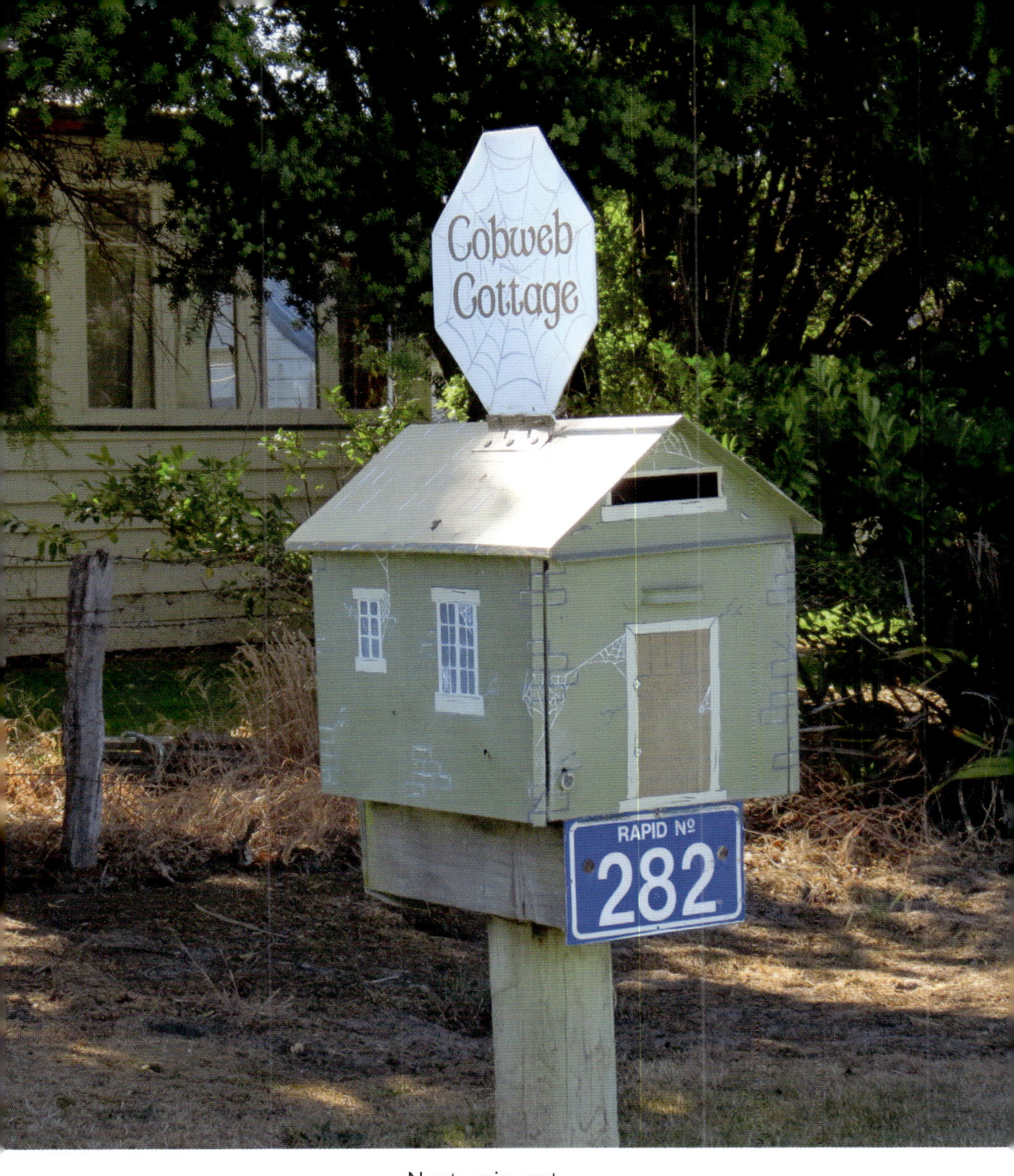

Nest or invest.

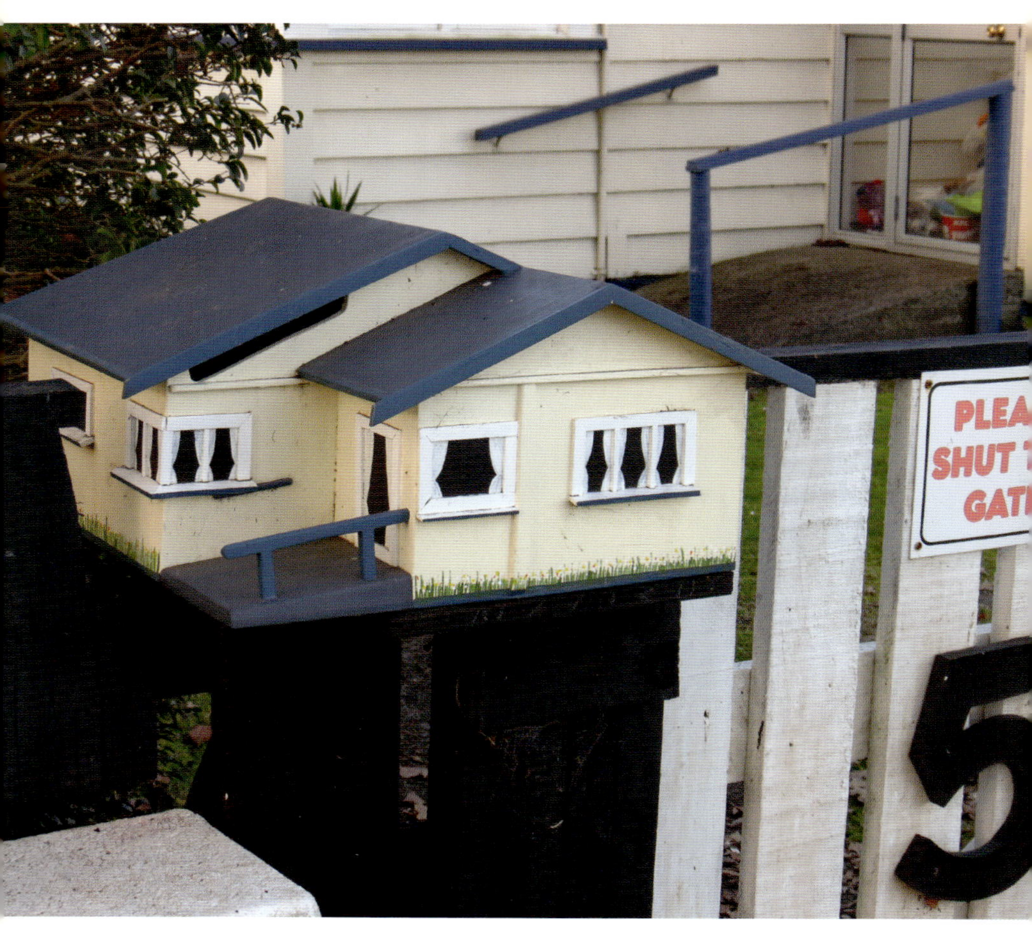

Honey, I'm shrinking the house.

IN THE KITCHEN

From fridges to breadmakers and microwave ovens, almost everything in the kitchen has the potential to be a letterbox, including the kitchen sink.

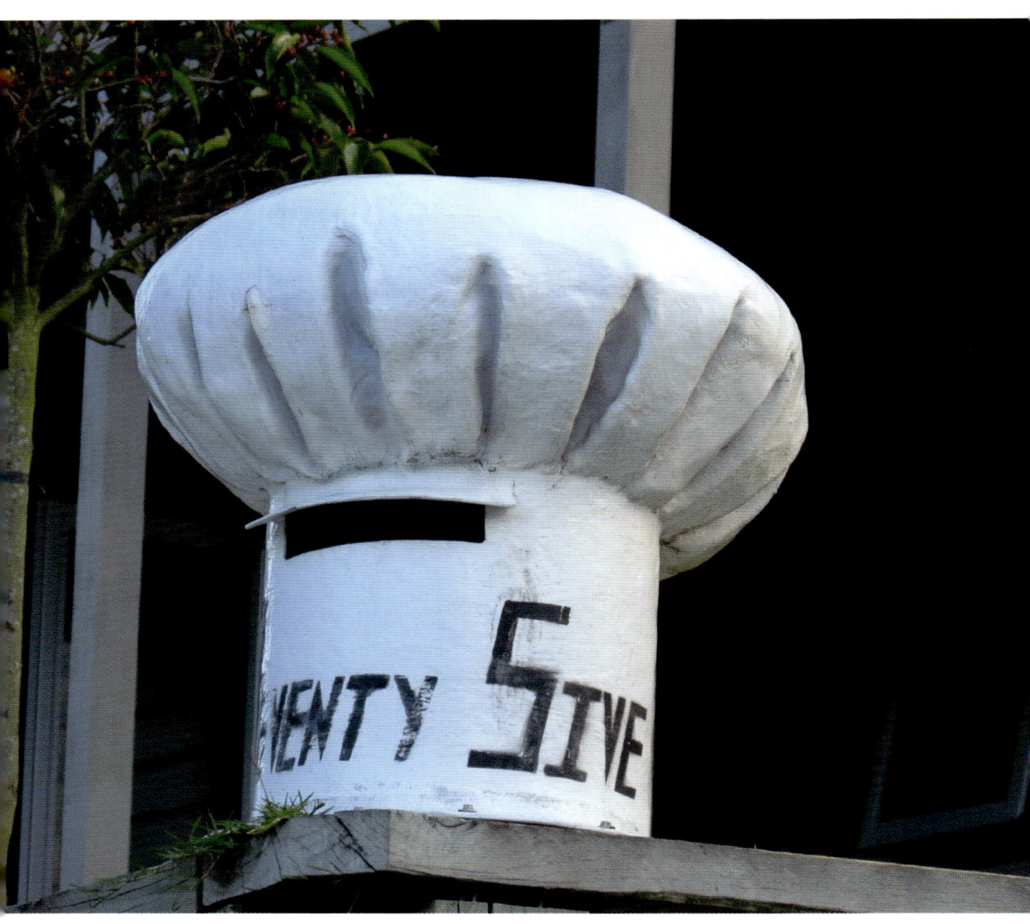

Home of a Master Chef.

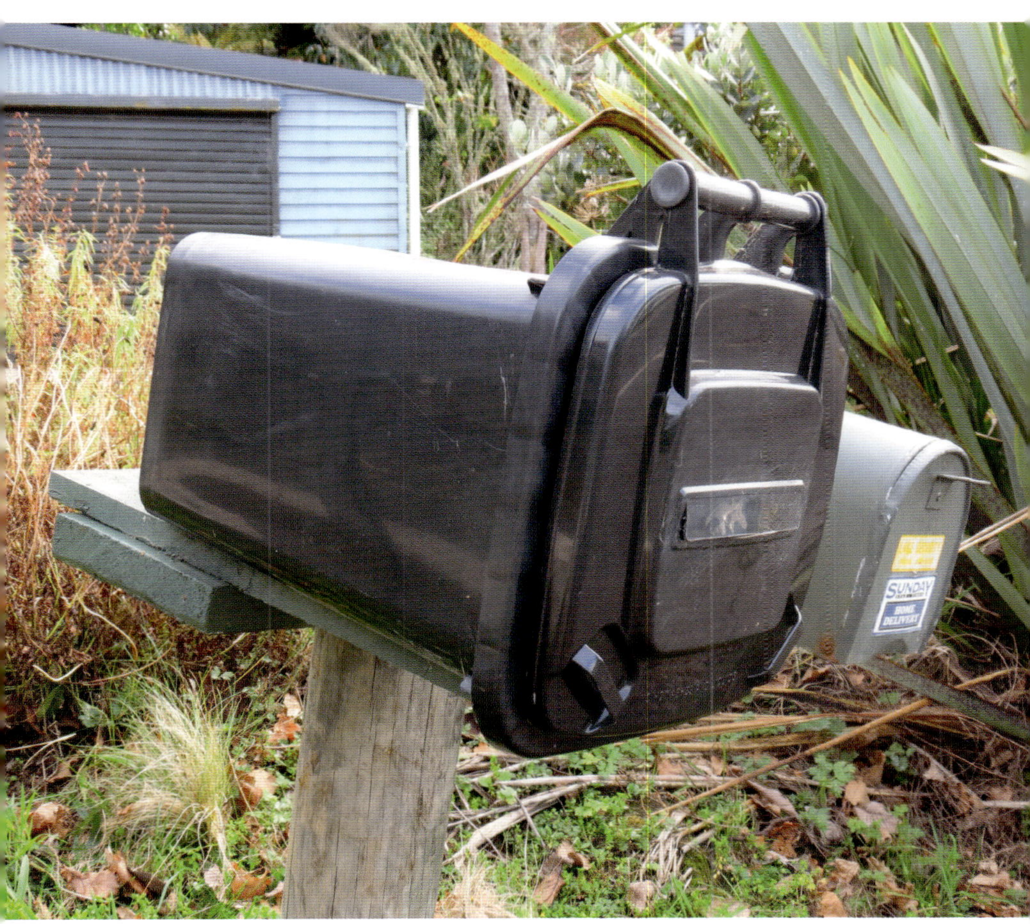

For the chef's scraps.

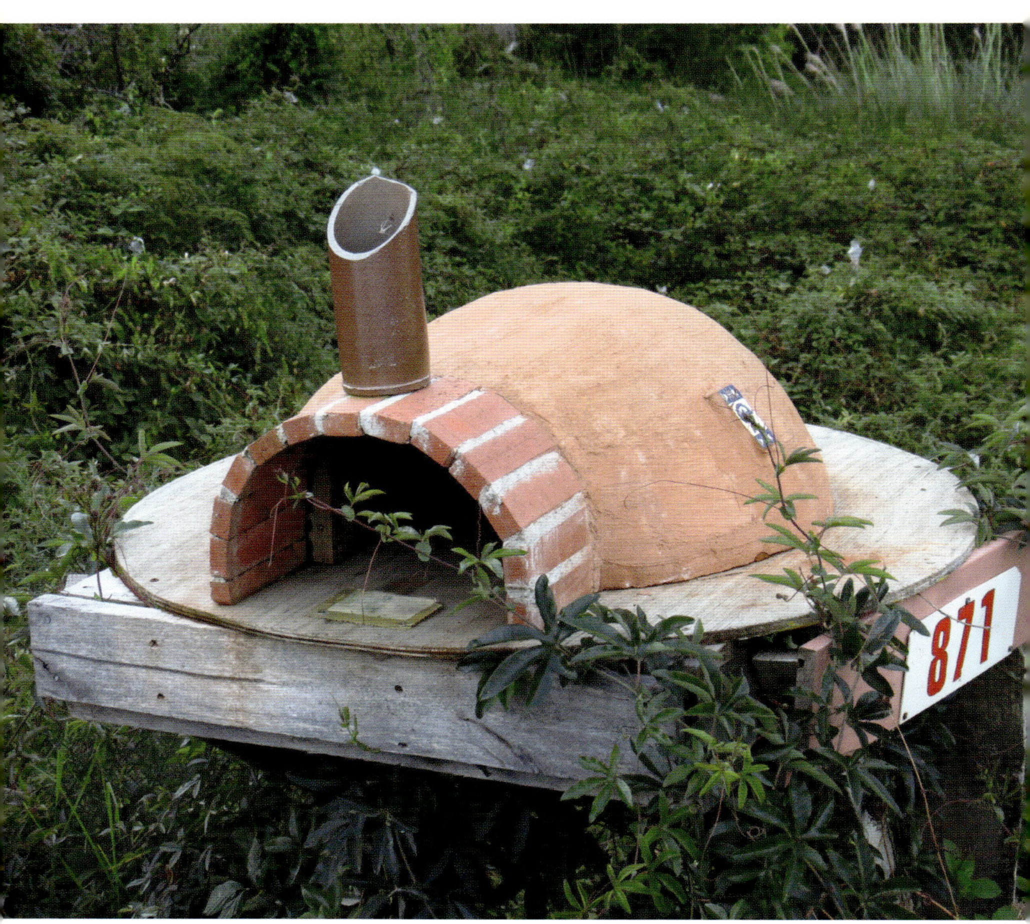

For pizza and mail deliveries?

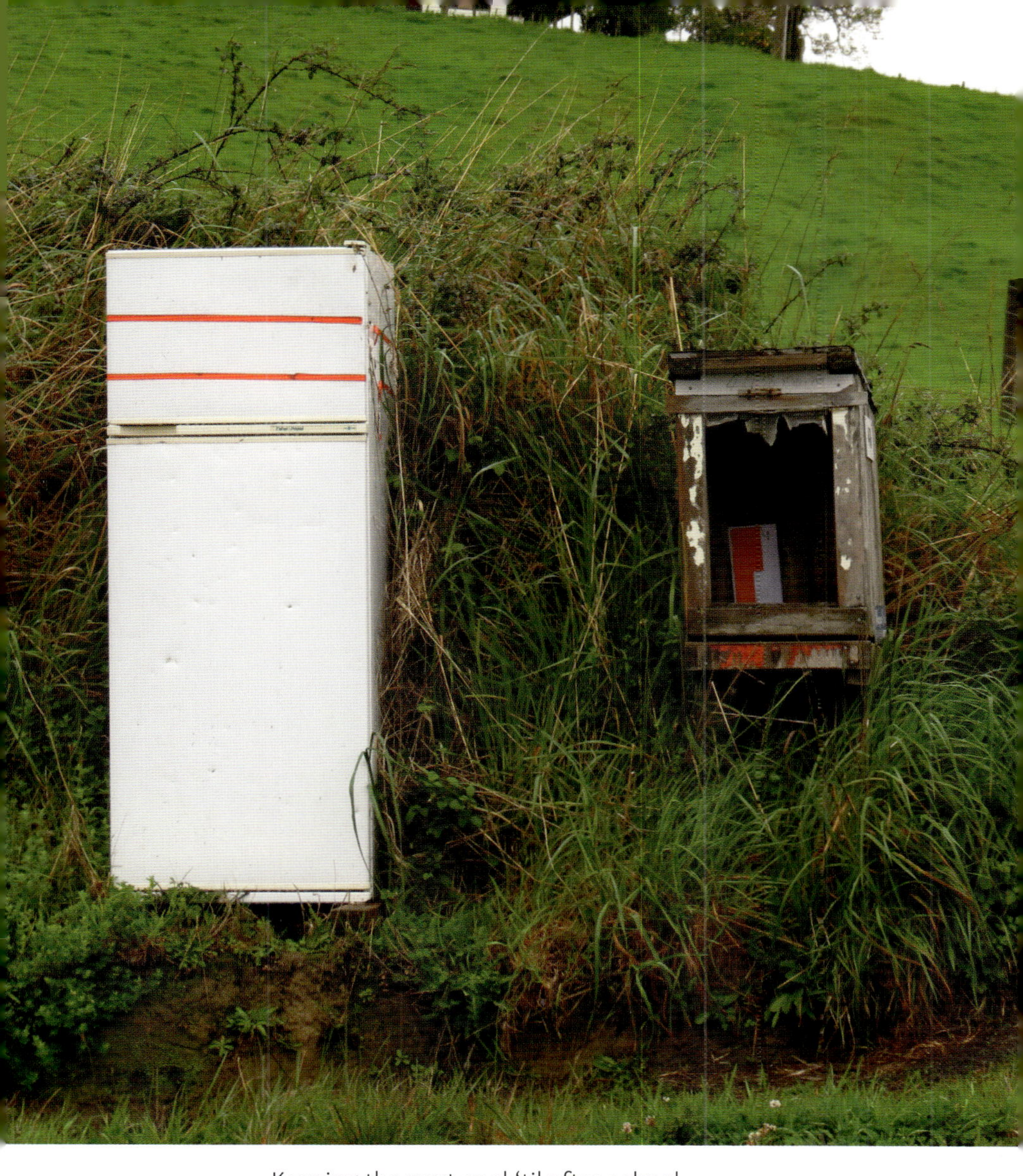

Keeping the post cool 'til after school.

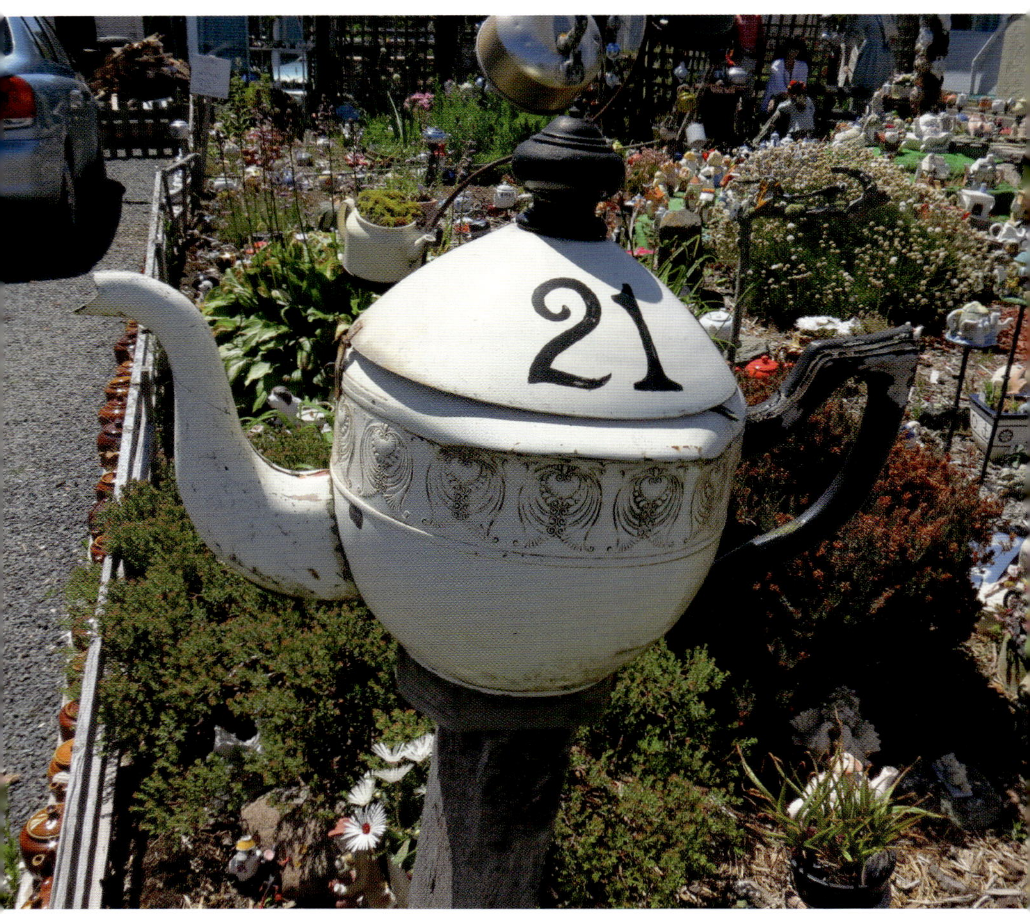

Tea for plenty more than two.

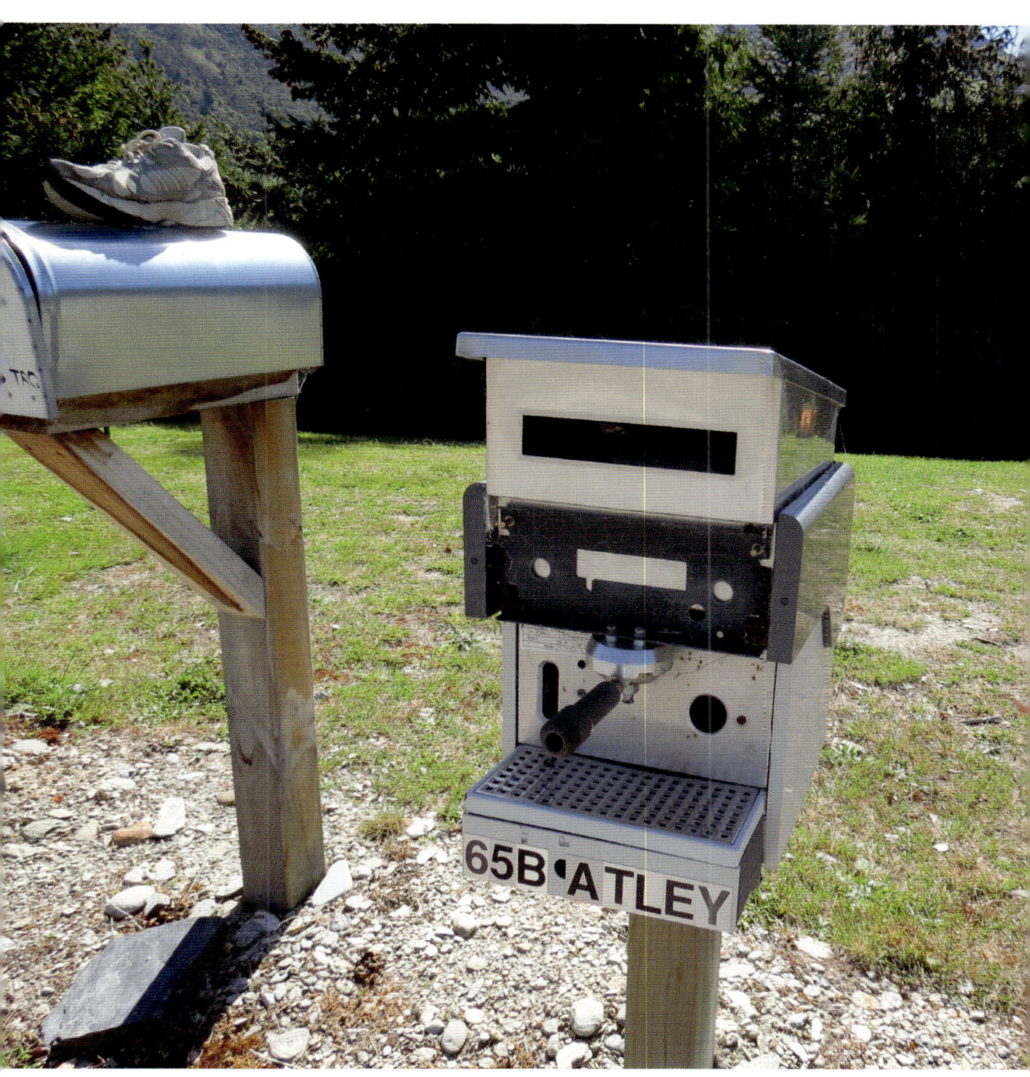

Coffee on the run.

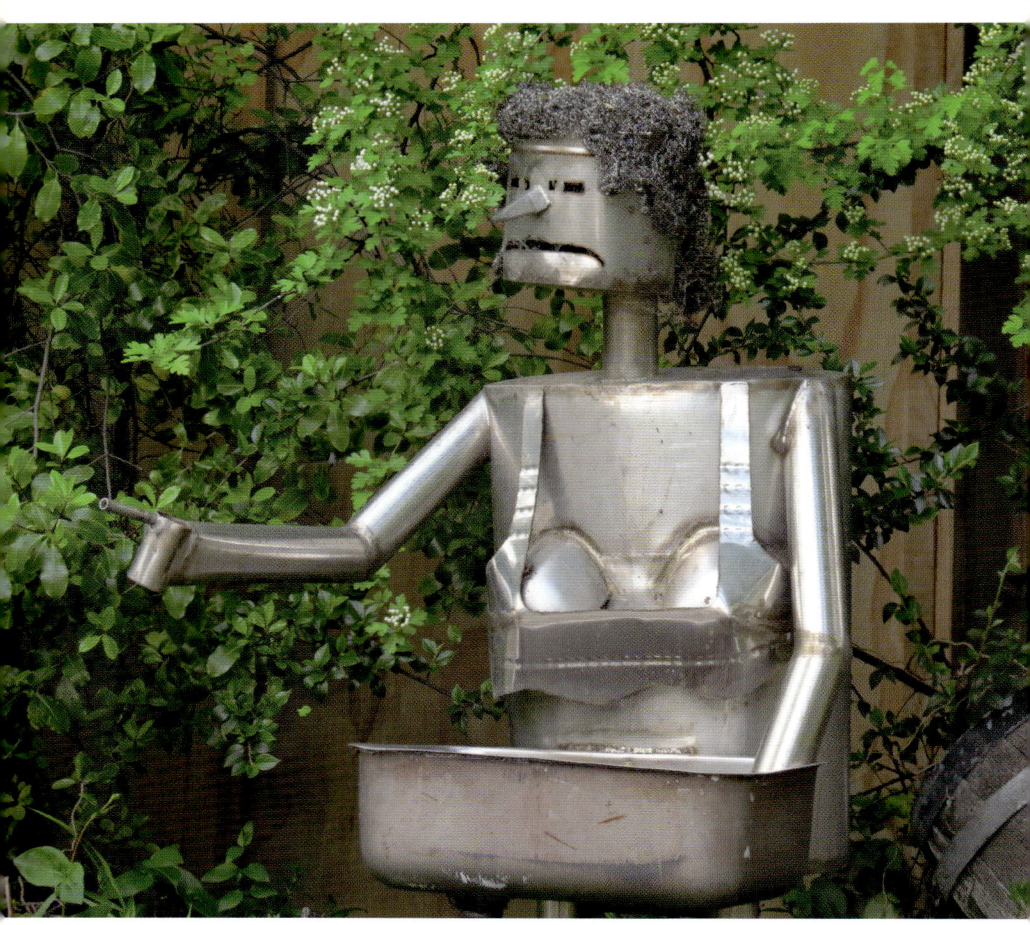

Metal maiden and the kitchen sink.

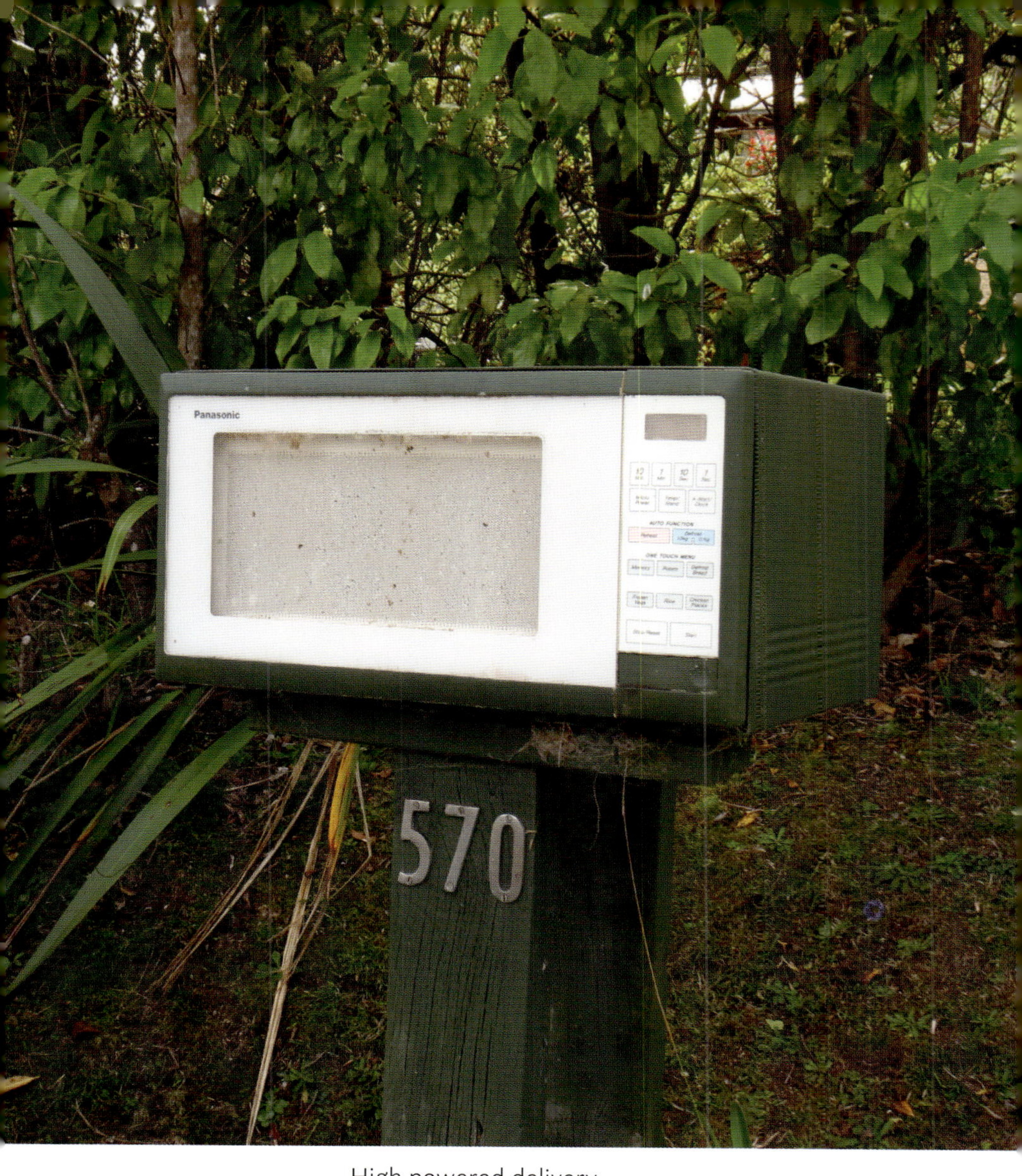

High powered delivery.

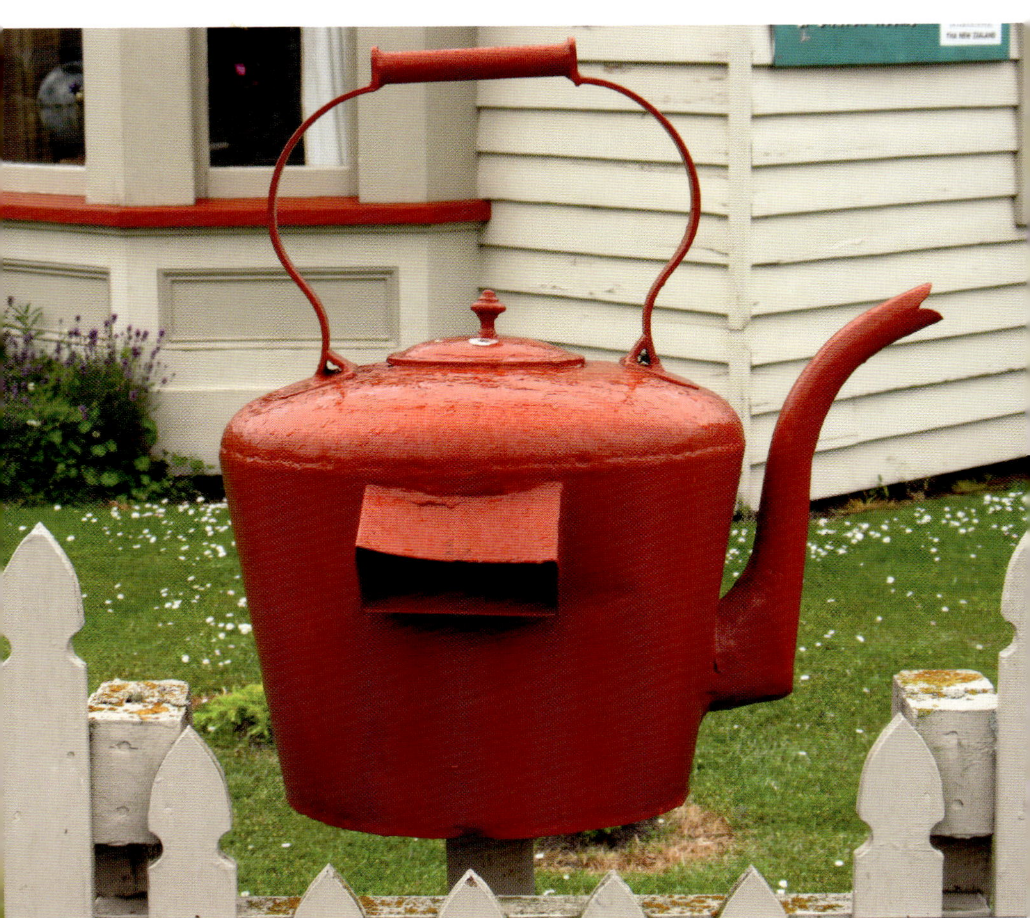

Whistle stop on the mail run.

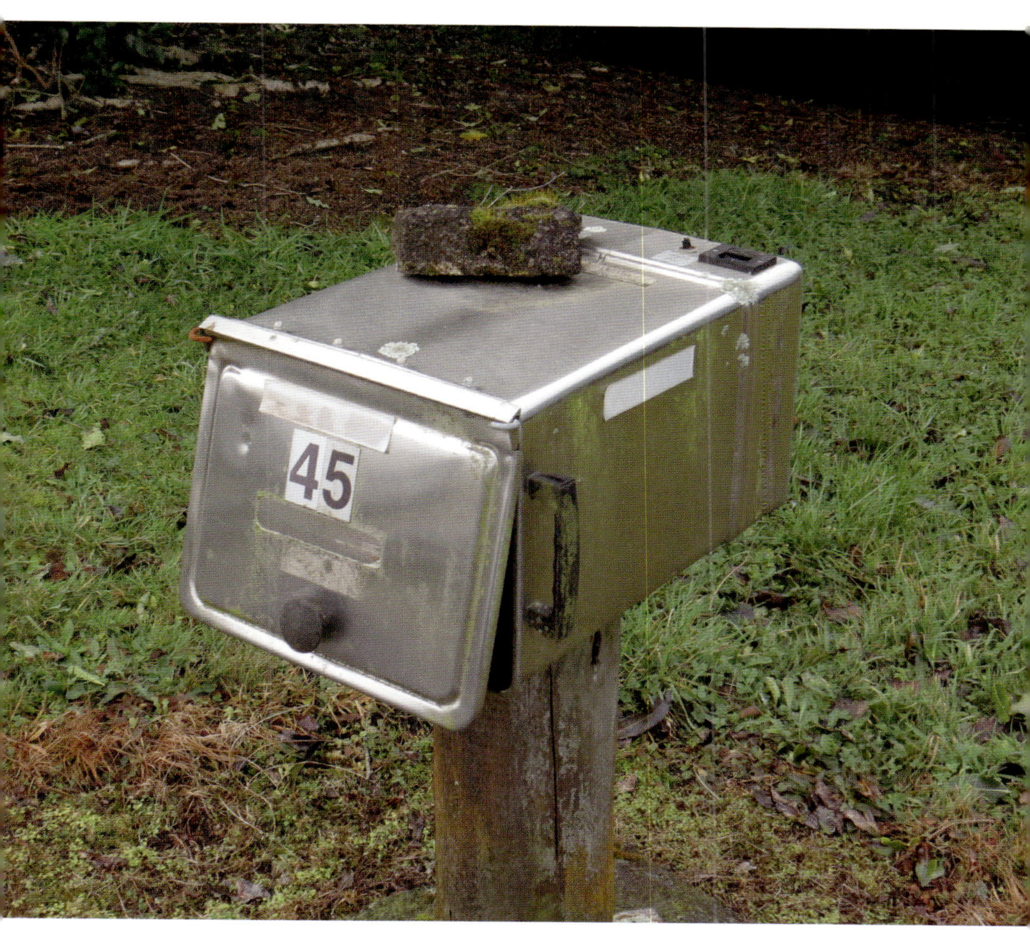

Give us this day our daily mail.

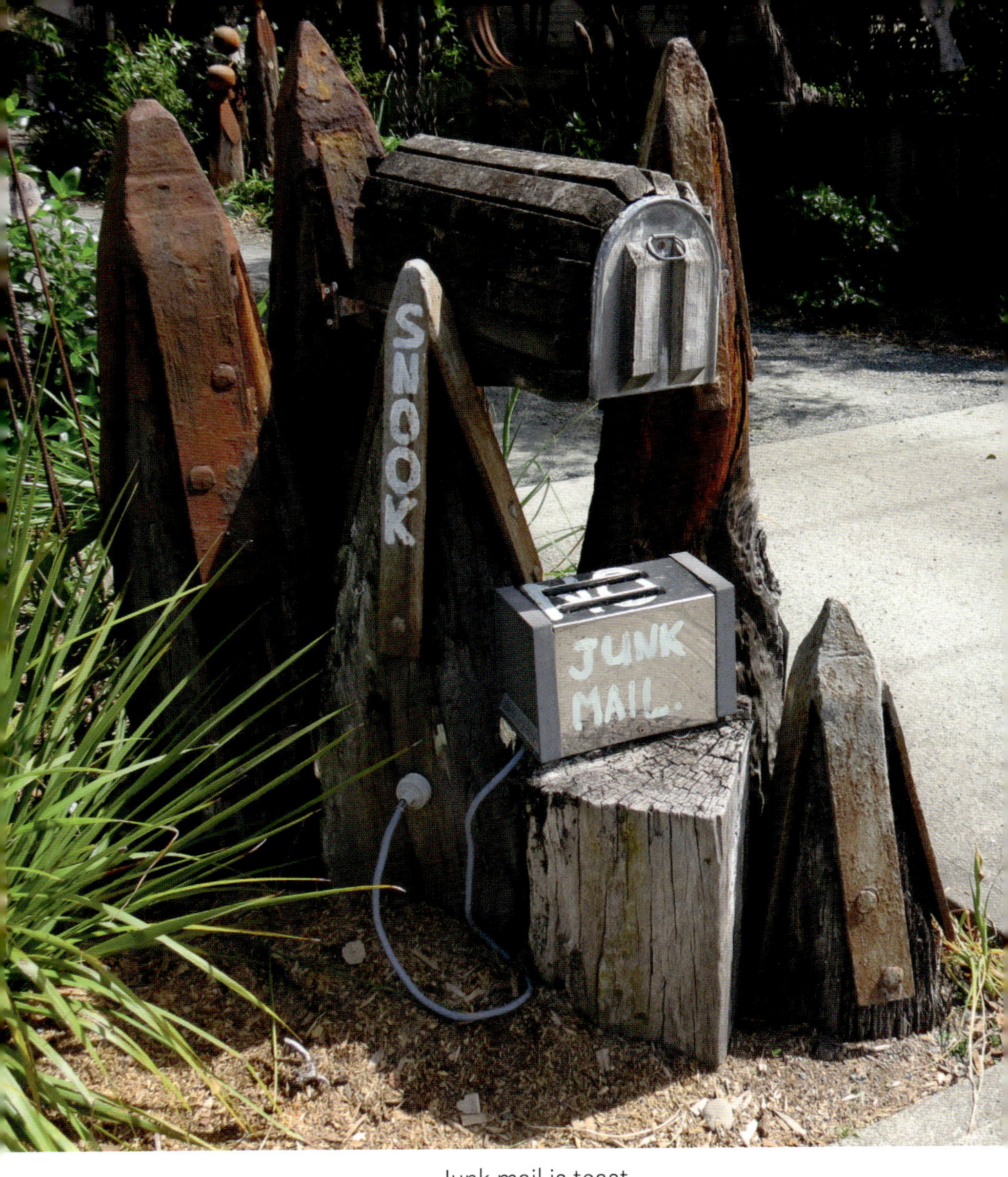

Junk mail is toast.

IN THE GARDEN

The traditional 'Kiwi quarter acre section' with its vegetable patch and flower gardens may be making way for more densely populated neighbourhoods, but Kiwis are still keen gardeners.

These garden-themed letterboxes give a green thumbs up to celebrating gardens and all that thrive within them.

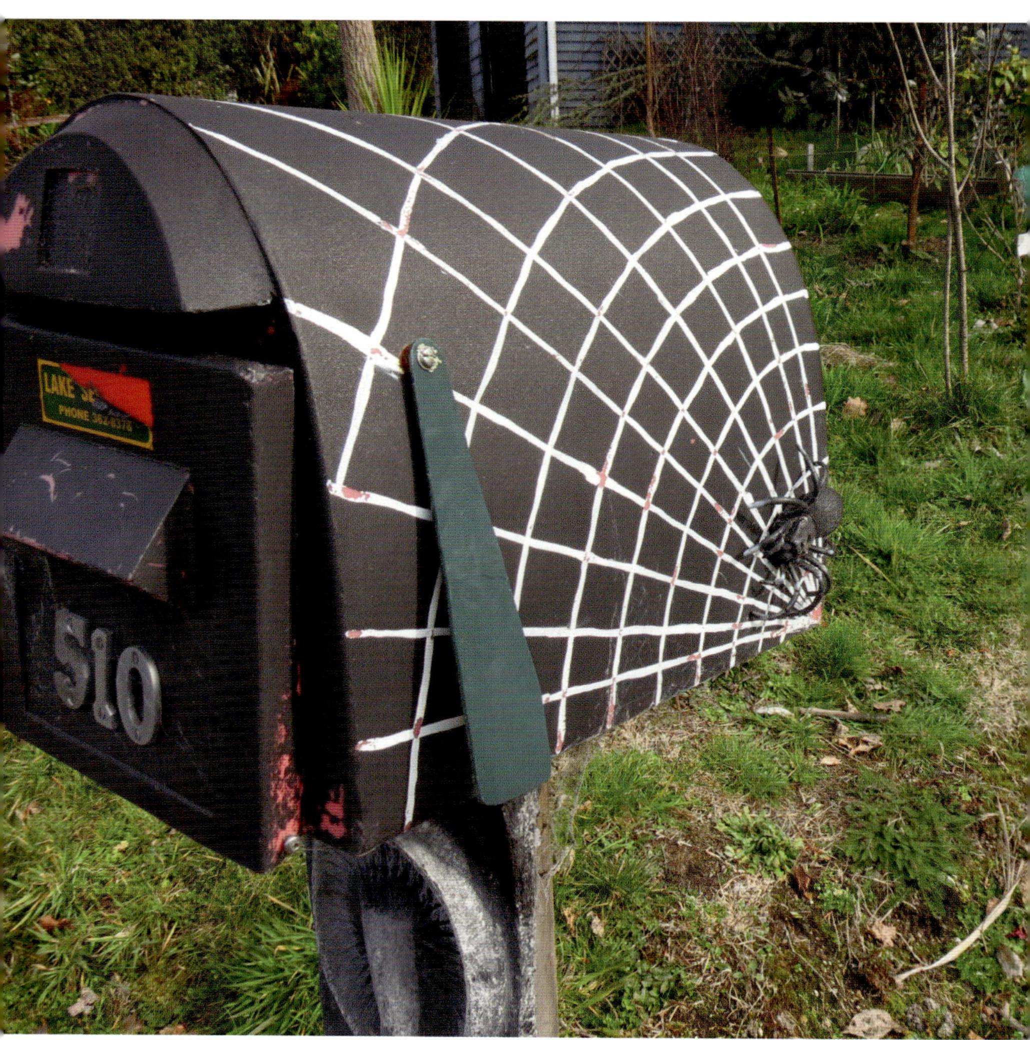

It's been a while between deliveries.

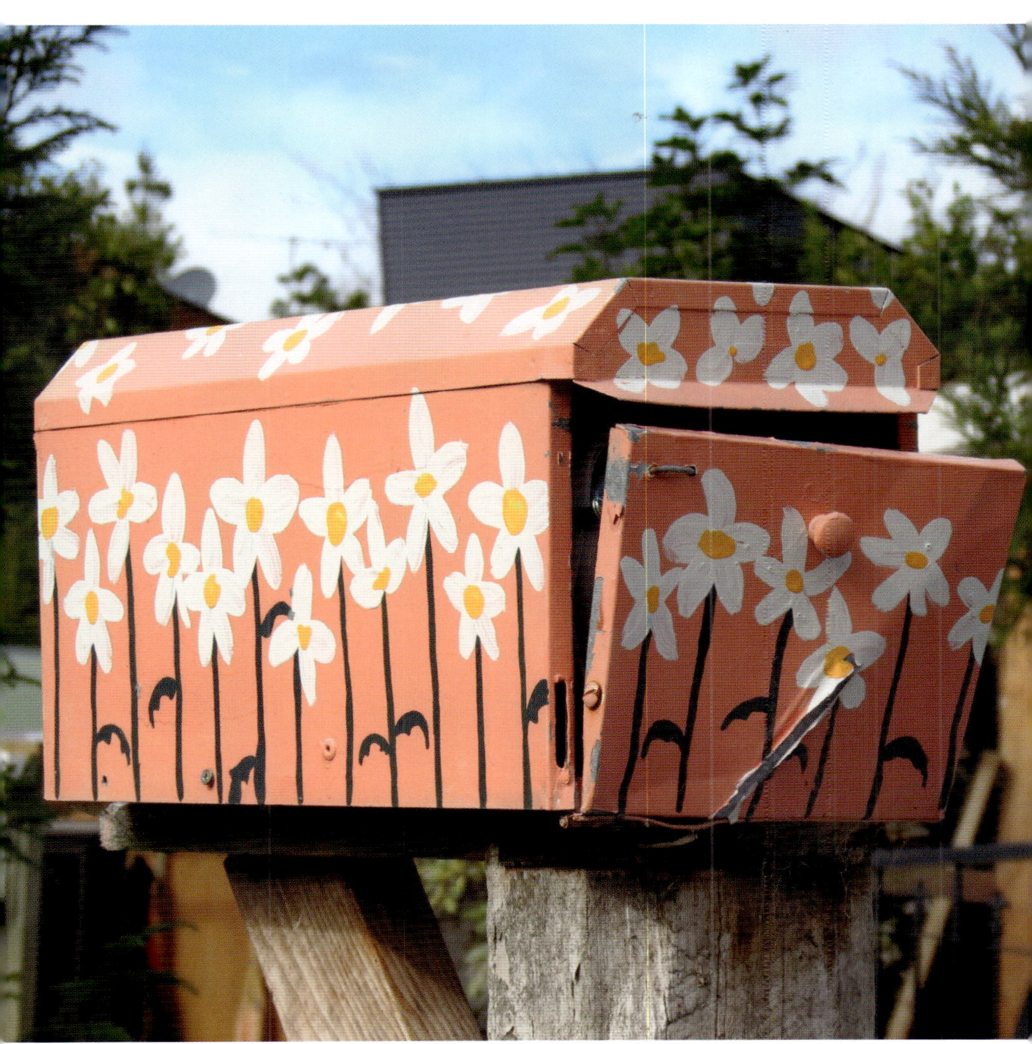

'Daisy, Daisy, send me your answer, do.'

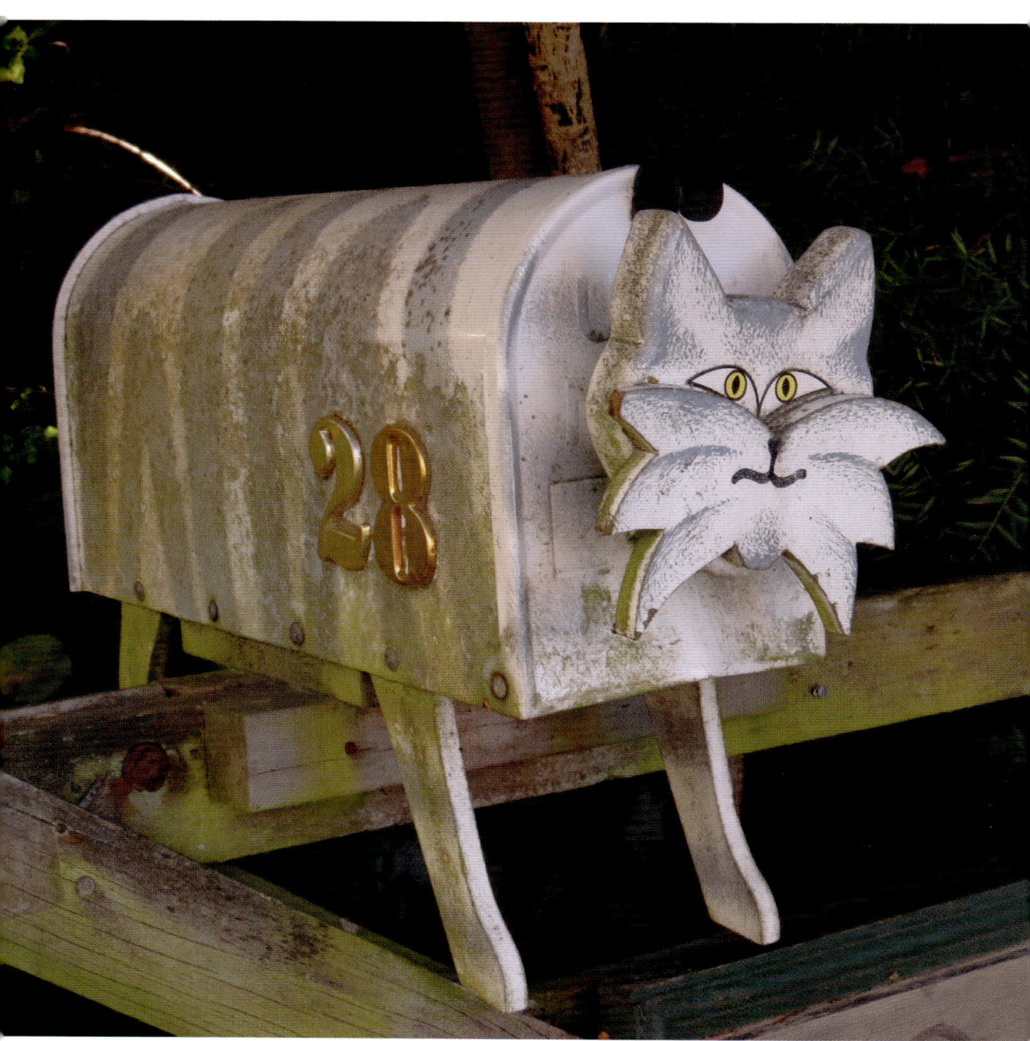

Purrfect place for the post.

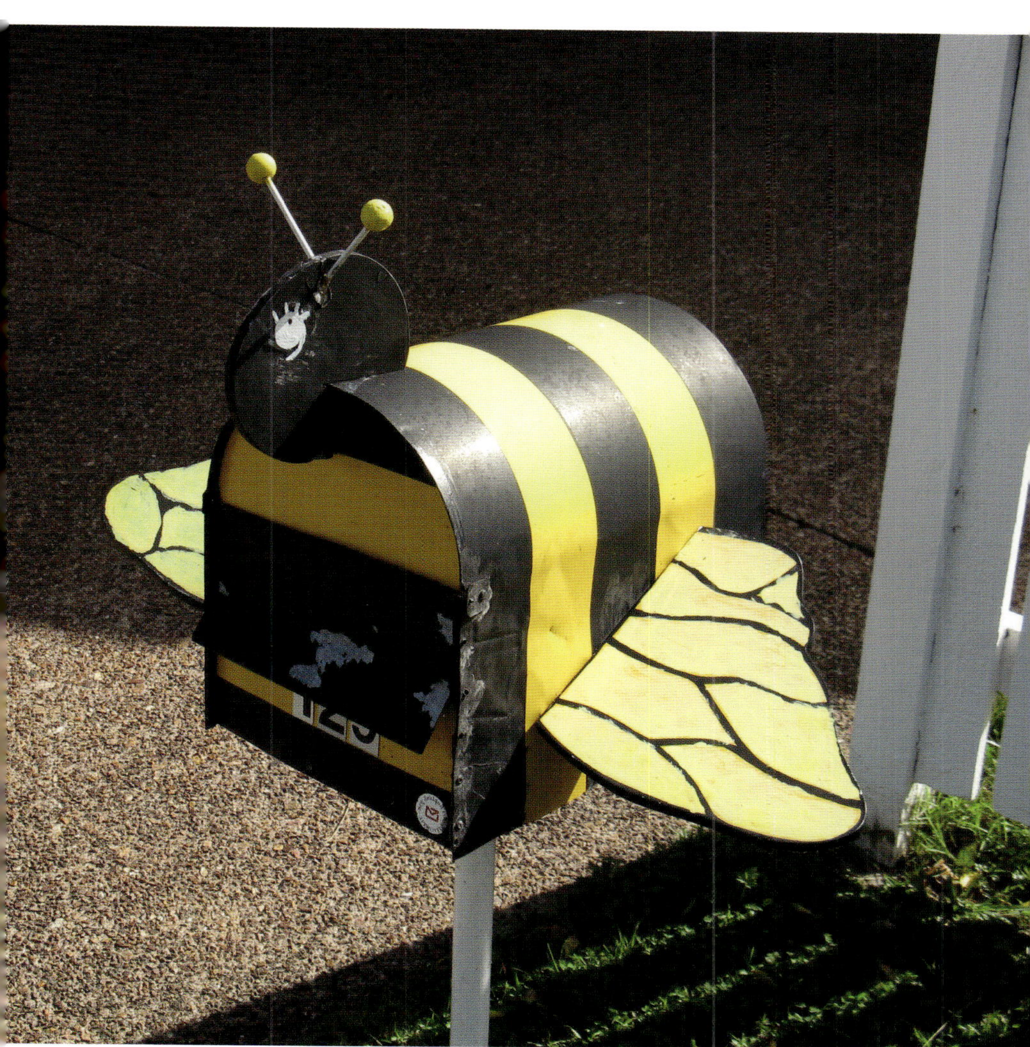

Abuzz with good news.

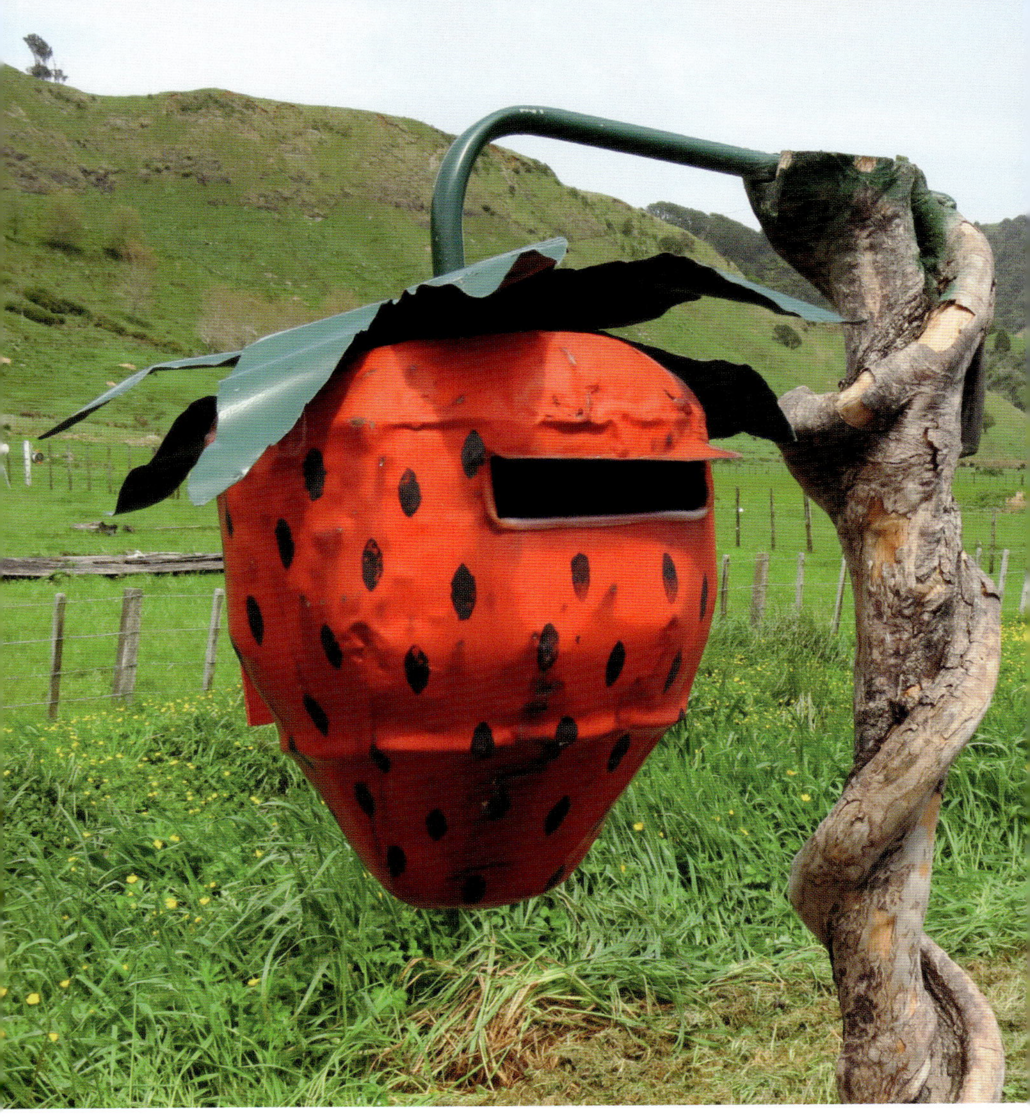

Pick me, postie.

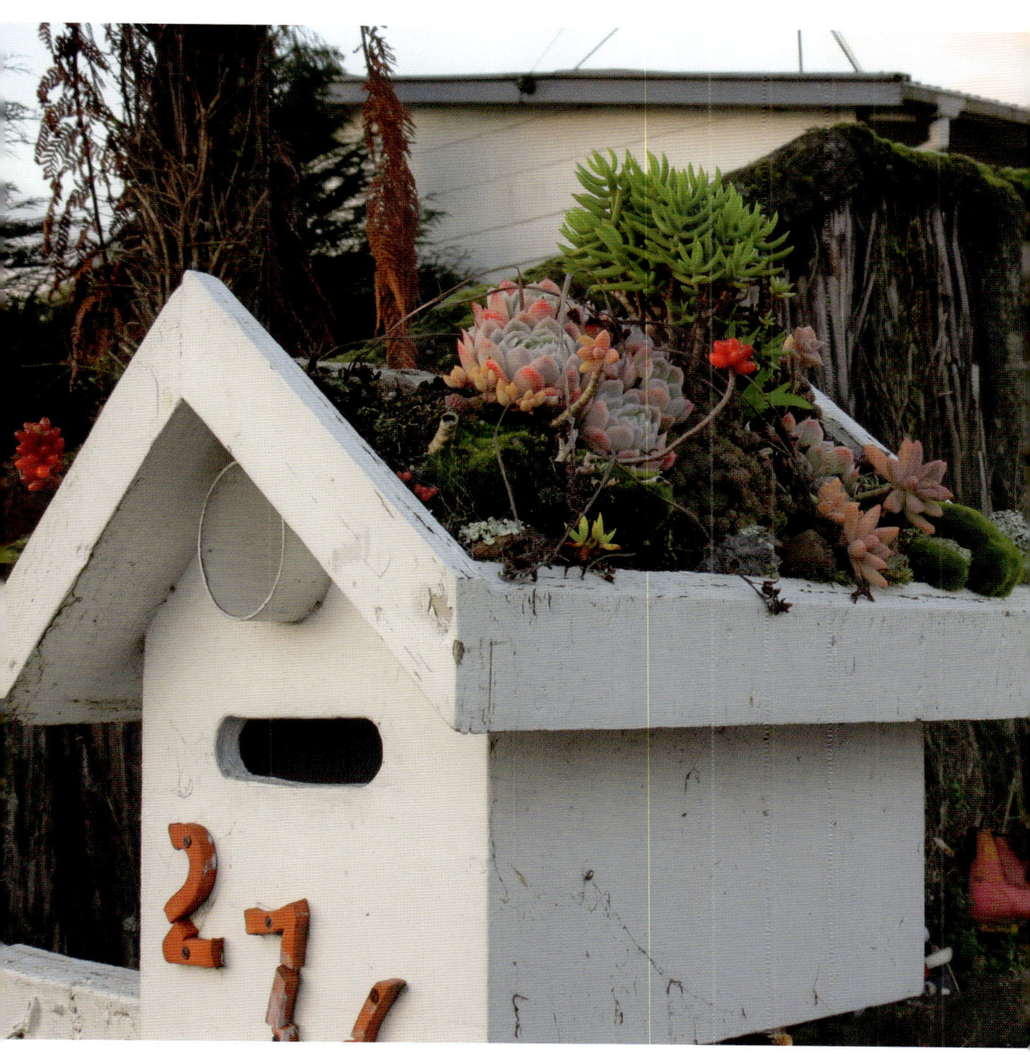

Bloom where you're planted.

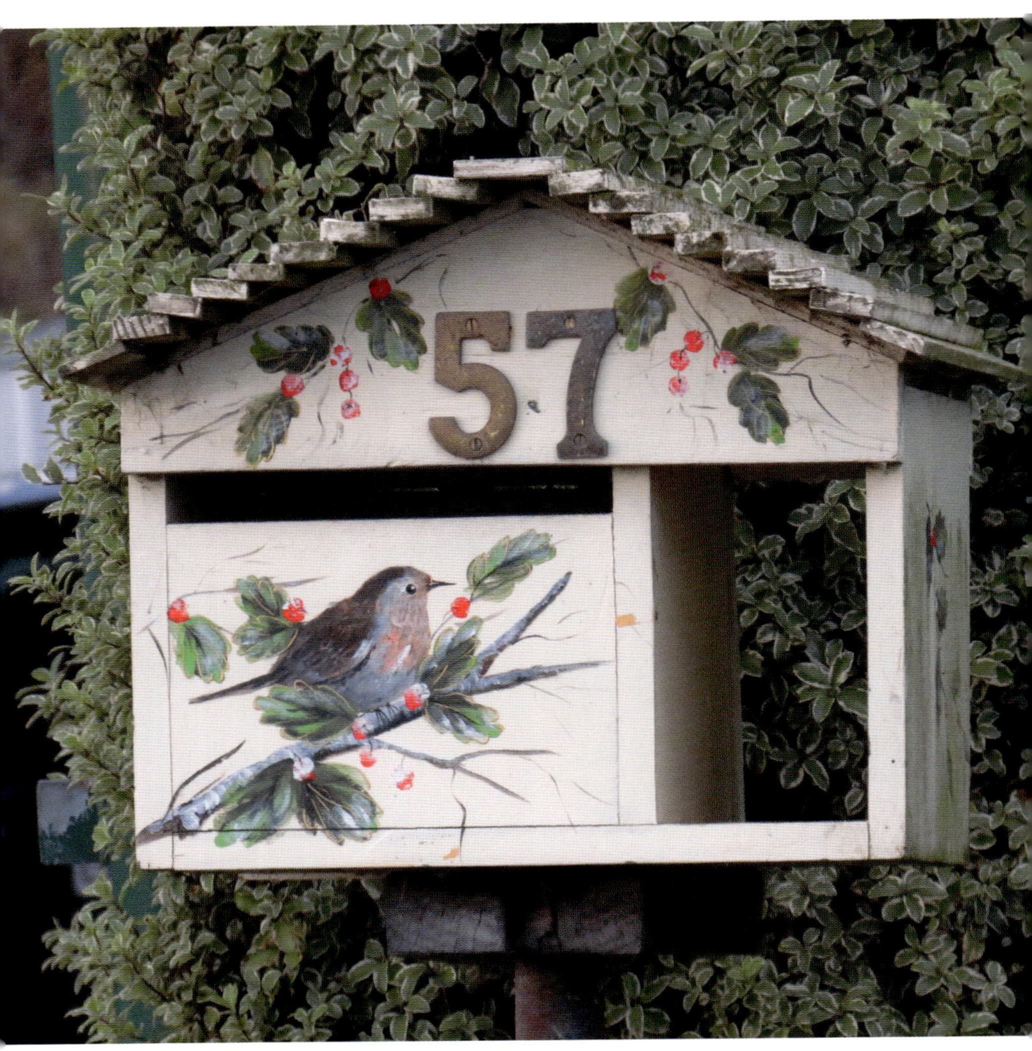

My best mate works for pigeon post.

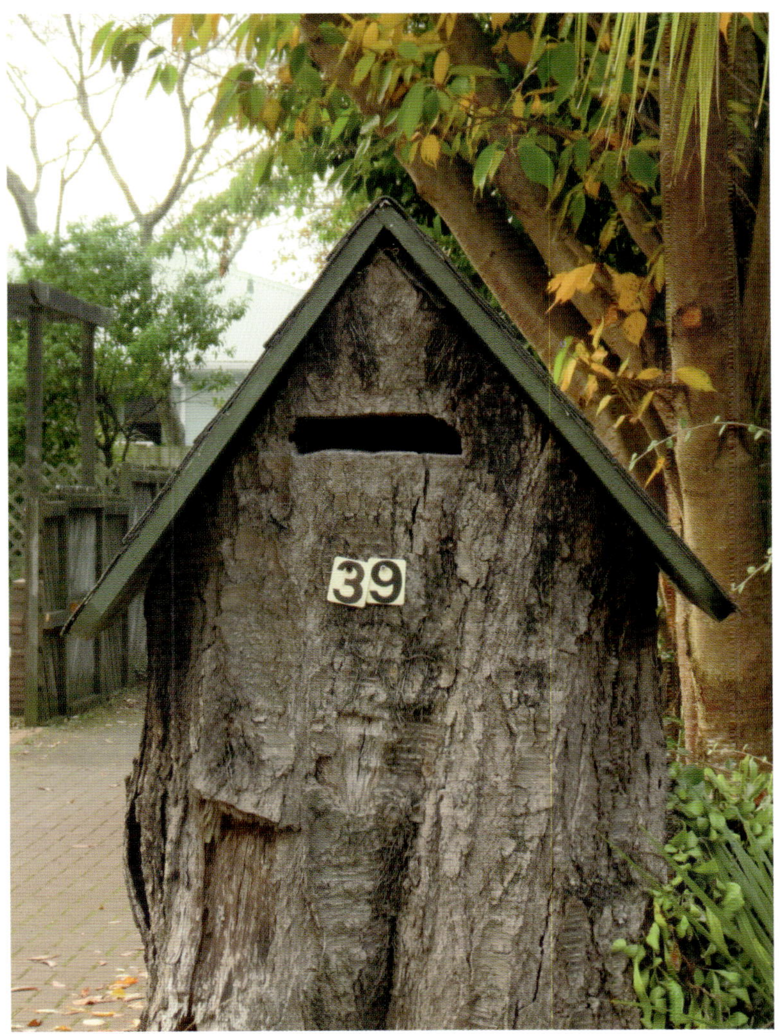

Stumping up with a sturdy letterbox.

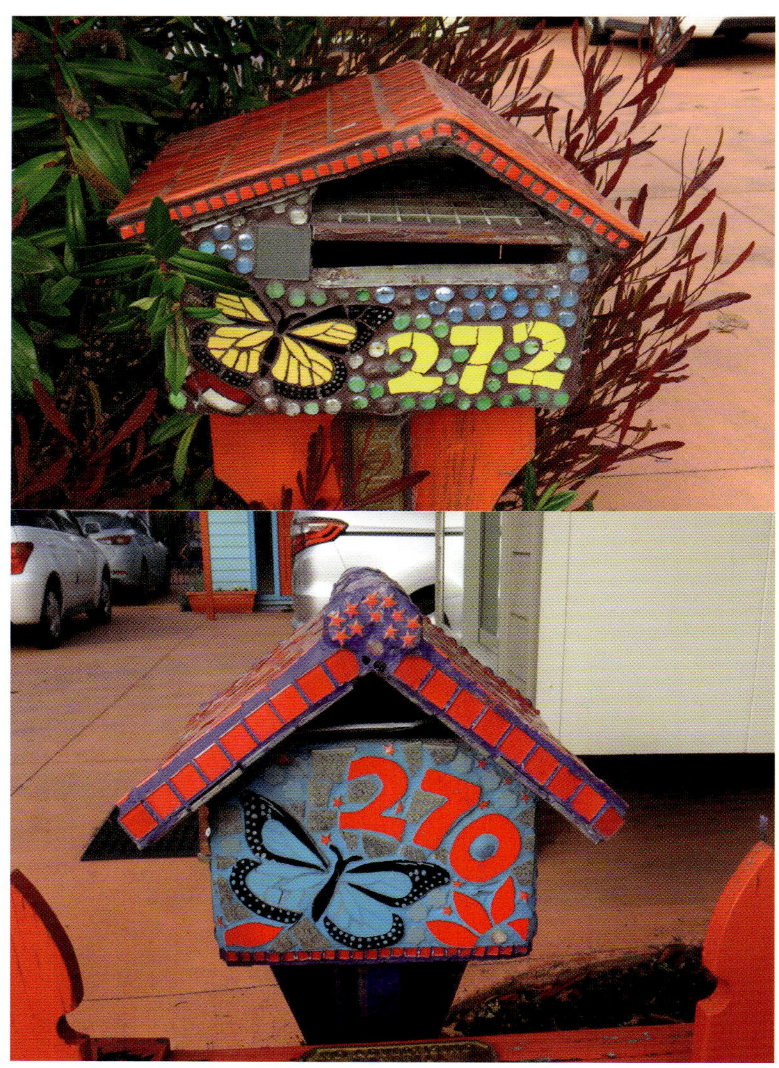

Mail drop courtesy of the Postman Butterfly.

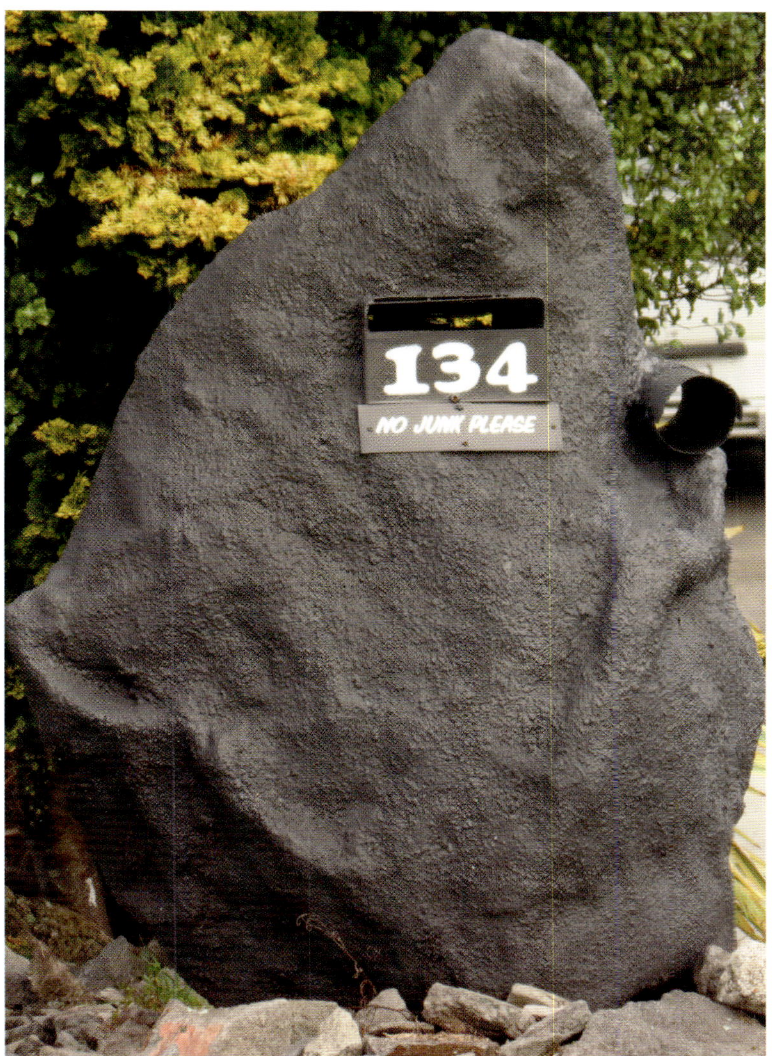

Rock on, postie.

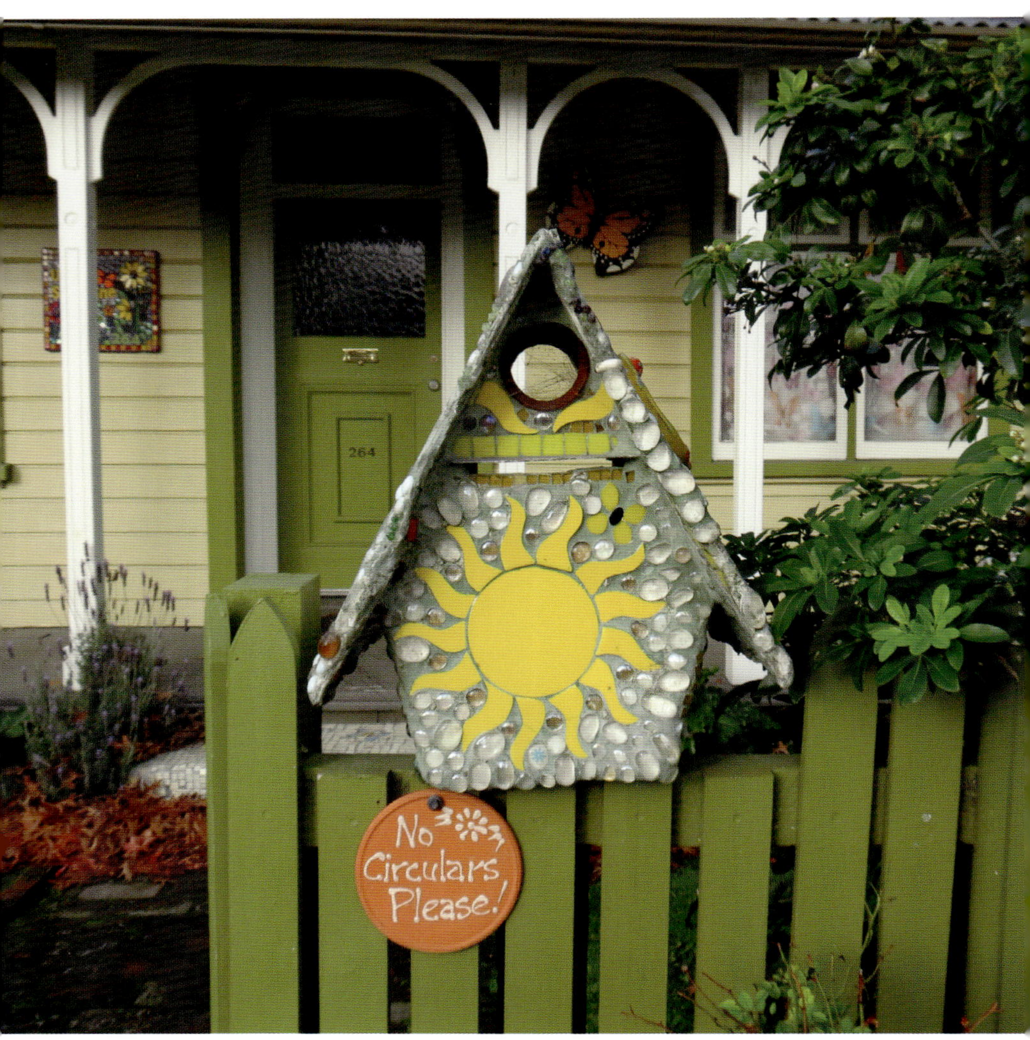

Here comes the sun.

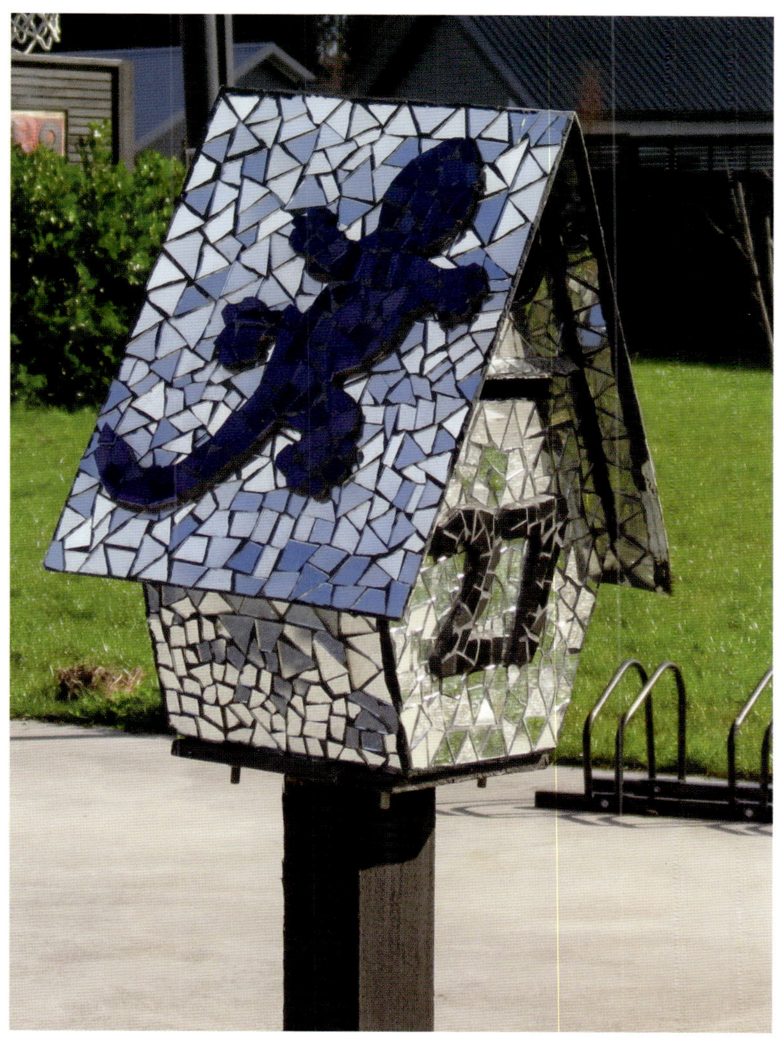

Flat out like a lizard.

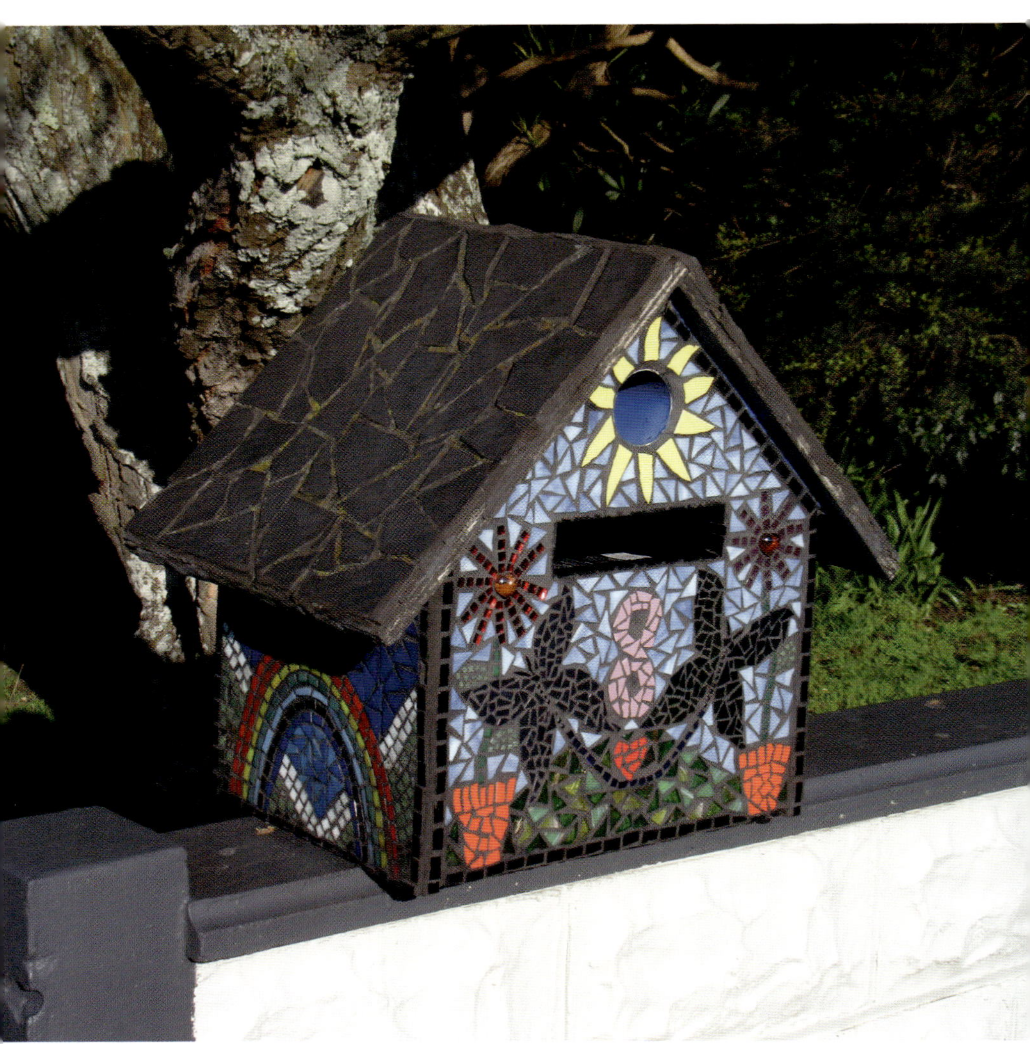

Solar-powered flowers at number 8.

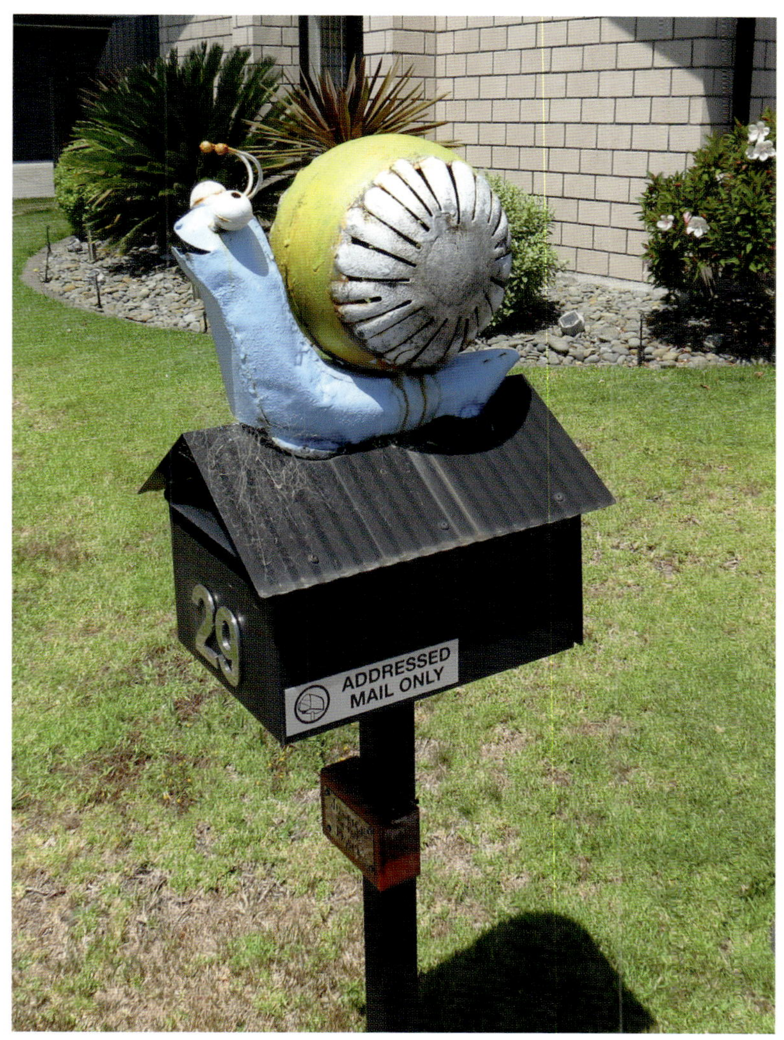

Snail mail.

TIKI TOUR

Why travel the short route when you can take the long way round, or as we Kiwis call it, a tiki tour.

The first official 'Tiki Tours' hit the road in 1946 and were low-cost bus tours run by the New Zealand Government Tourist Bureau. Initially Tiki Tours were based around staying at government-owned hotels, but by 1966 the network expanded, and Tiki Tours could take you around the whole country.

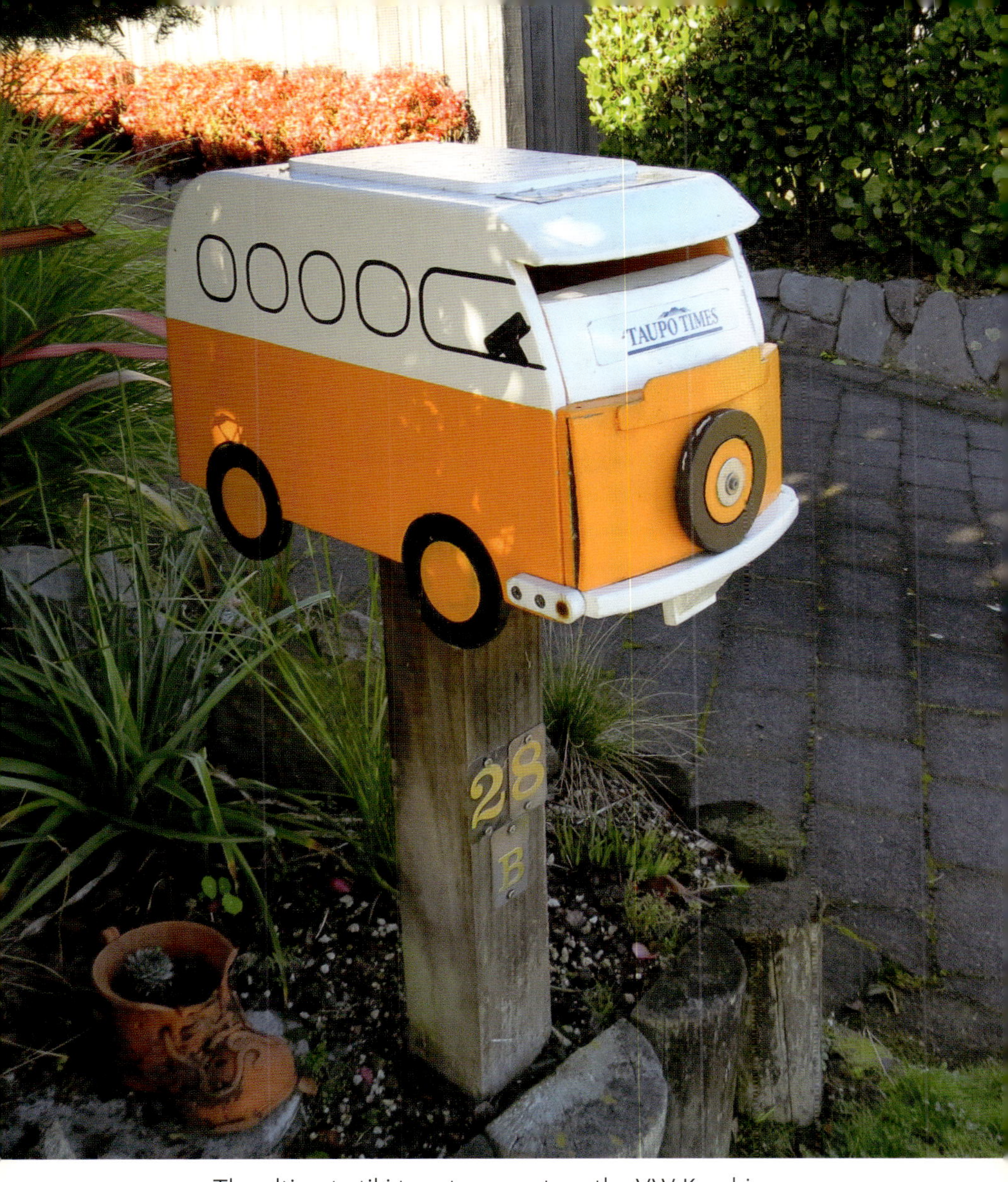

The ultimate tiki tour transport — the VW Kombi.

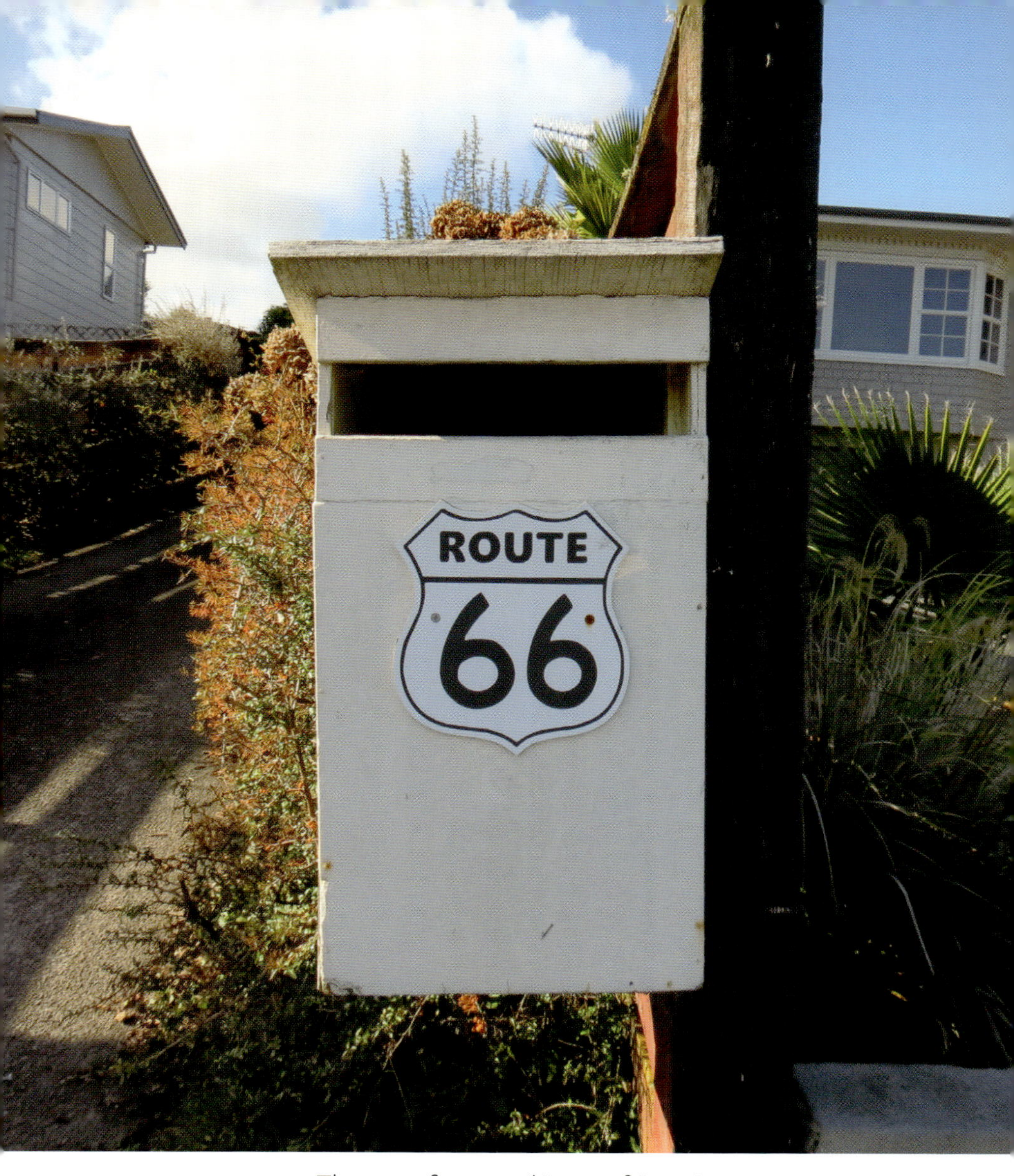

The most famous tiki tour of America.

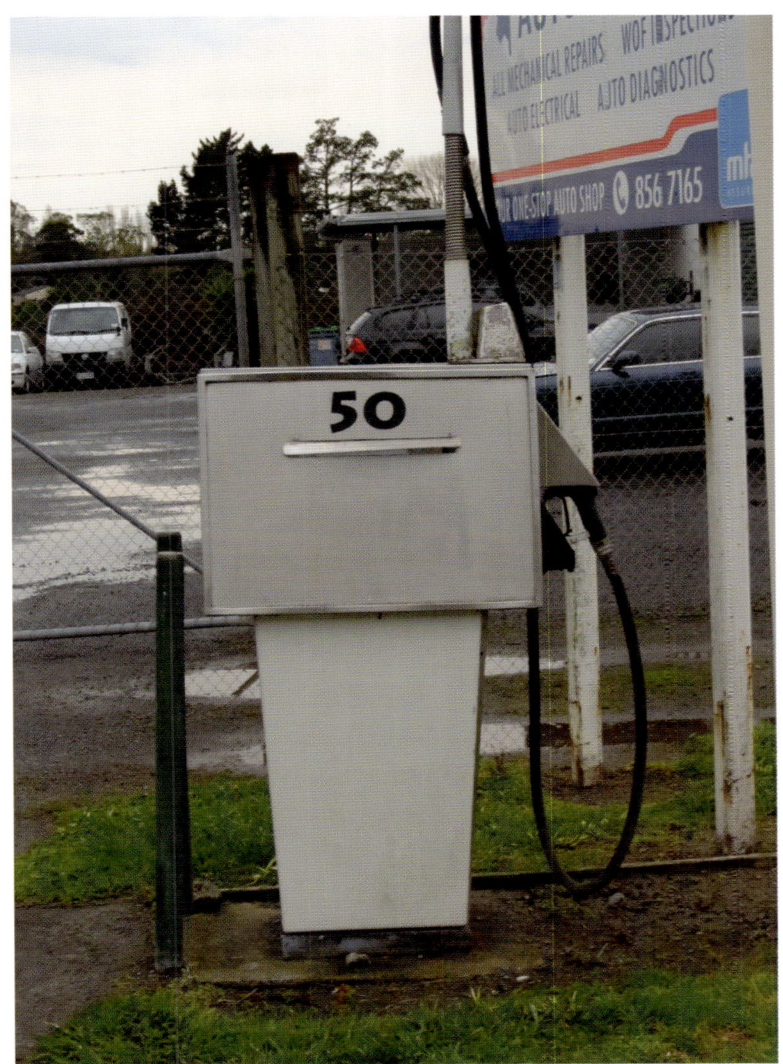

Fuel up for the tour.

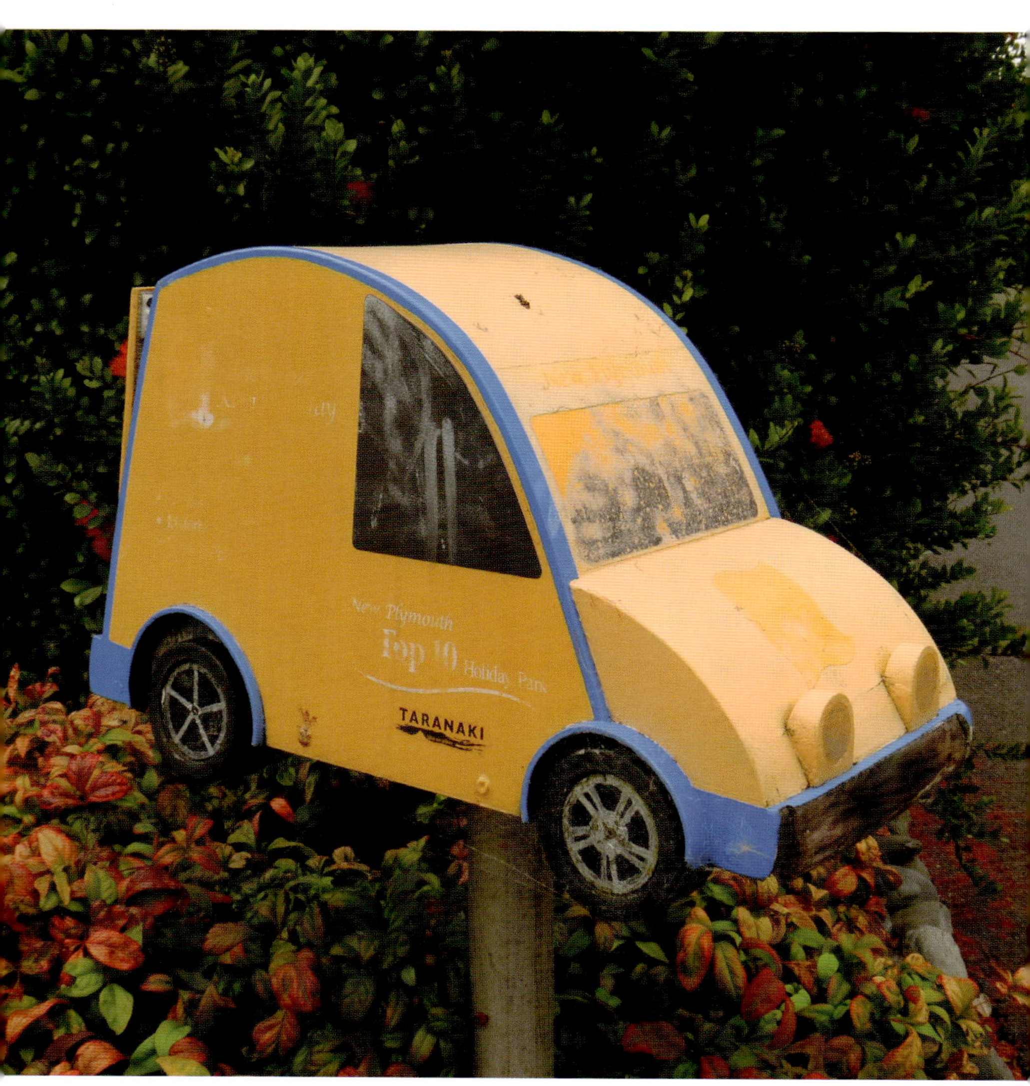

Closer to home — tiki tour through Taranaki.

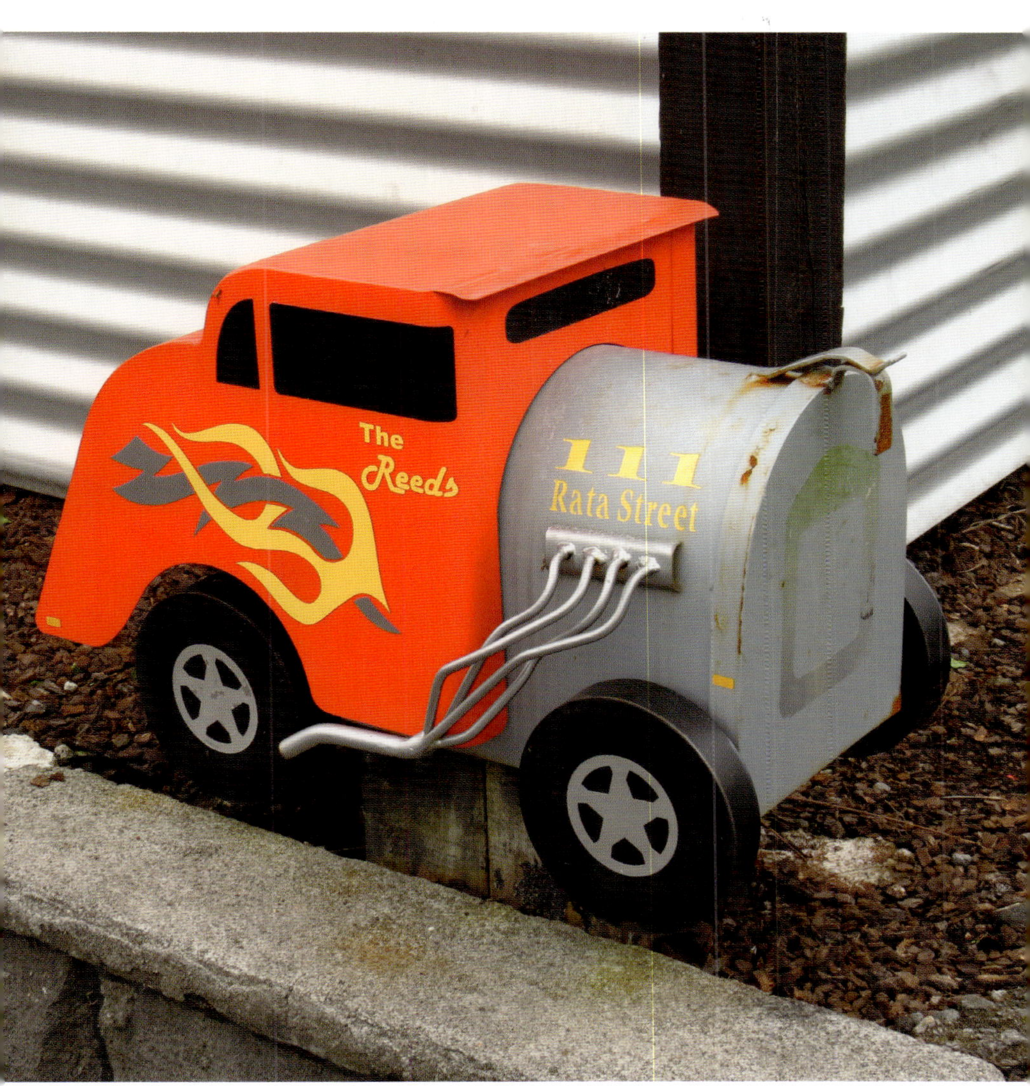

Beach Hop here we come.

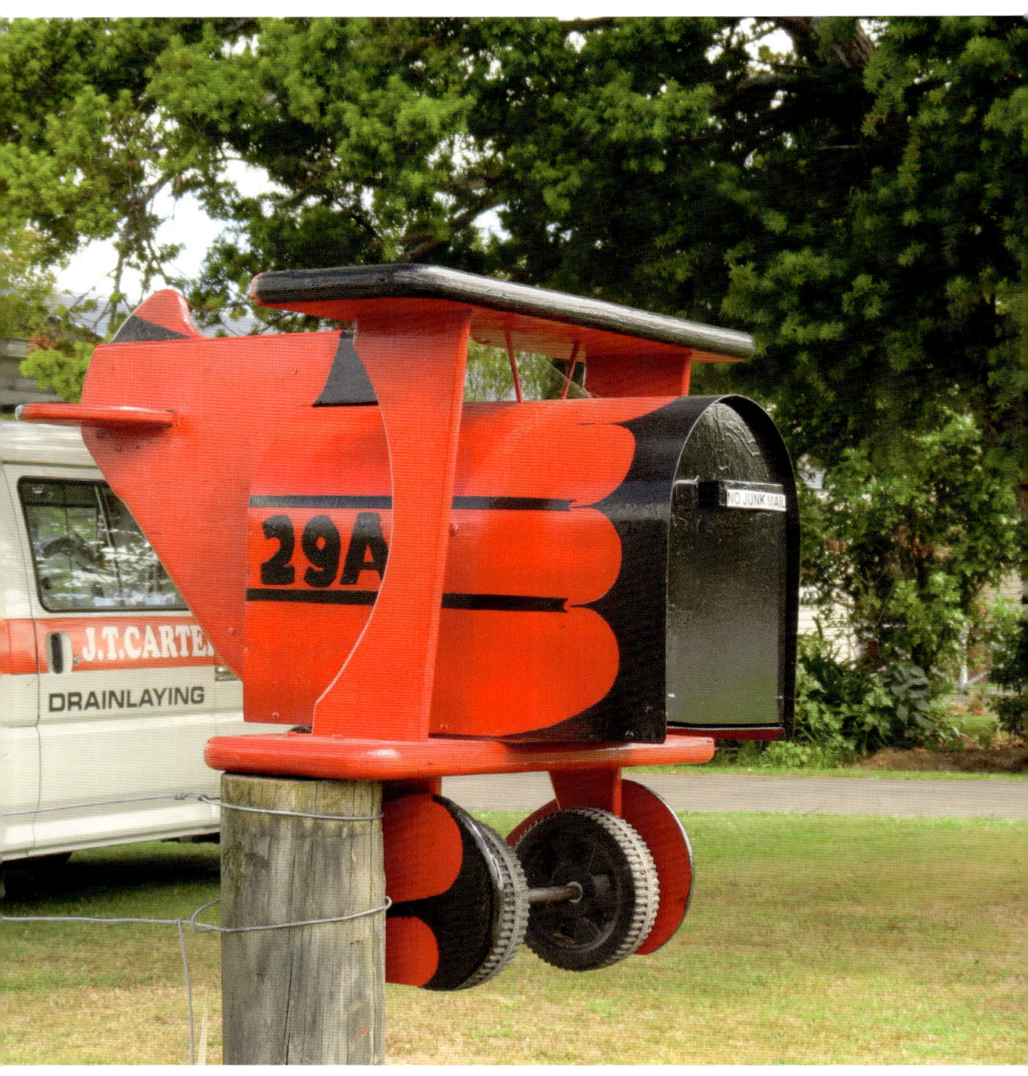

Take to the skies for a scenic tour.

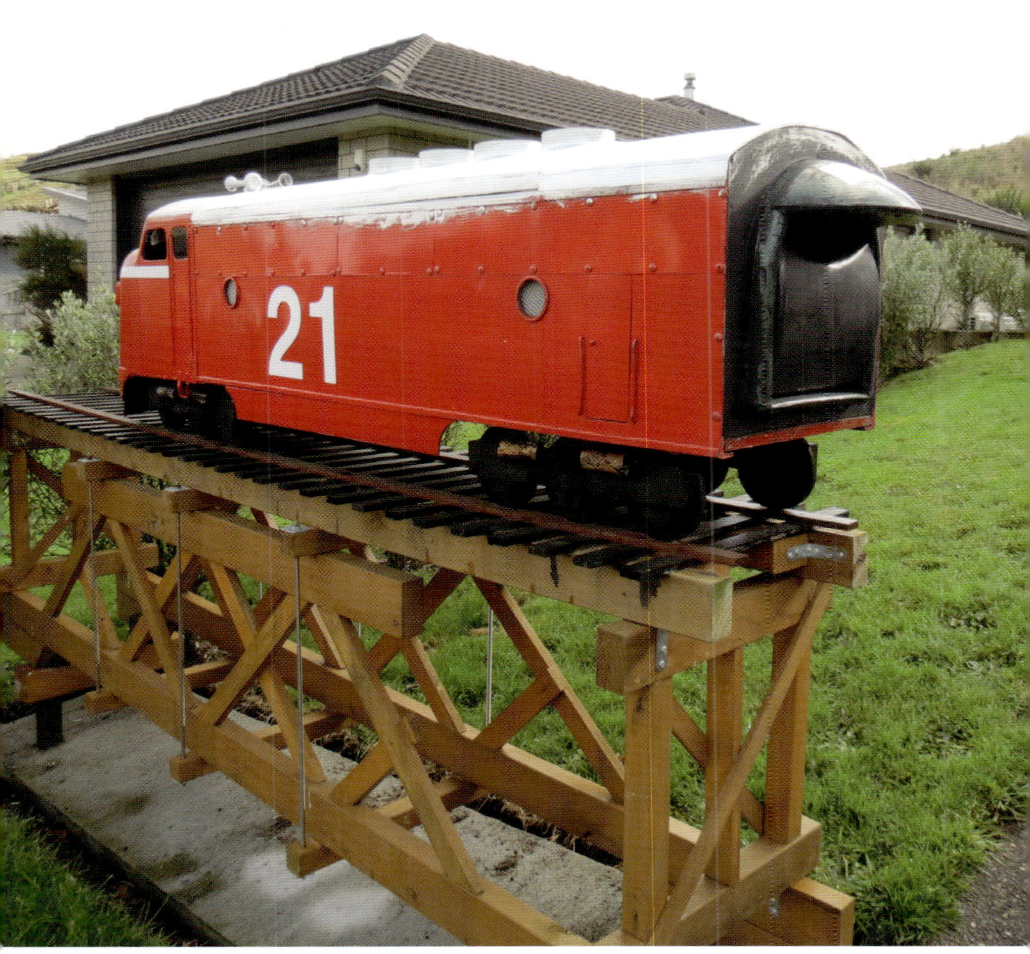

On track for an express delivery.

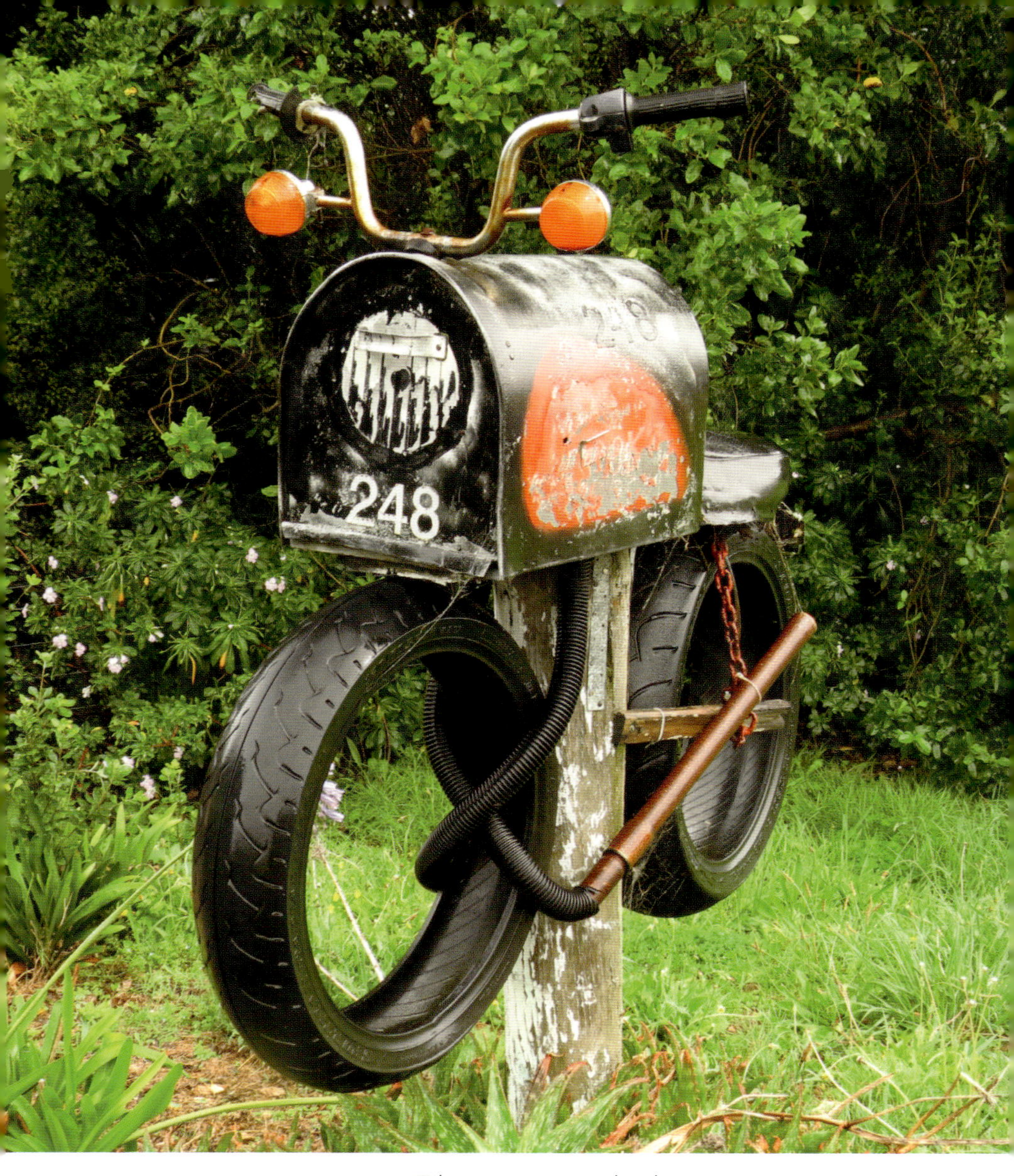

Tiki tour on two wheels.

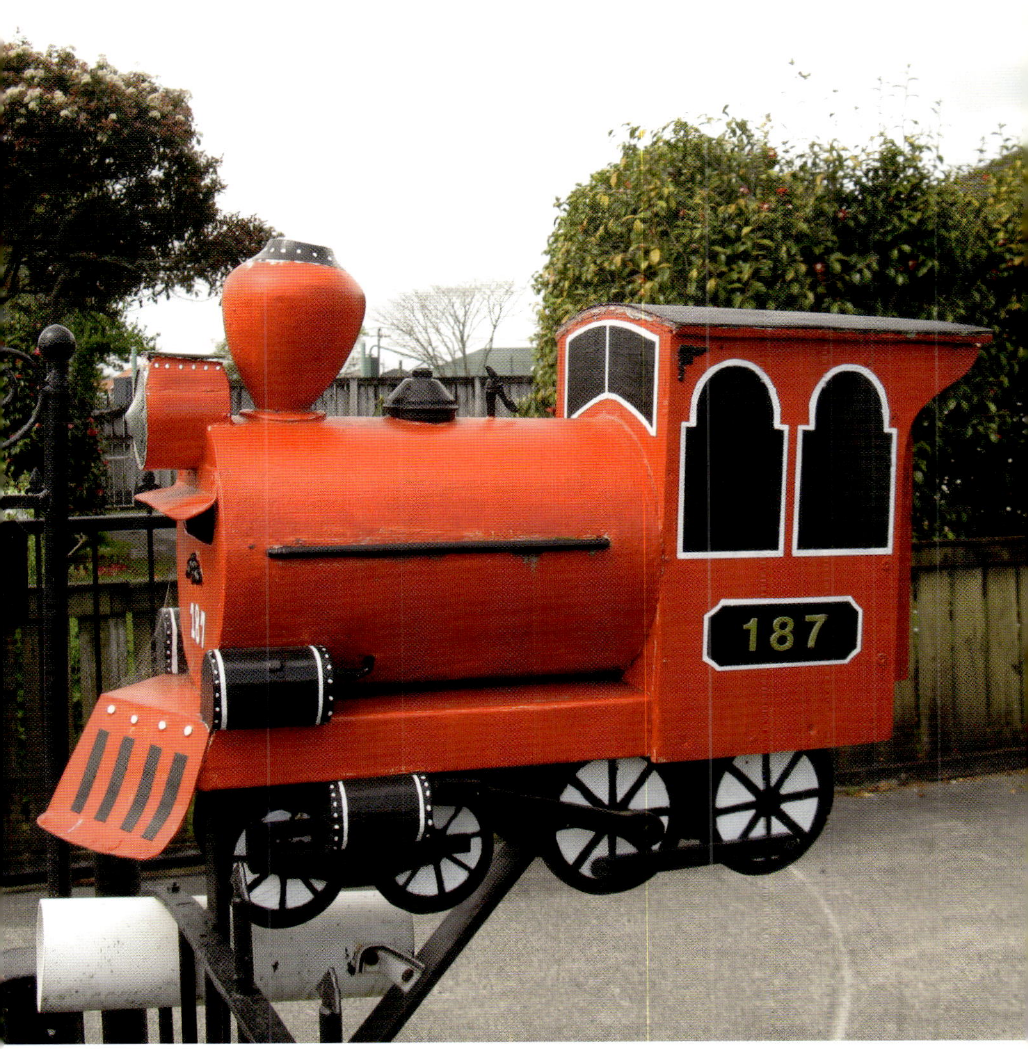

The little steam engine that could . . . collect the mail.

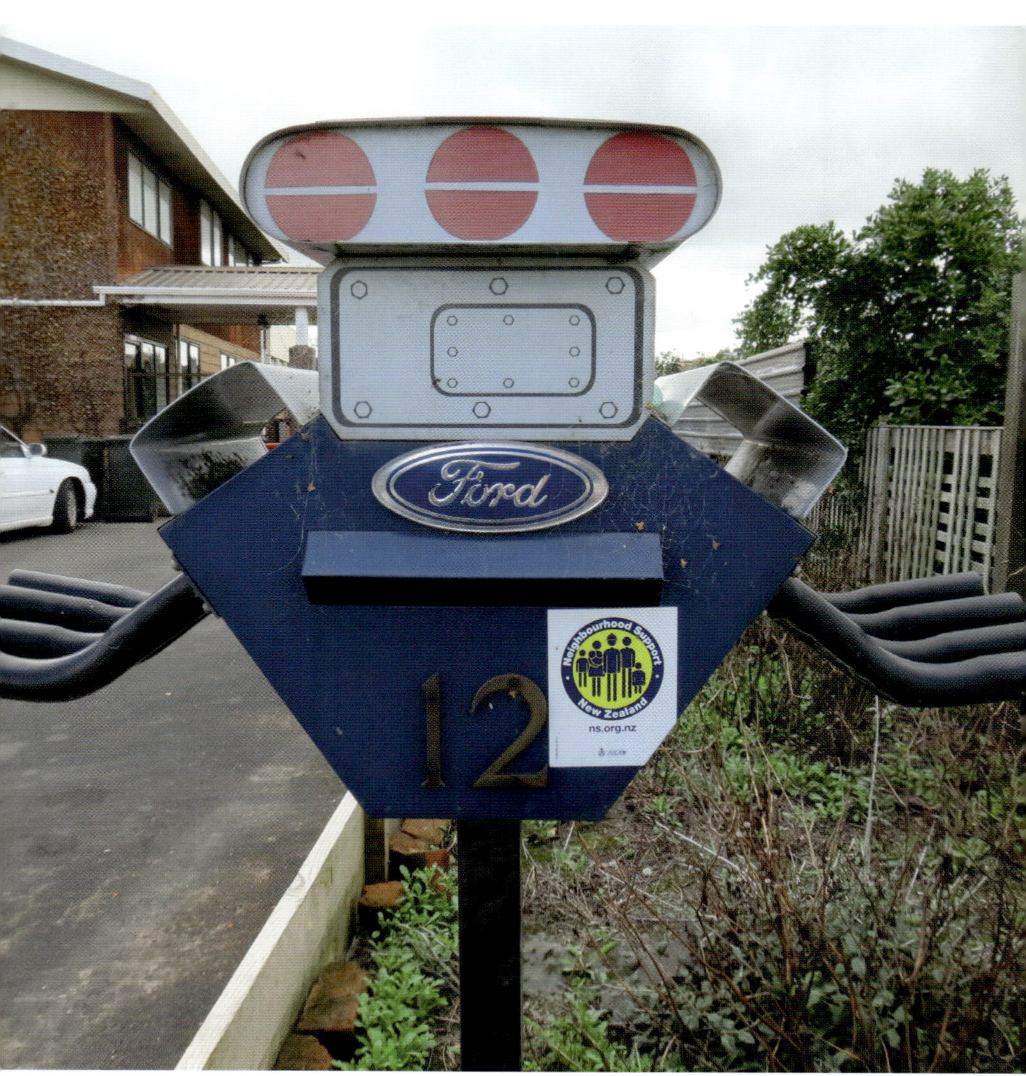

Ford is the tiki tourer of choice at number 12.

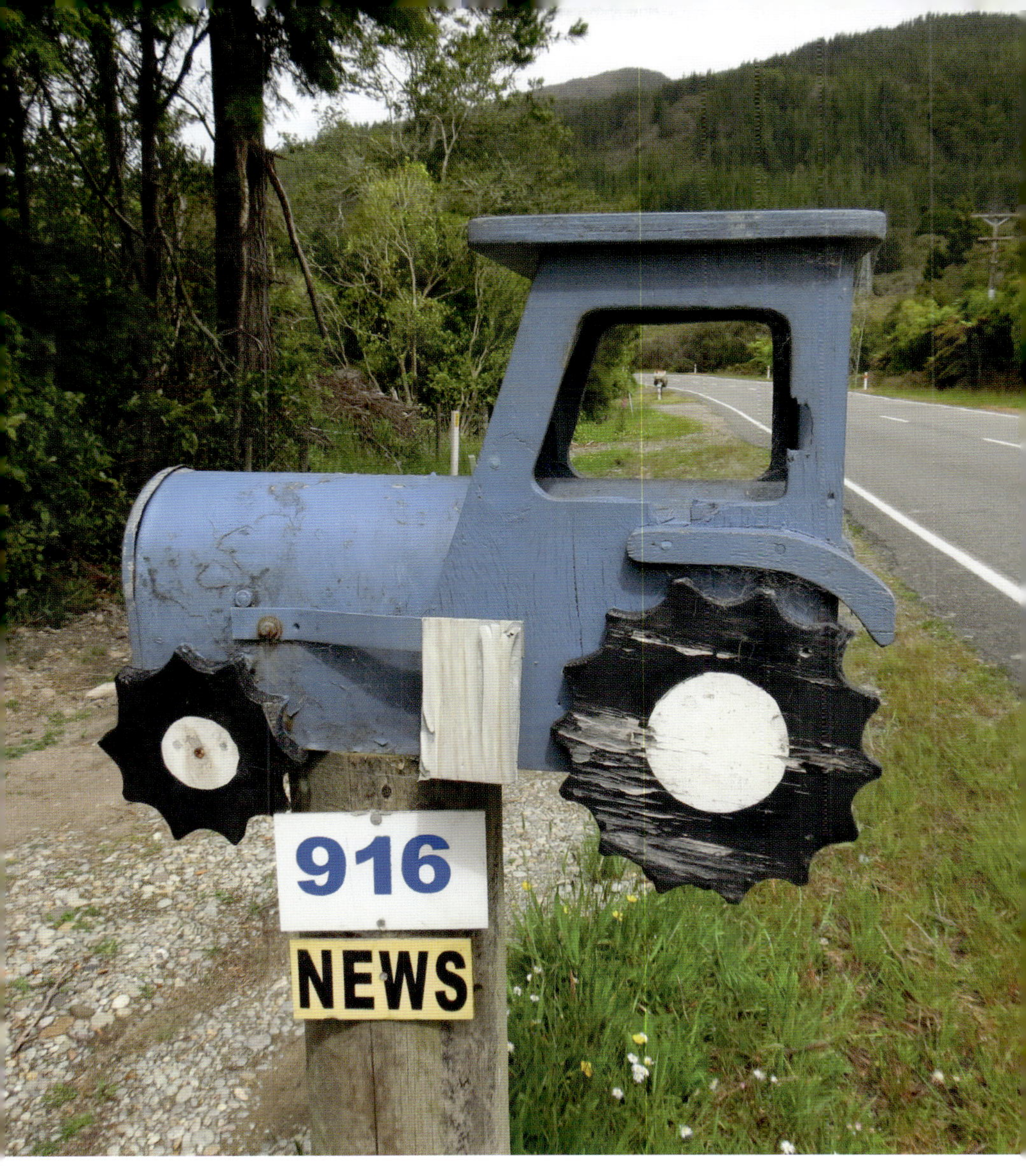

Out in the wop wops.

REUSE & REPURPOSE

The reuse and repurpose ethos is flourishing at the front gates of New Zealand properties. It seems no item is exempt from being turned into a letterbox, whether it's an engine block, clothes dryer or a dive tank.

There is also some classic Kiwi ingenuity at play here: 'She'll be right, there'll be something in the back shed I can use to make a letterbox.' Followed closely by 'Why would I pay for something I can make myself?'

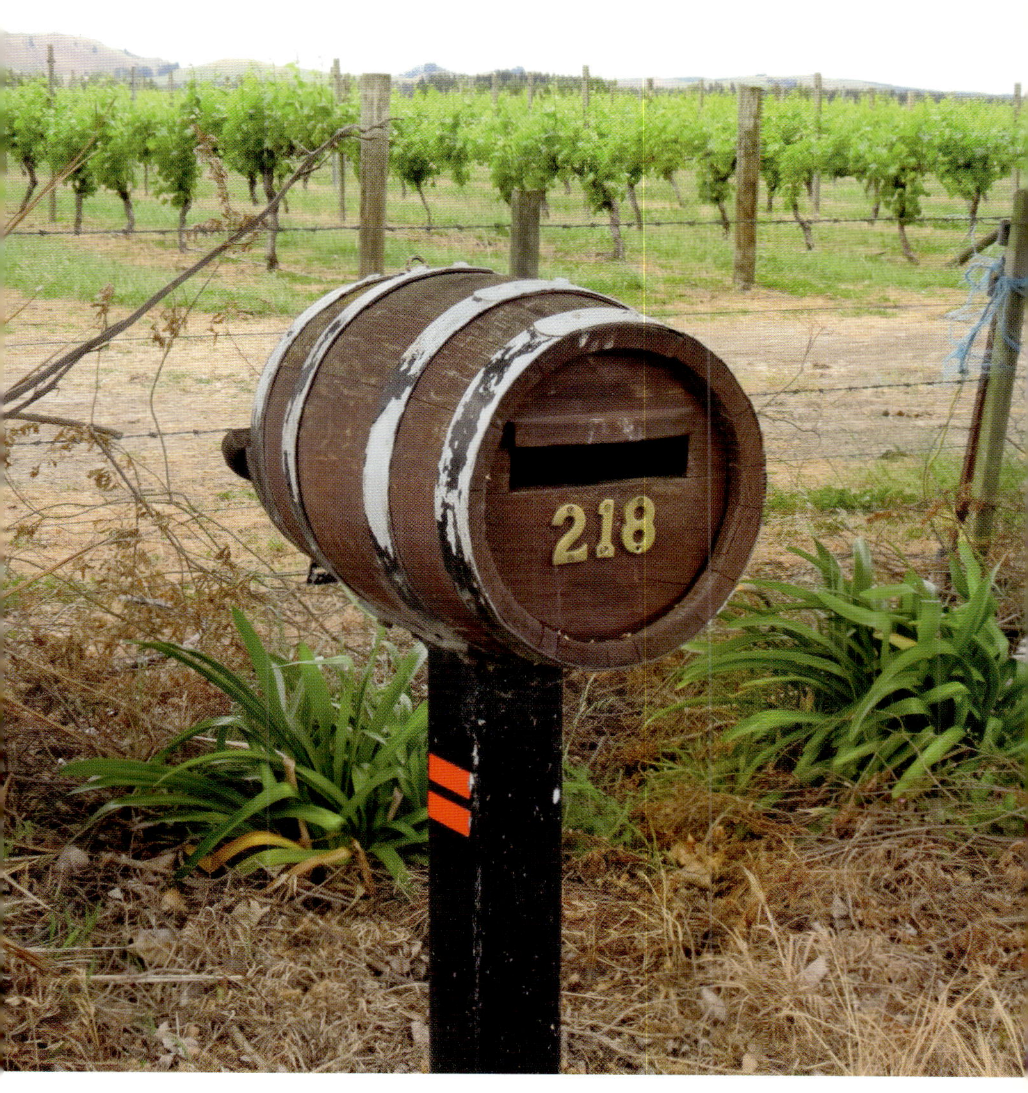

Cheers, Postie!

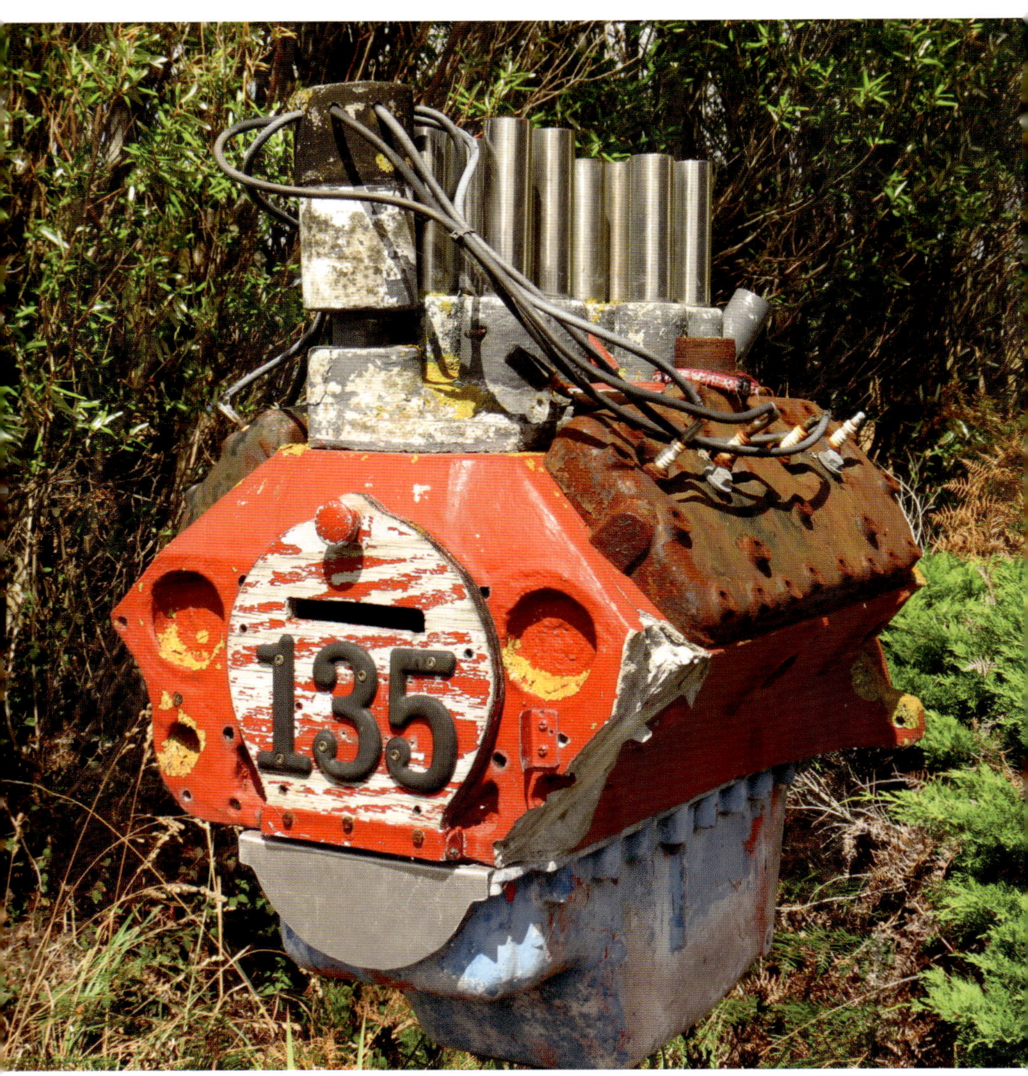

Revved up to collect the mail.

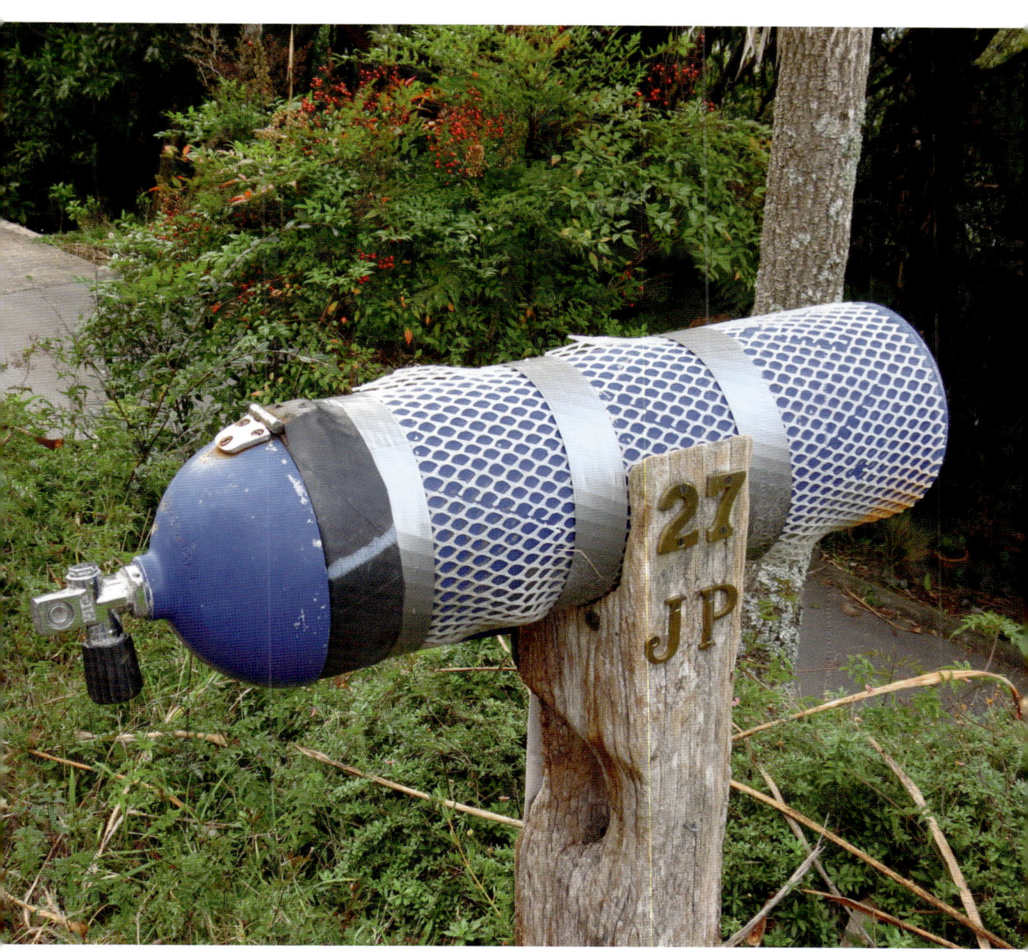

Delivery down under.

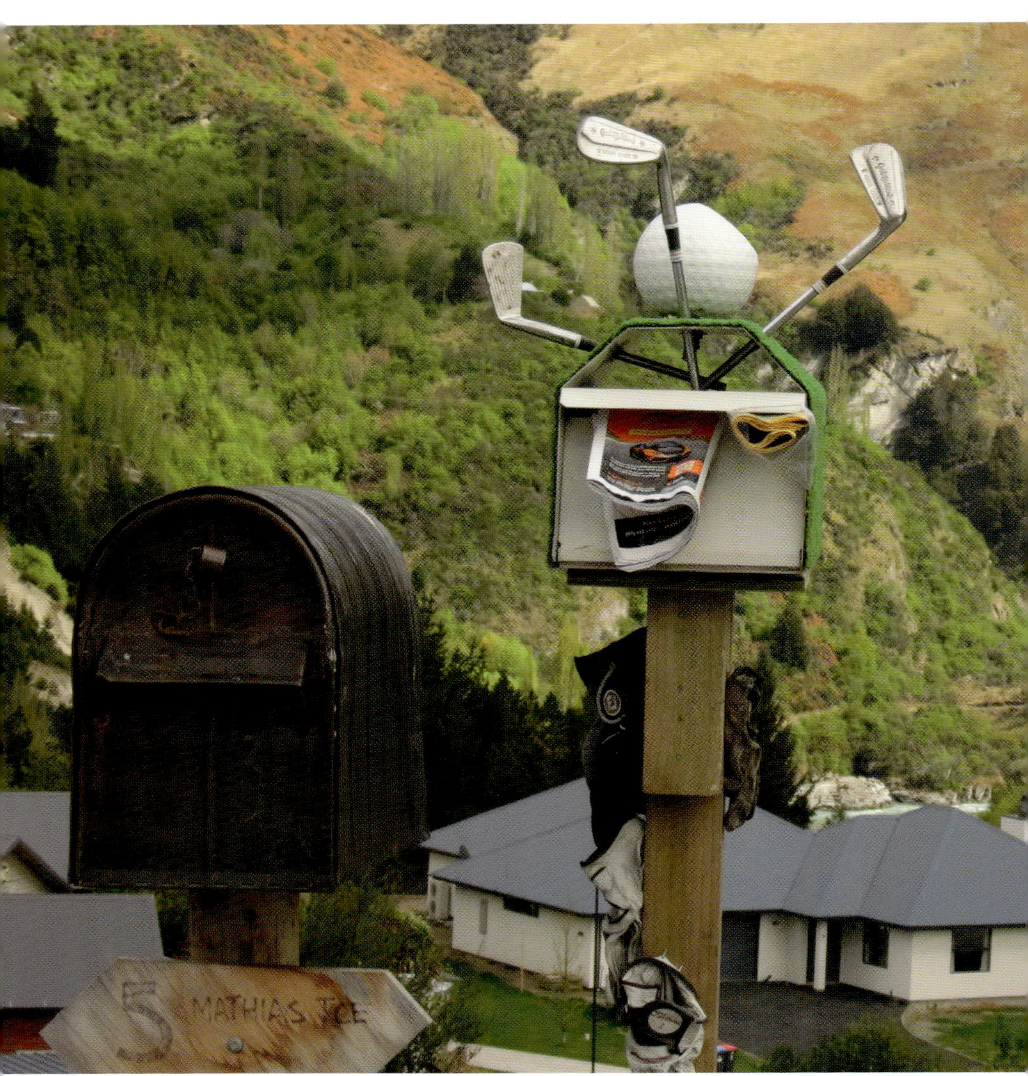

Teed off with junk mail.

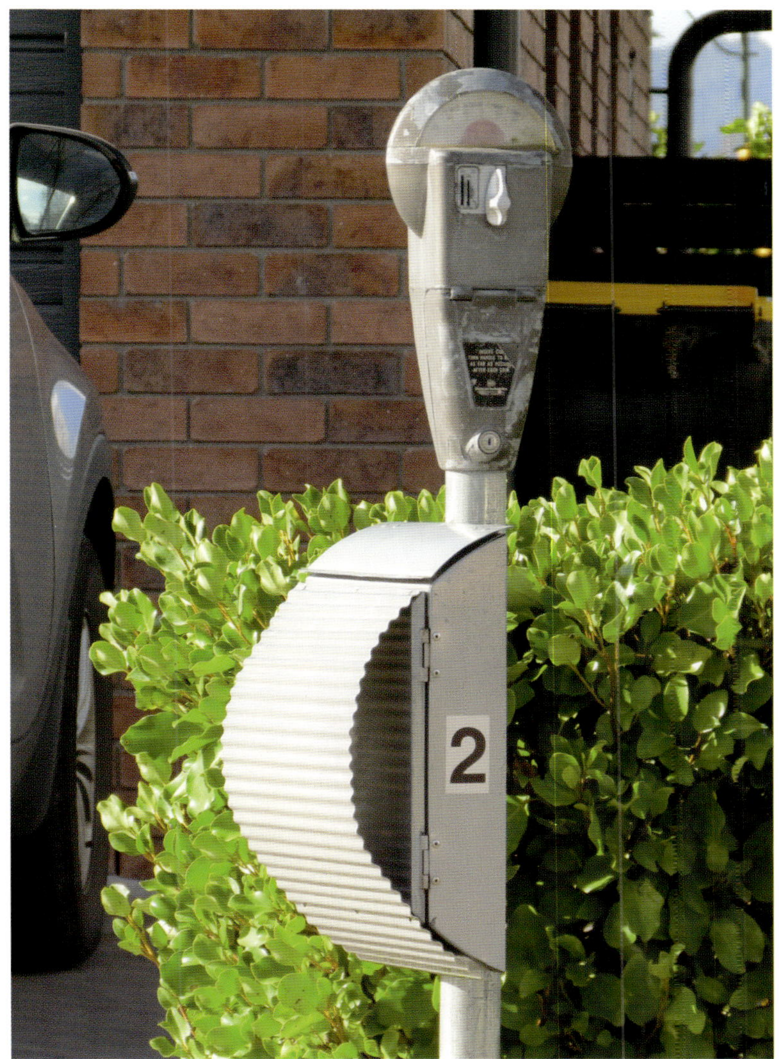

Time's ticking for the traditional letterbox.

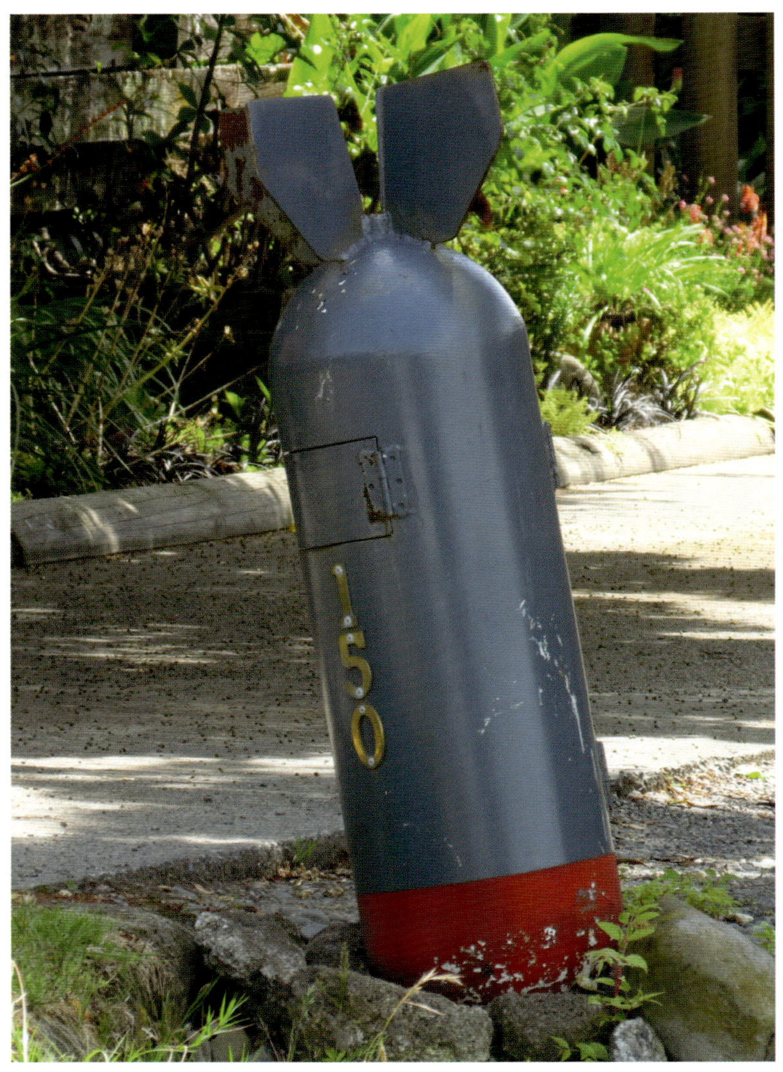

Potentially explosive mail drop!

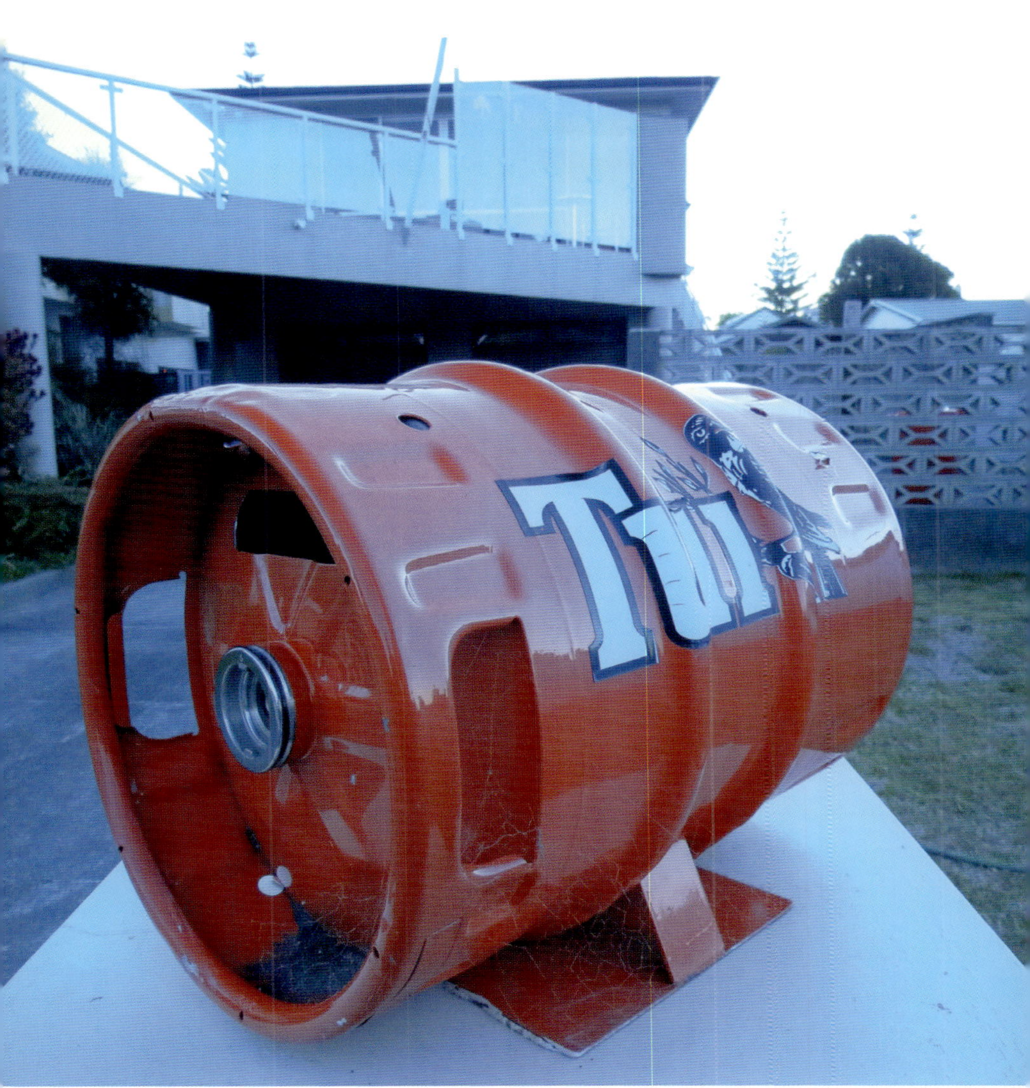

The cheque is in the post — Yeah right!

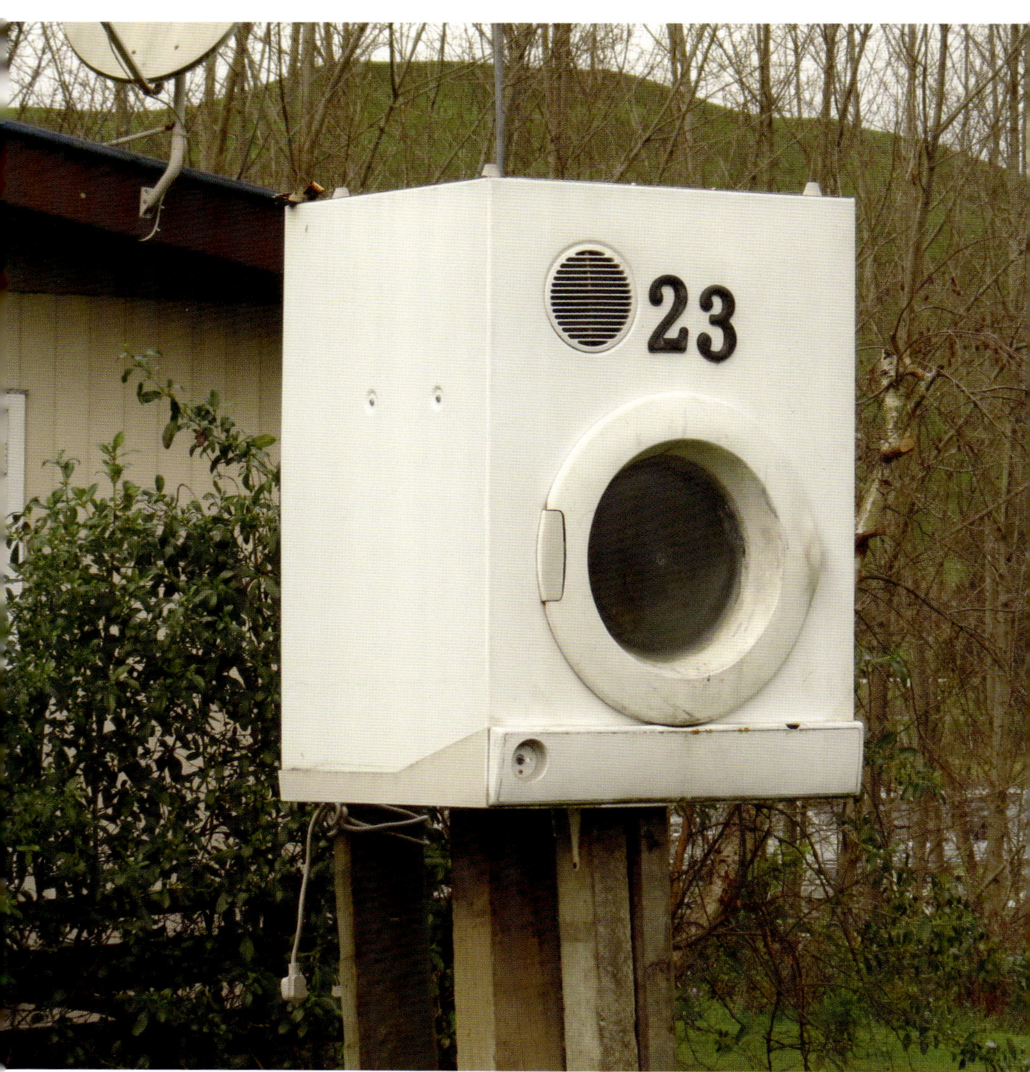

A different kind of hot mail.

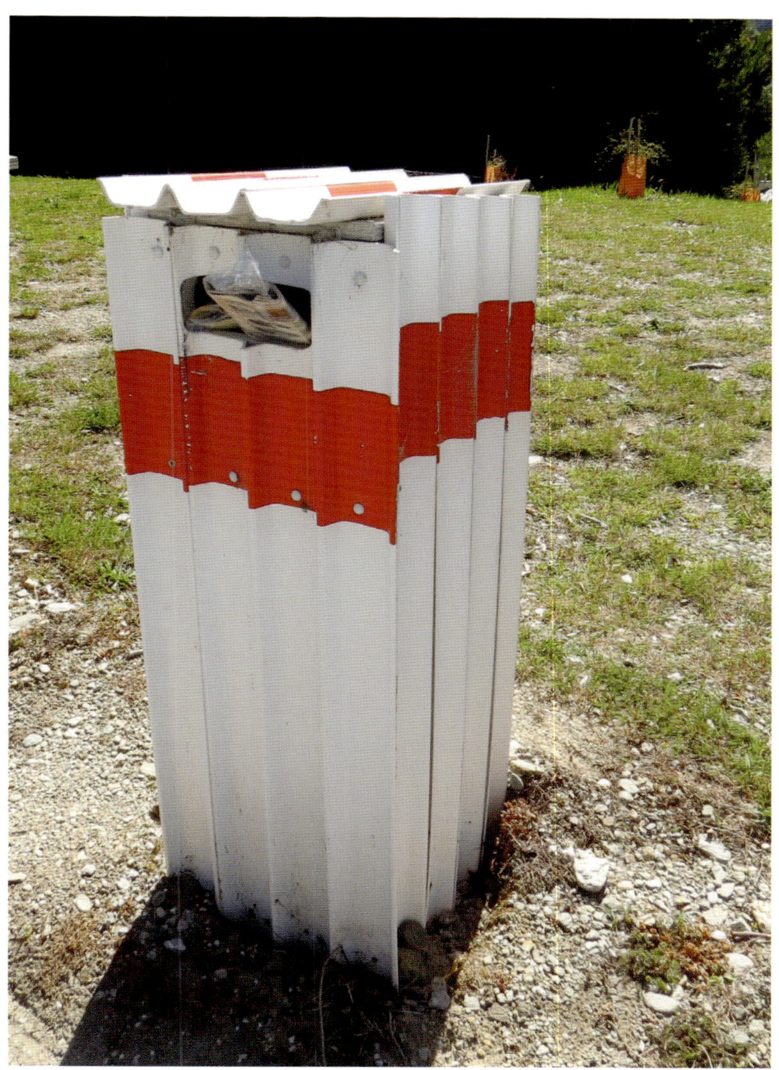

The postie's sure to spot this one at night.

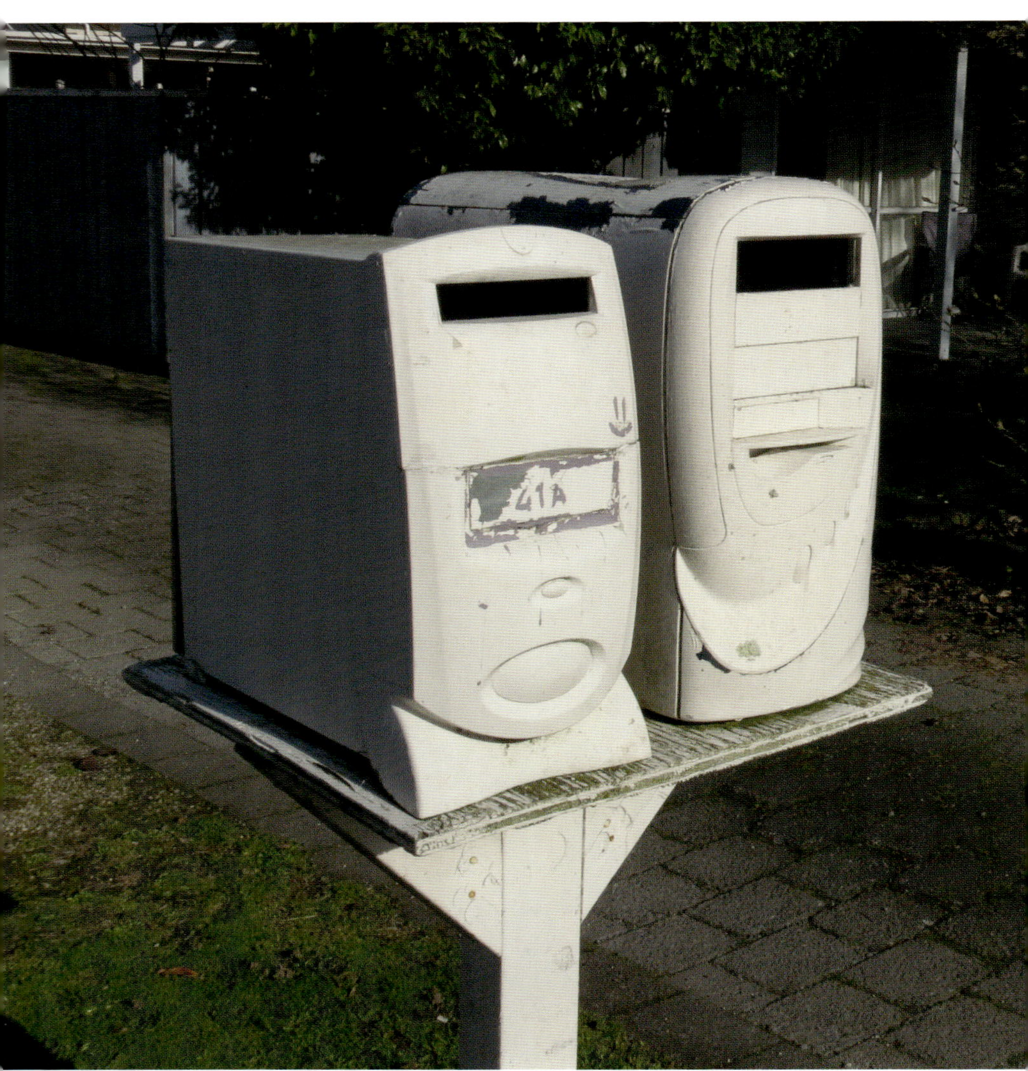

Sign of the times — email versus snail mail.

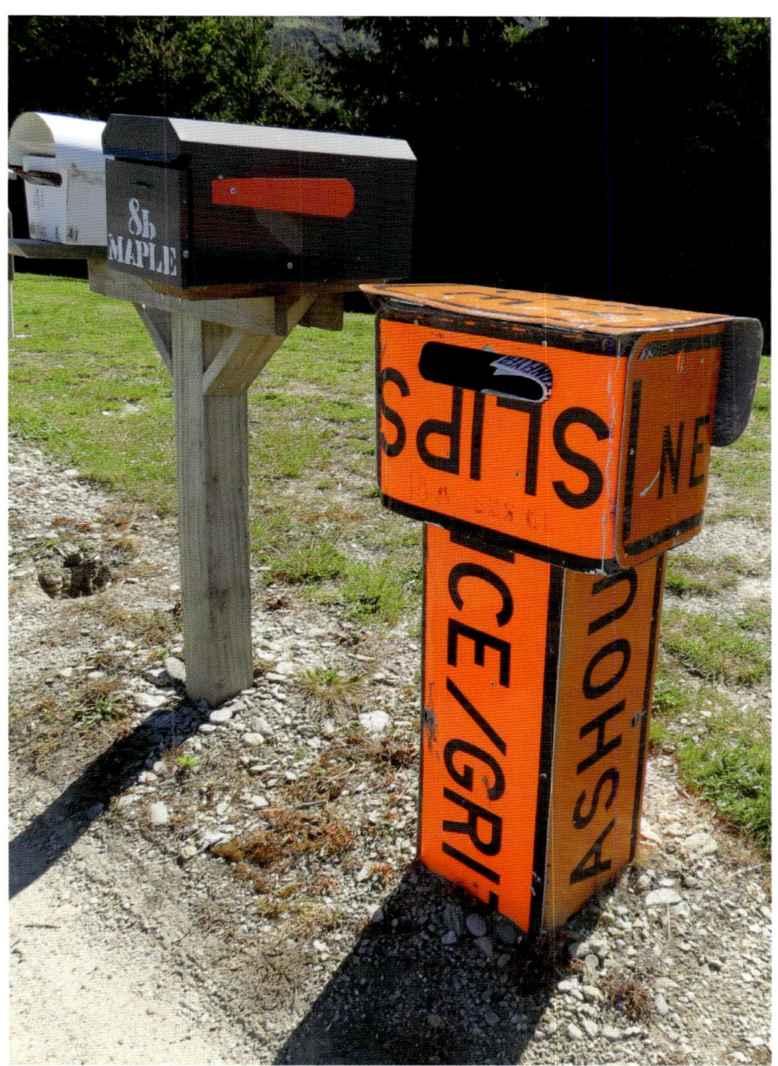

The letterbox equivalent of the hi-vis vest.

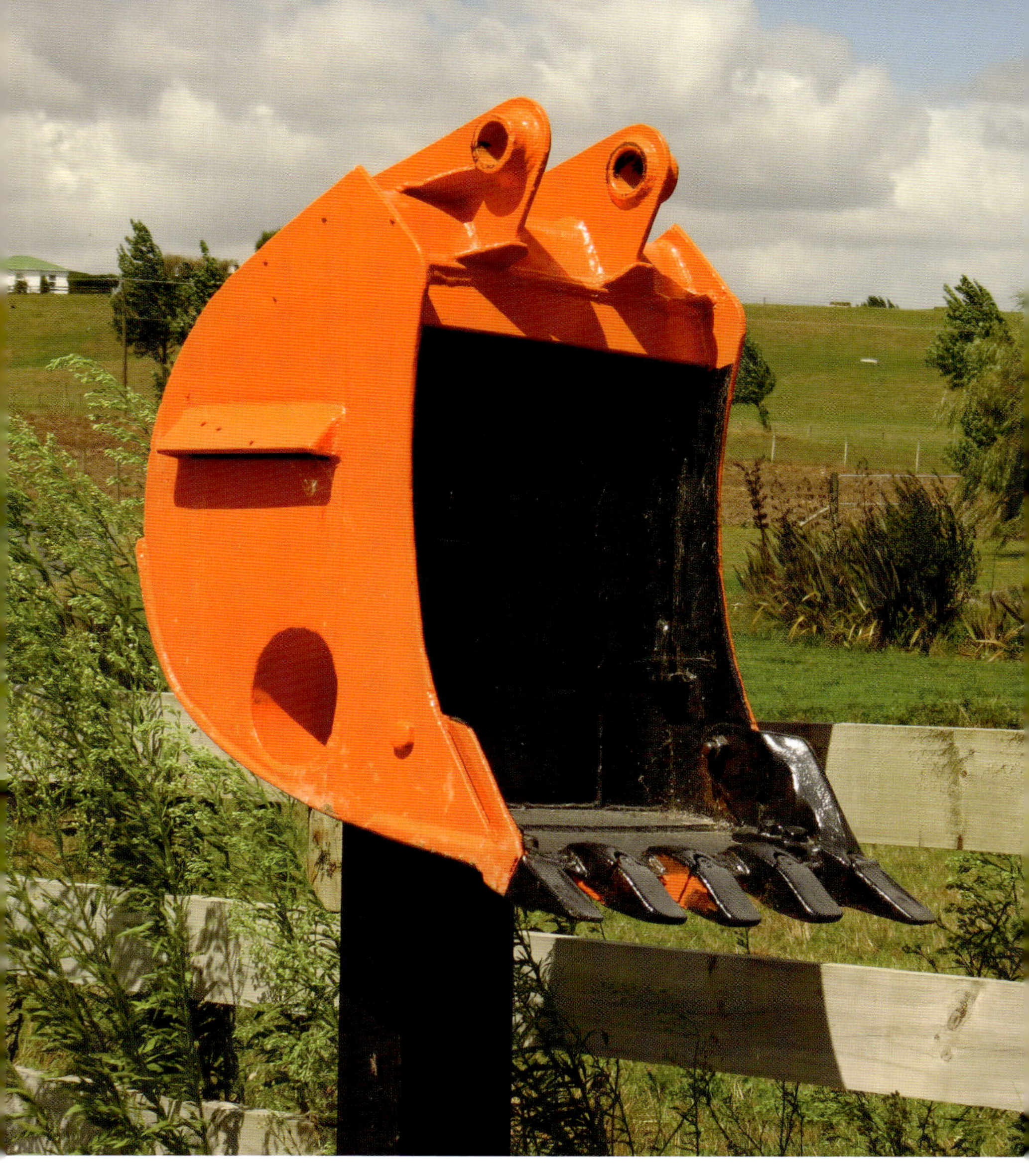

Digging the delivery.

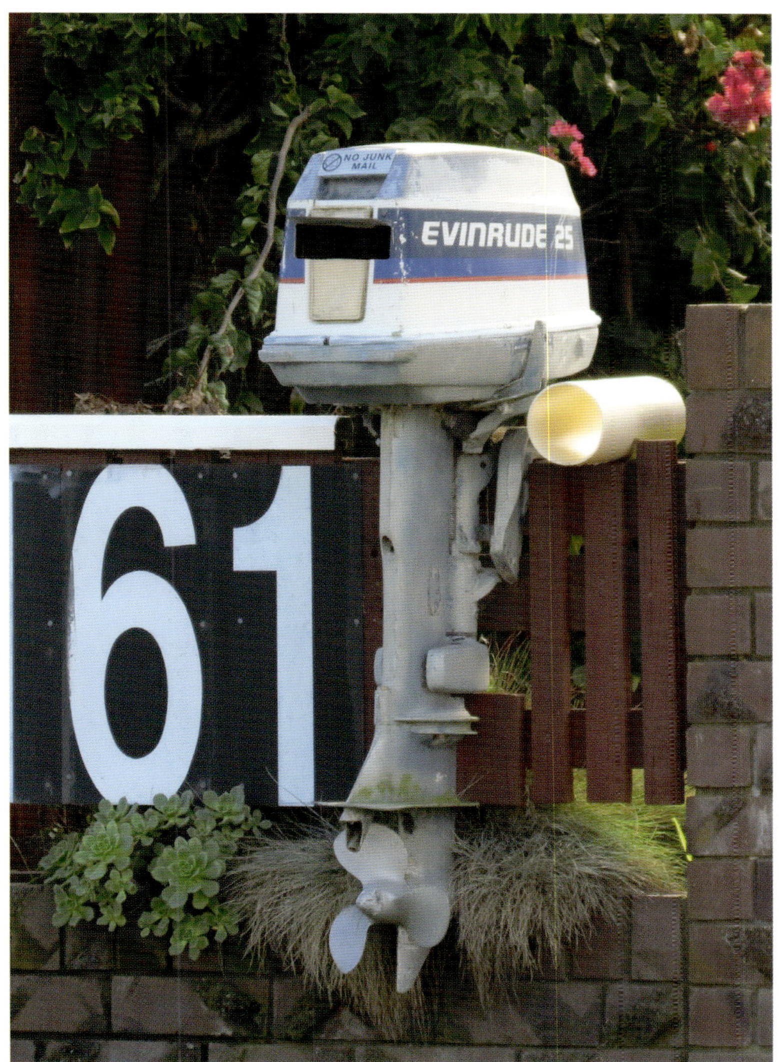

Propelled to collect the post.

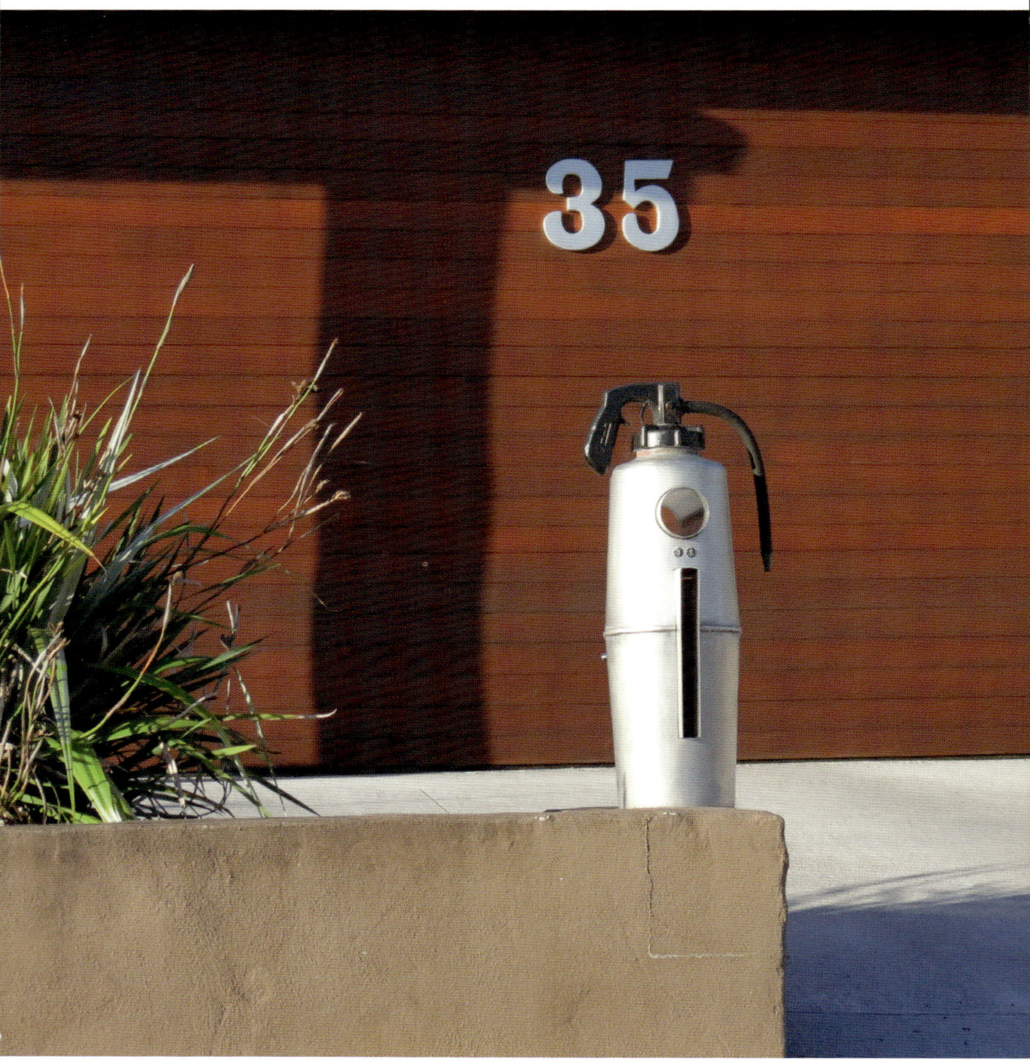

Prepared for a red-hot delivery.

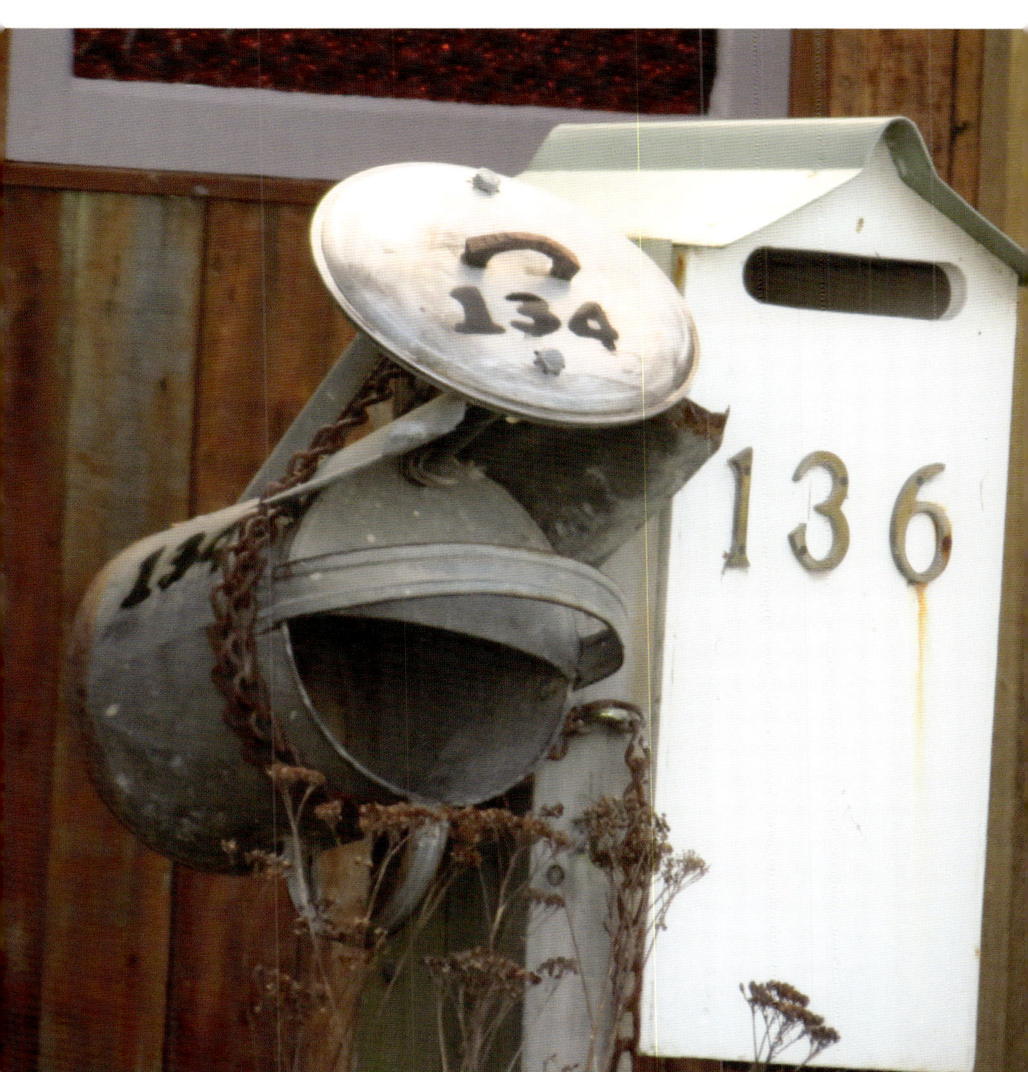

A watering can awaits the Postie van.

KIWIANA

What do jandals, sheep, All Blacks and the kiwi bird have in common? They are all New Zealand icons that have over time helped form part of our national identity, collectively known as Kiwiana.

Kiwiana is what makes us Kiwis unique and it has been celebrated with letterboxes from Rerewhakaaitu to Ranfurly.

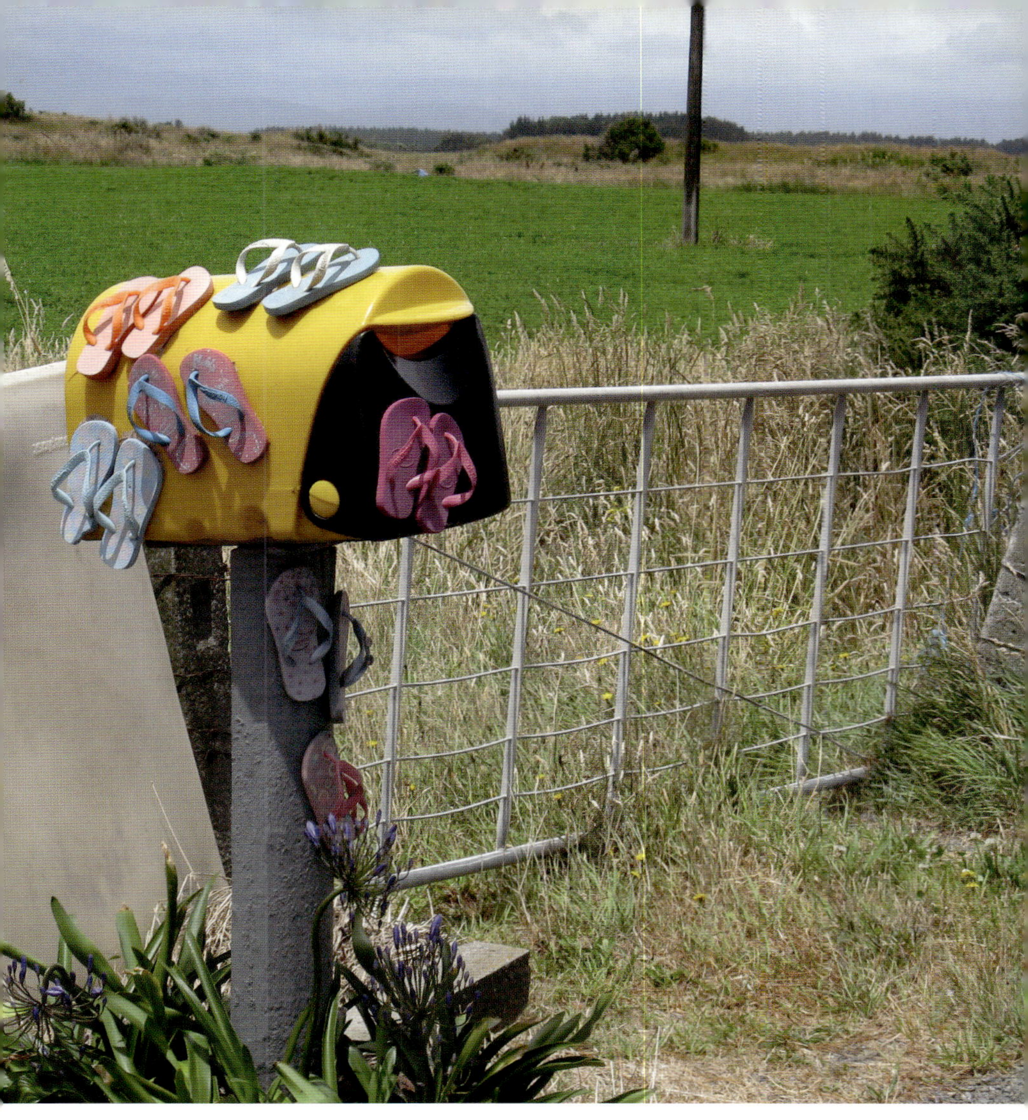

The Kiwi summer footwear of choice when it's not bare feet.

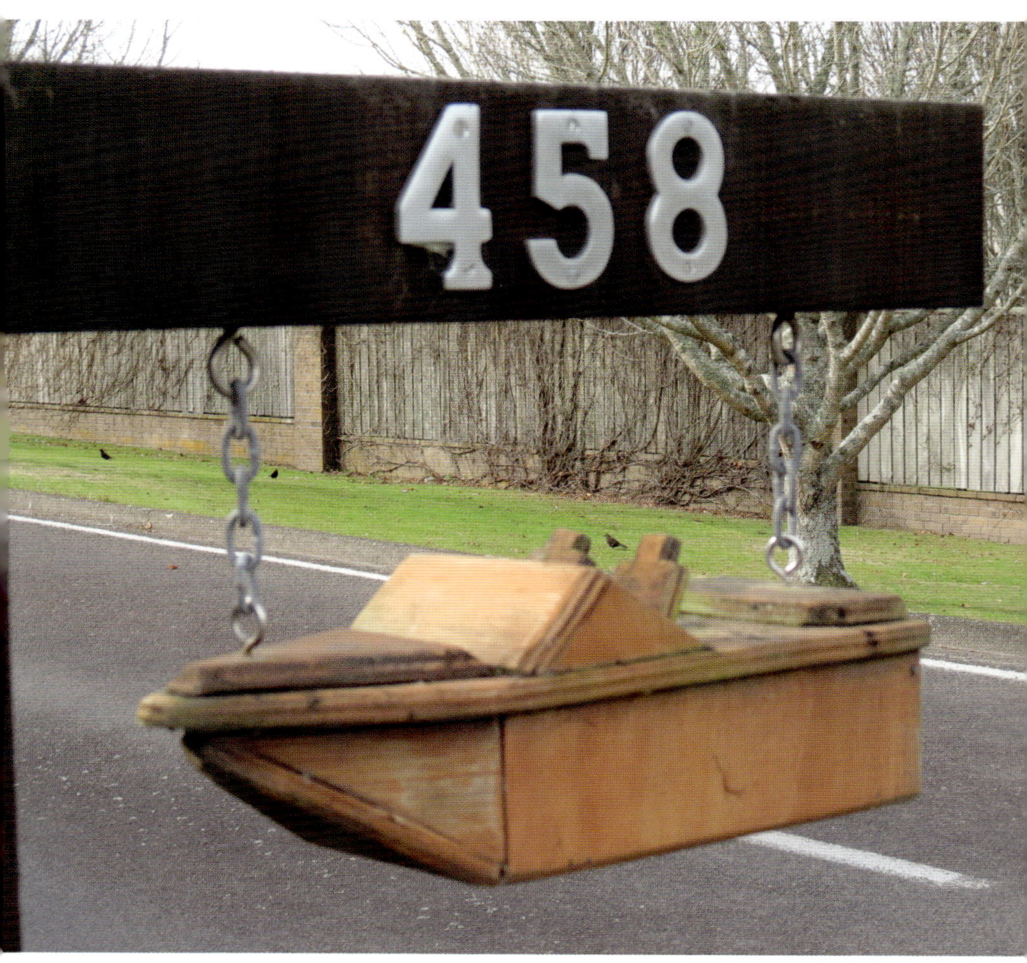

Make a quick getaway in a Hamilton jet boat.

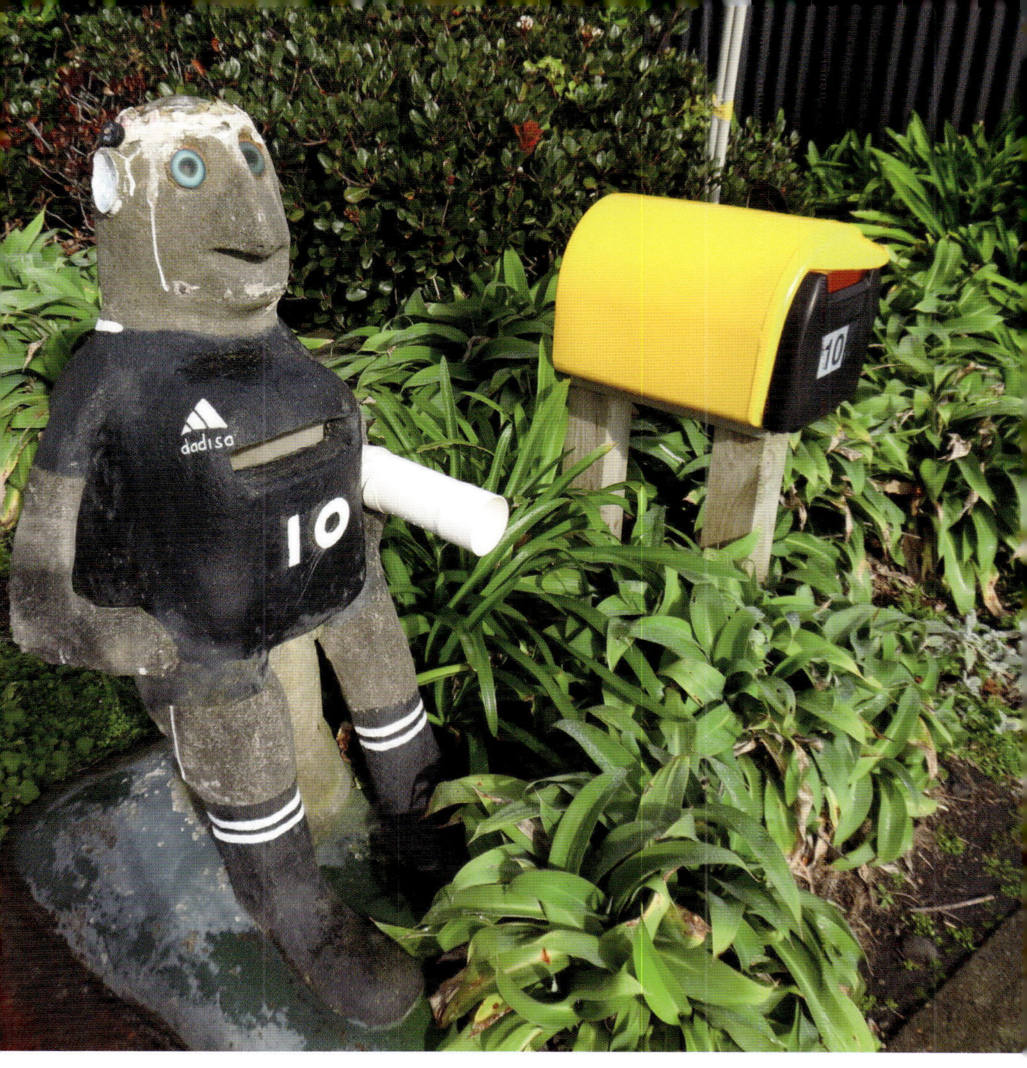

This has got to be former No. 10, Dan Carter, right?
The resemblance is uncanny!

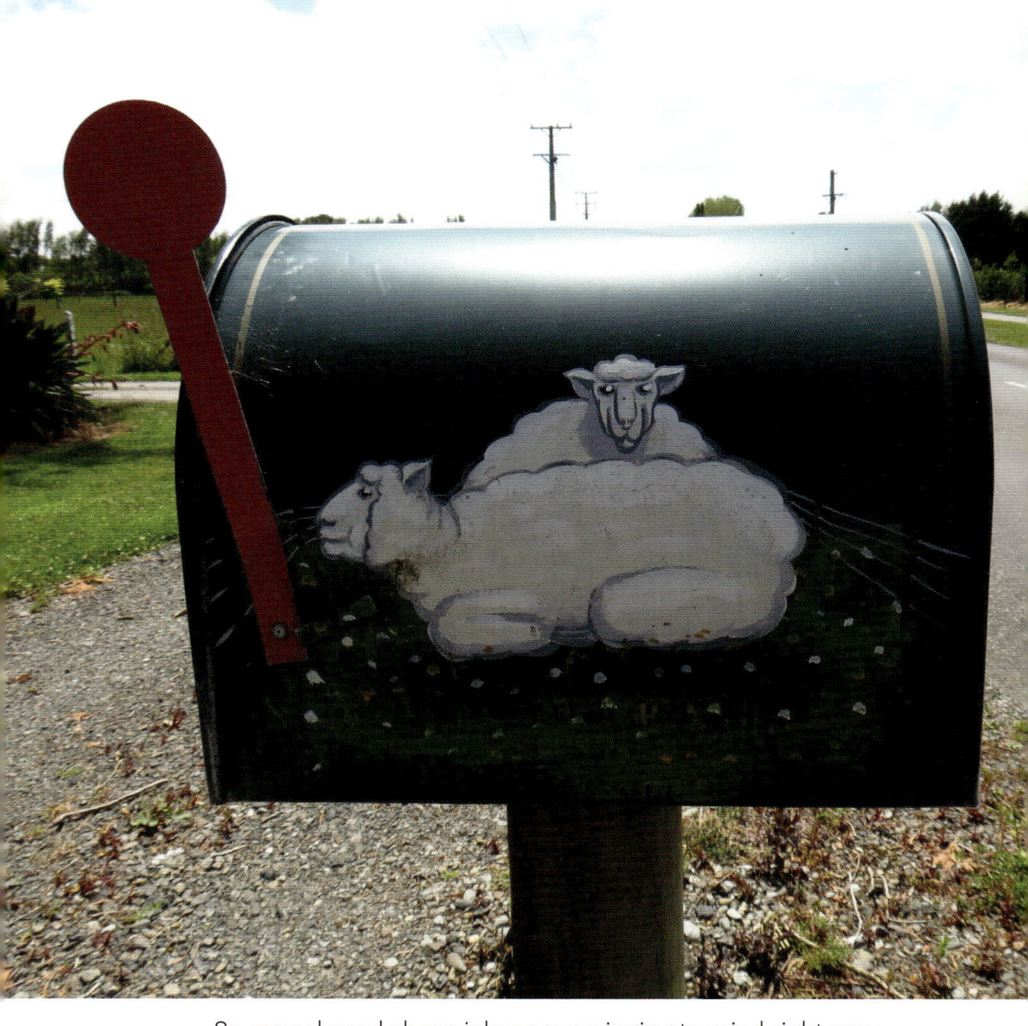

So many baaad sheep jokes are springing to mind right now.

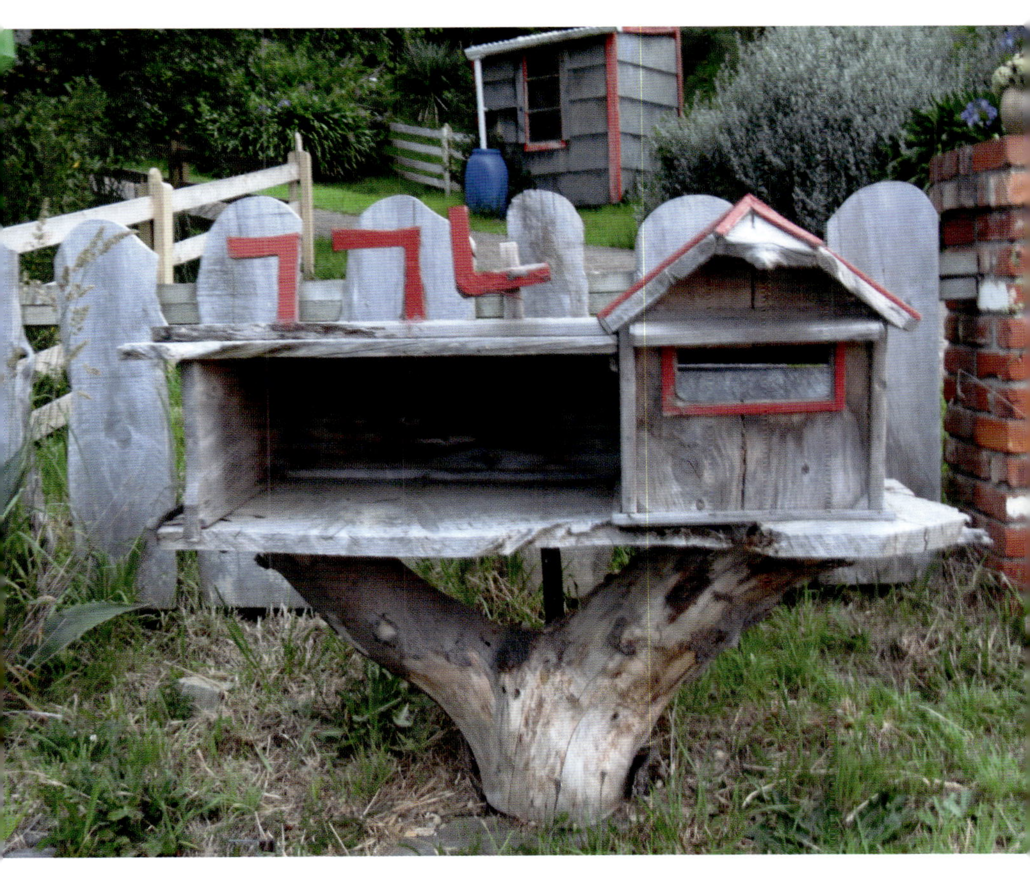

DIY is in our DNA, so says one of our major hardware chains.

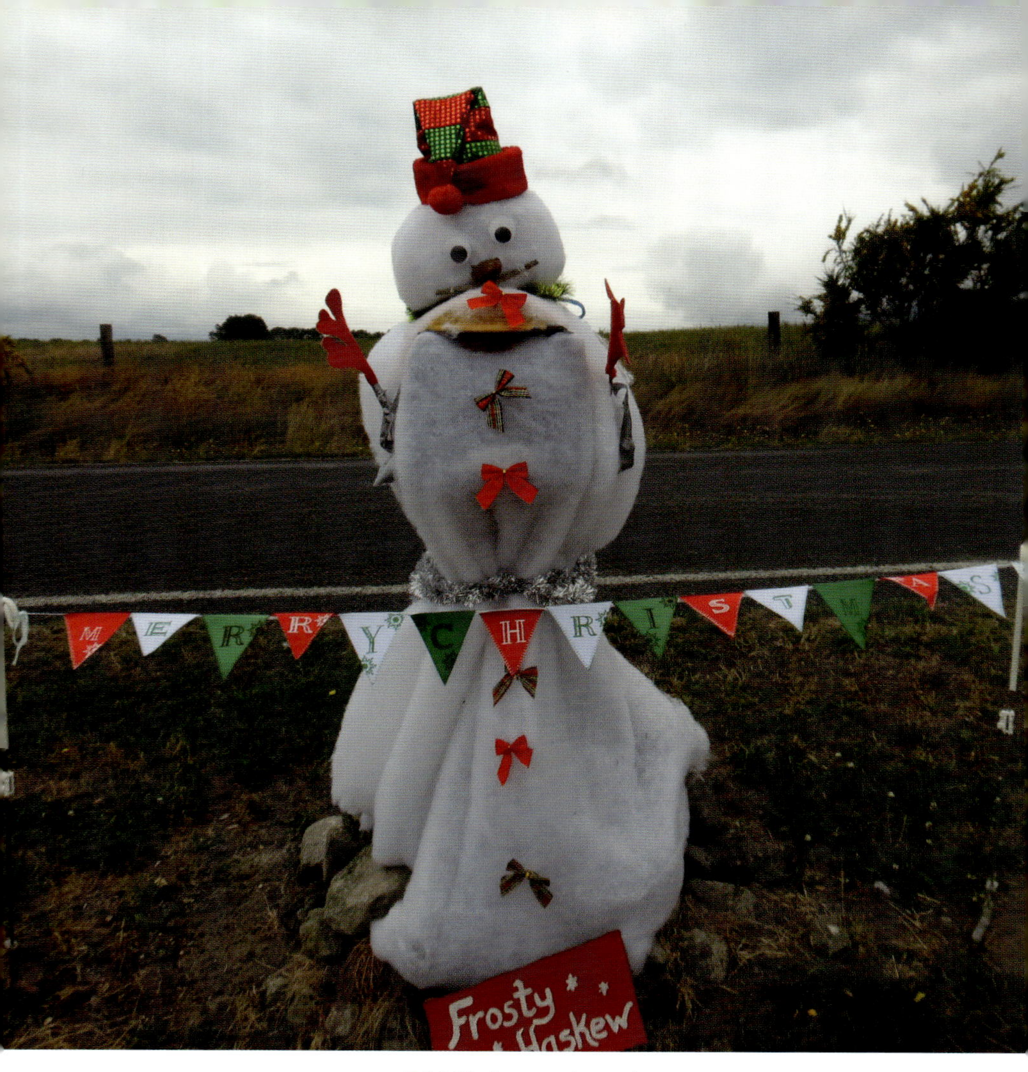

DIY Christmas letterbox.

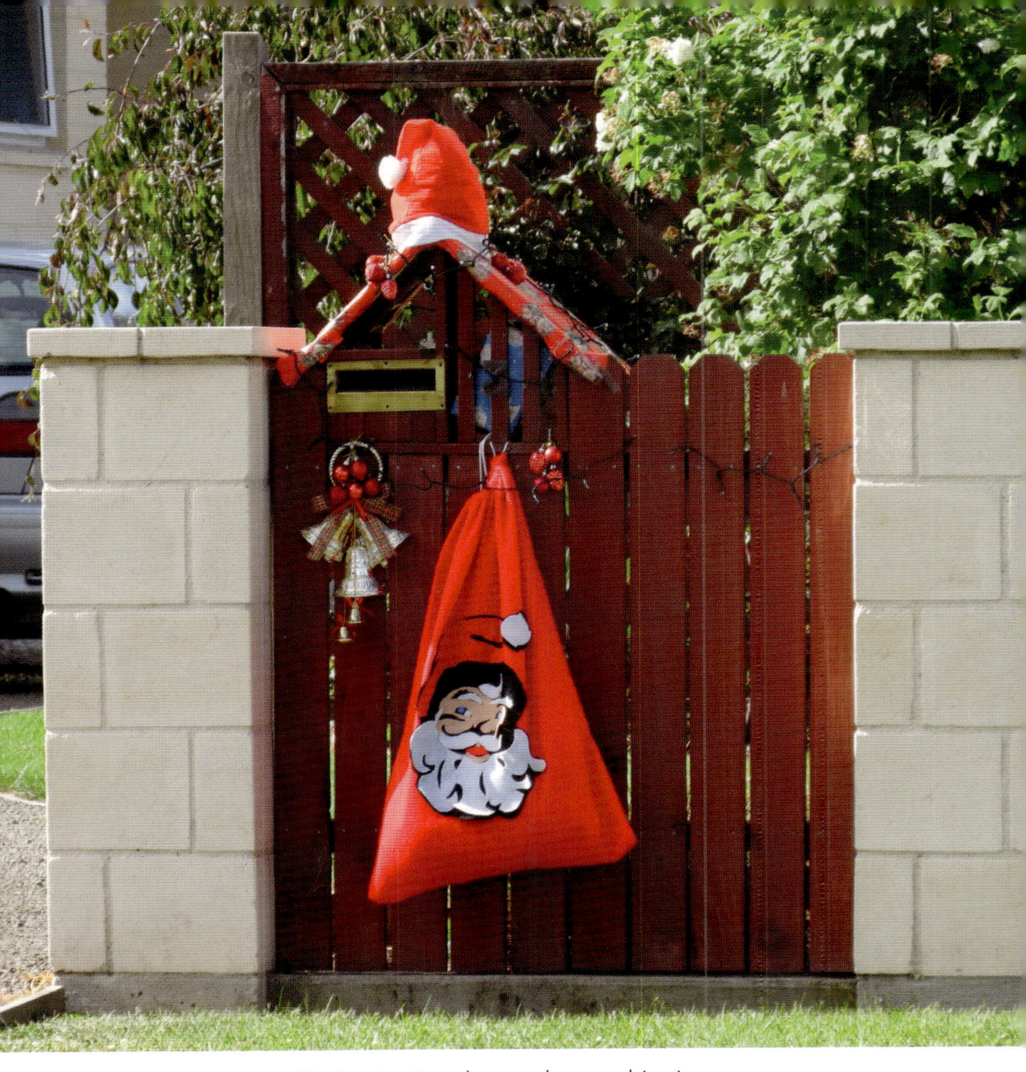

Oi, Santa! You dropped something!

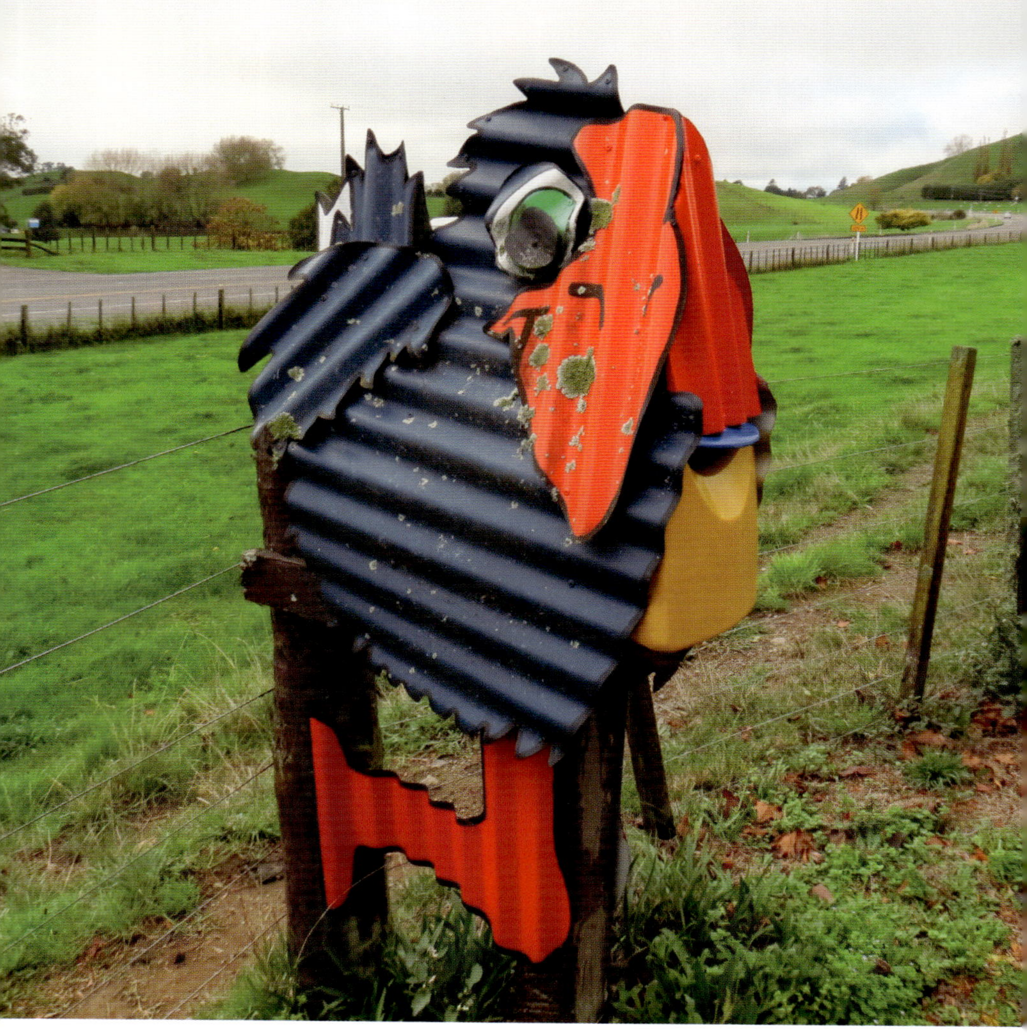

Corrugated iron is 'Kiwi as' and has many practical uses. It can also be used to turn letterboxes into works of art.

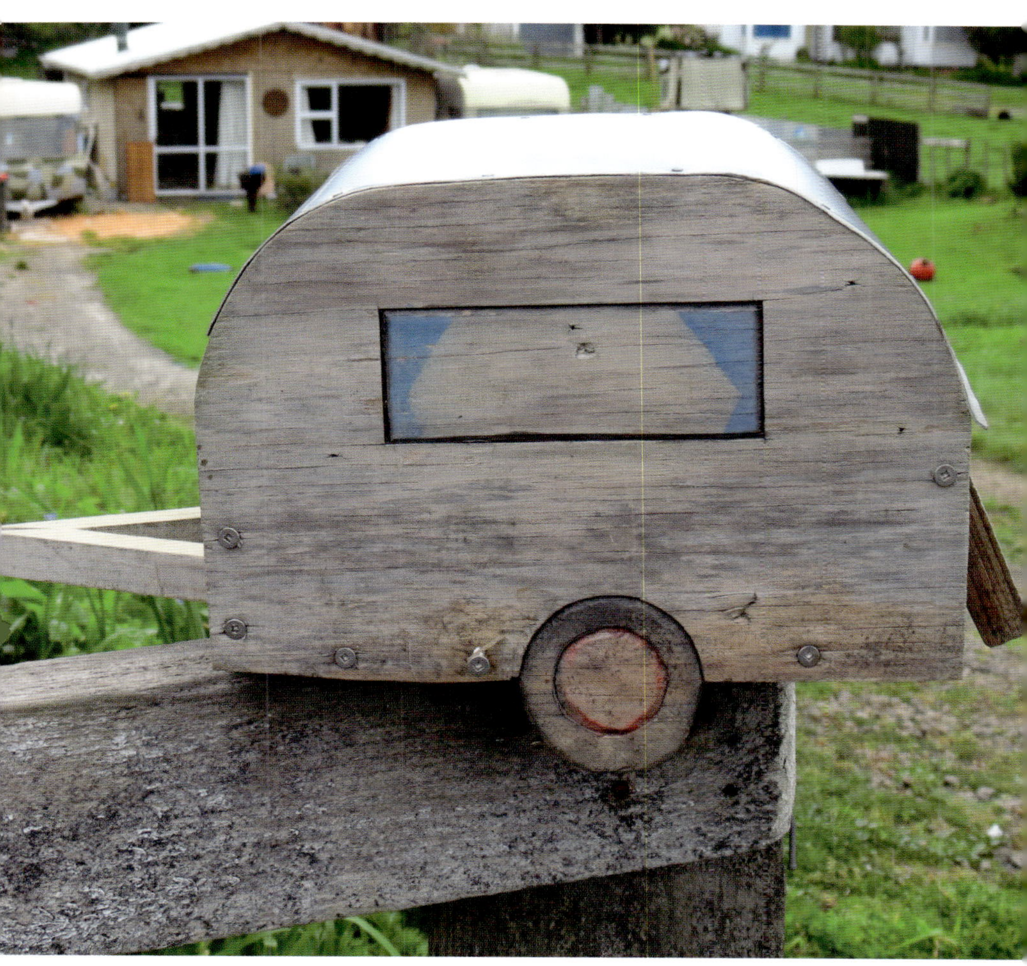

Caravanning is a Kiwi Christmas holiday tradition for many.

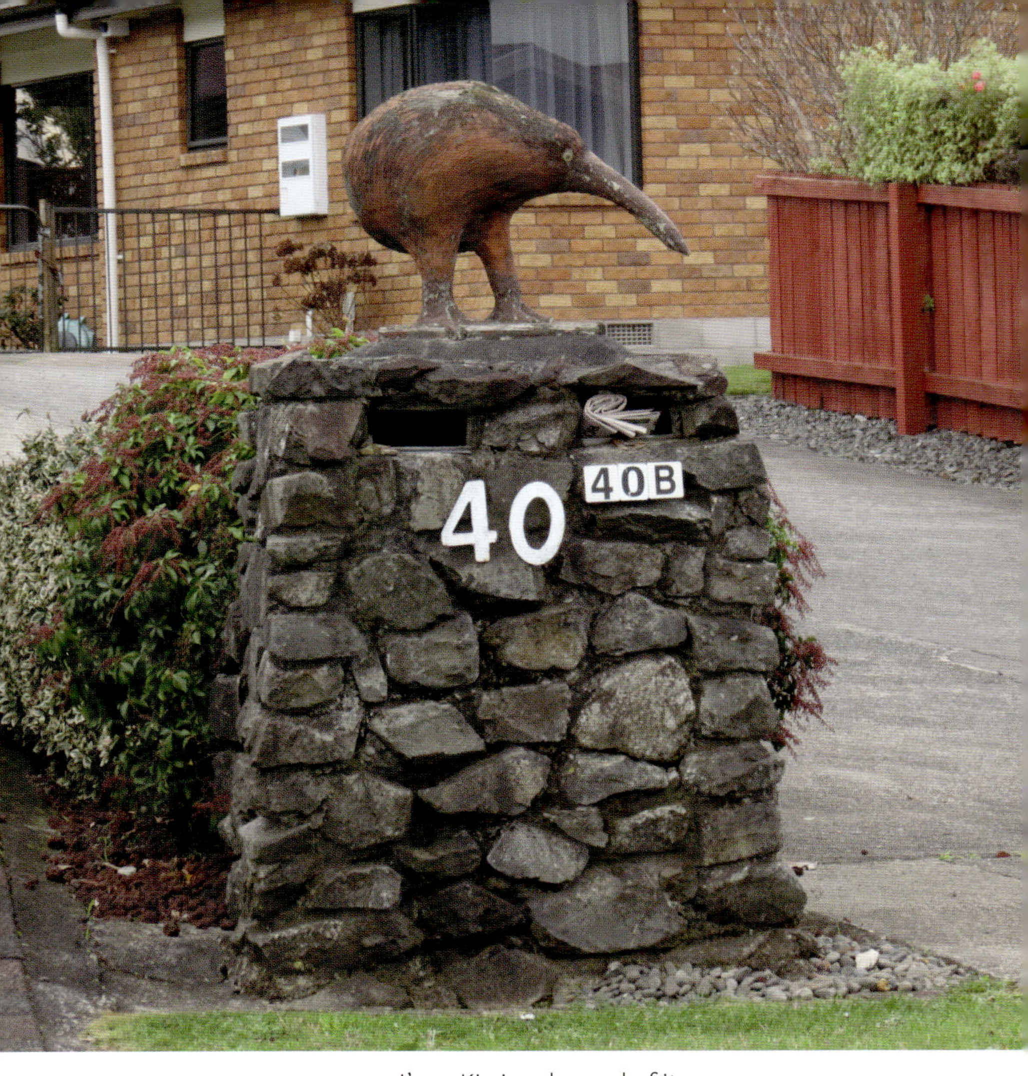

I'm a Kiwi and proud of it.

CRAFTY KIWIS

The letterboxes on the following pages have been made by crafty Kiwis kind enough to put their masterpieces on the roadside for everyone to enjoy.

These fine creations are all examples of, or relate to, the visual and decorative arts like painting, drawing, sculpting and mosaics. Stand by for fan mail!

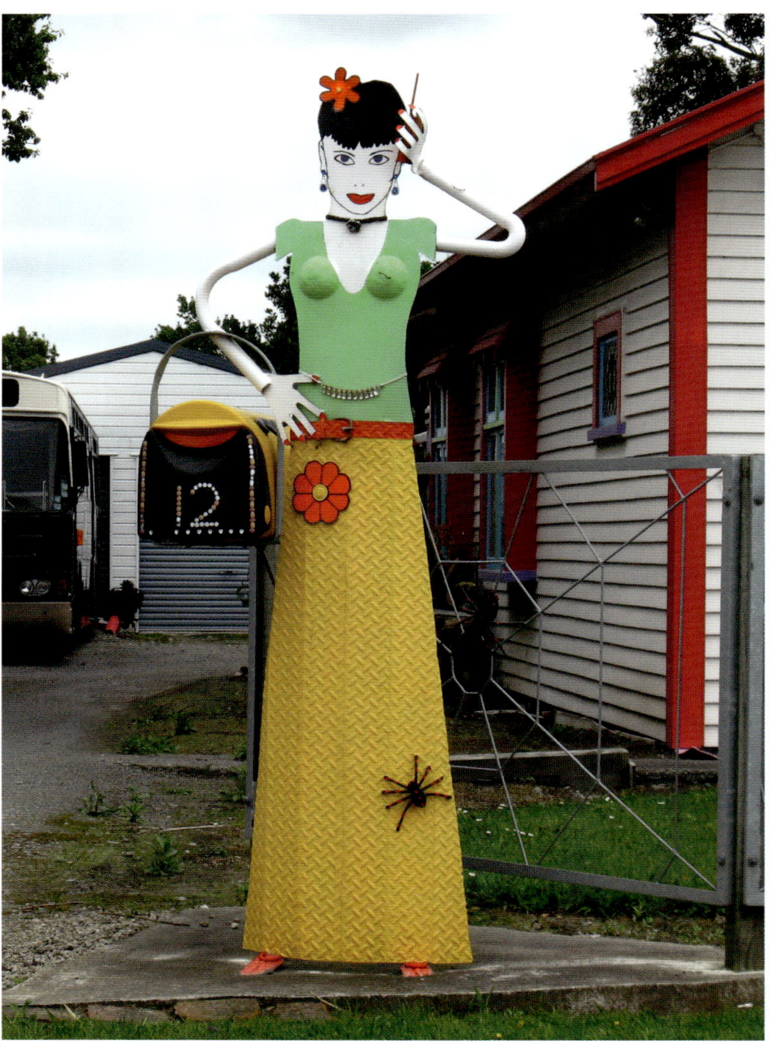

'Wow, my entry into the Wearable Arts Show has been accepted! Thanks, I'll see you there.'

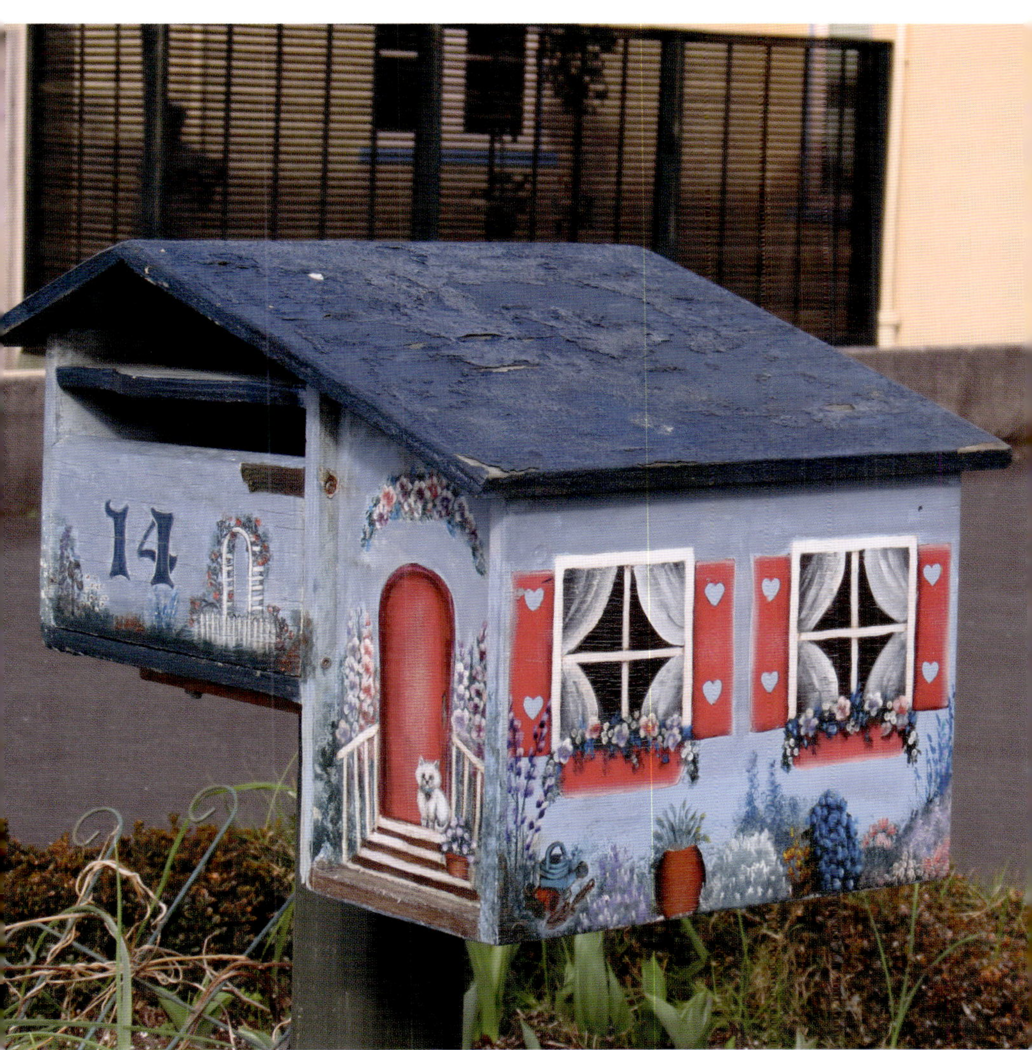

Blooming beautiful paint job.

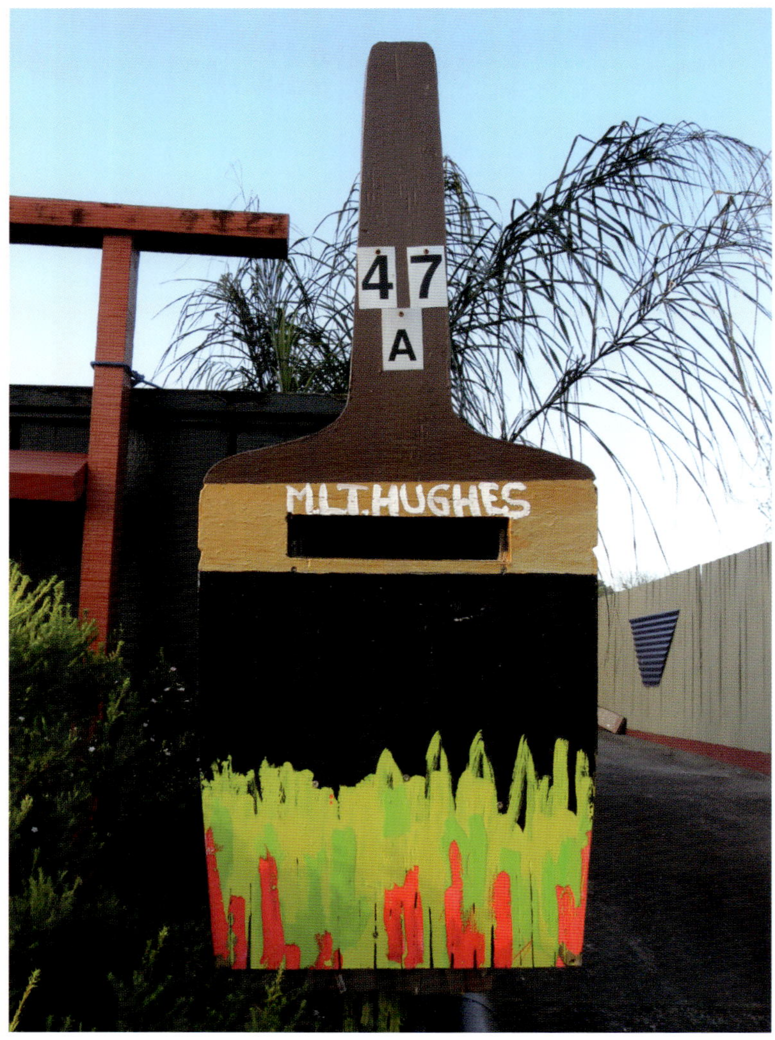

Let's paint the town yellow, pink and green.

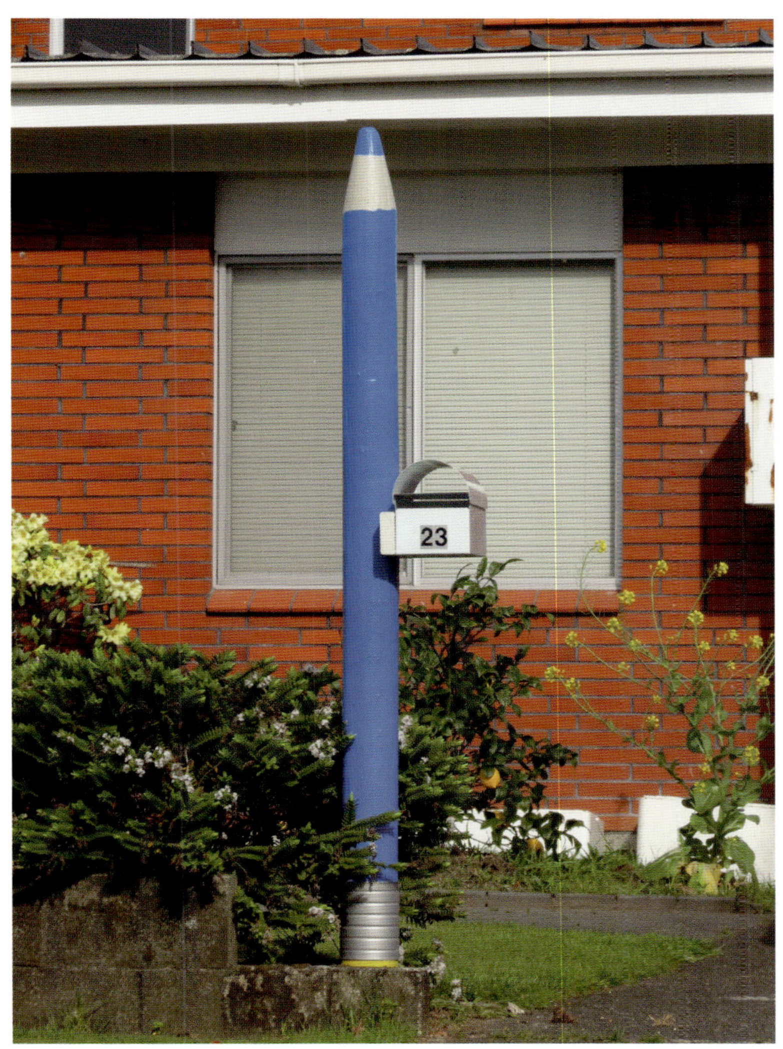

Pencil me in.

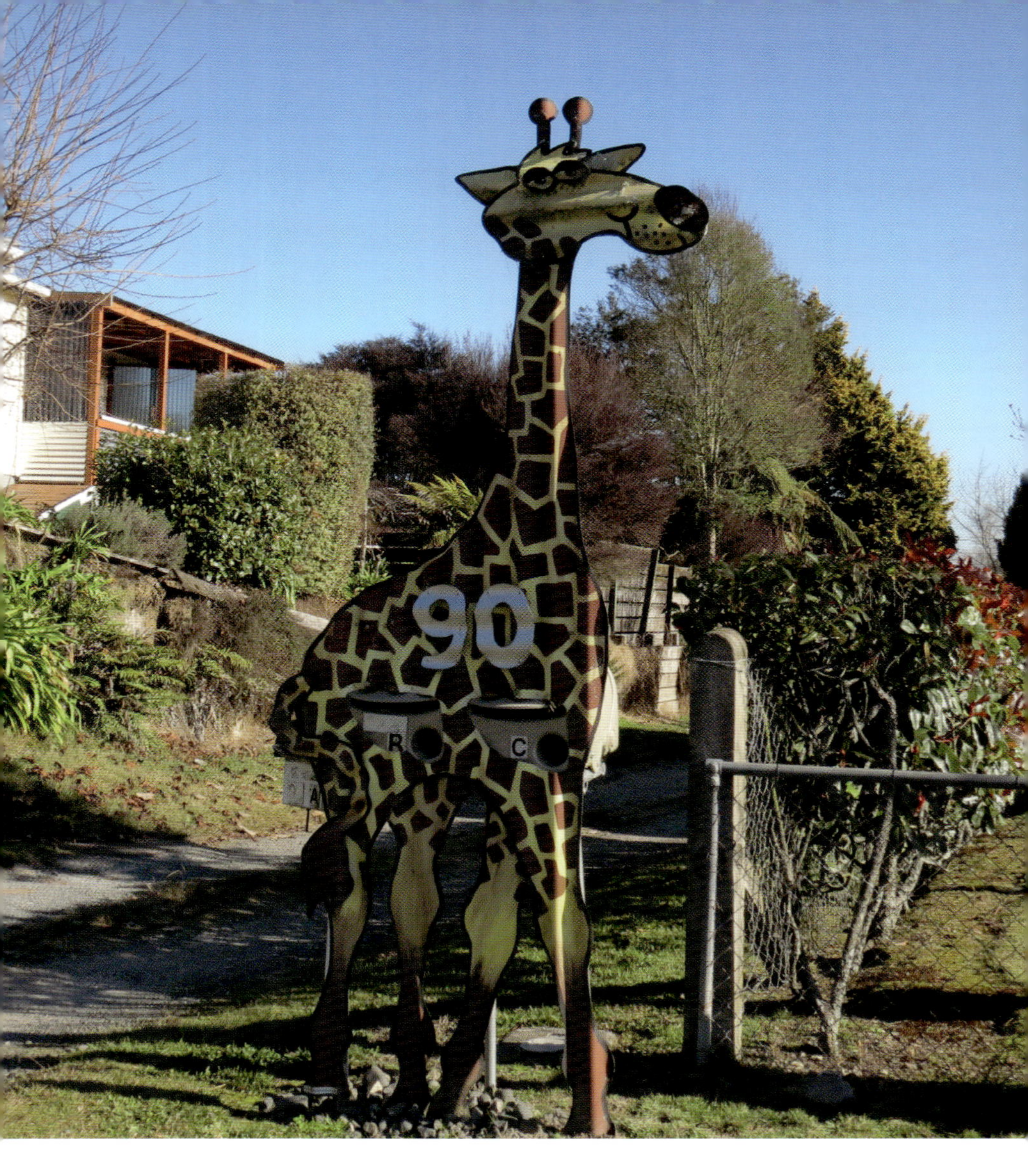

Tall order in corrugated iron.

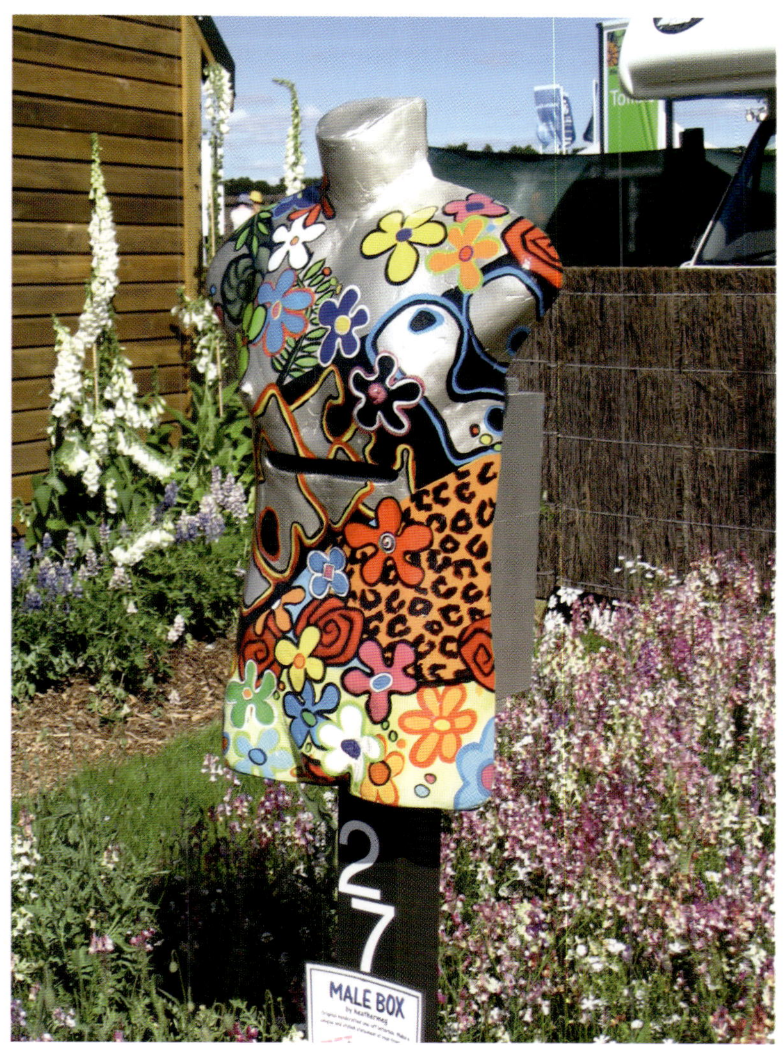

Male box in full flower.

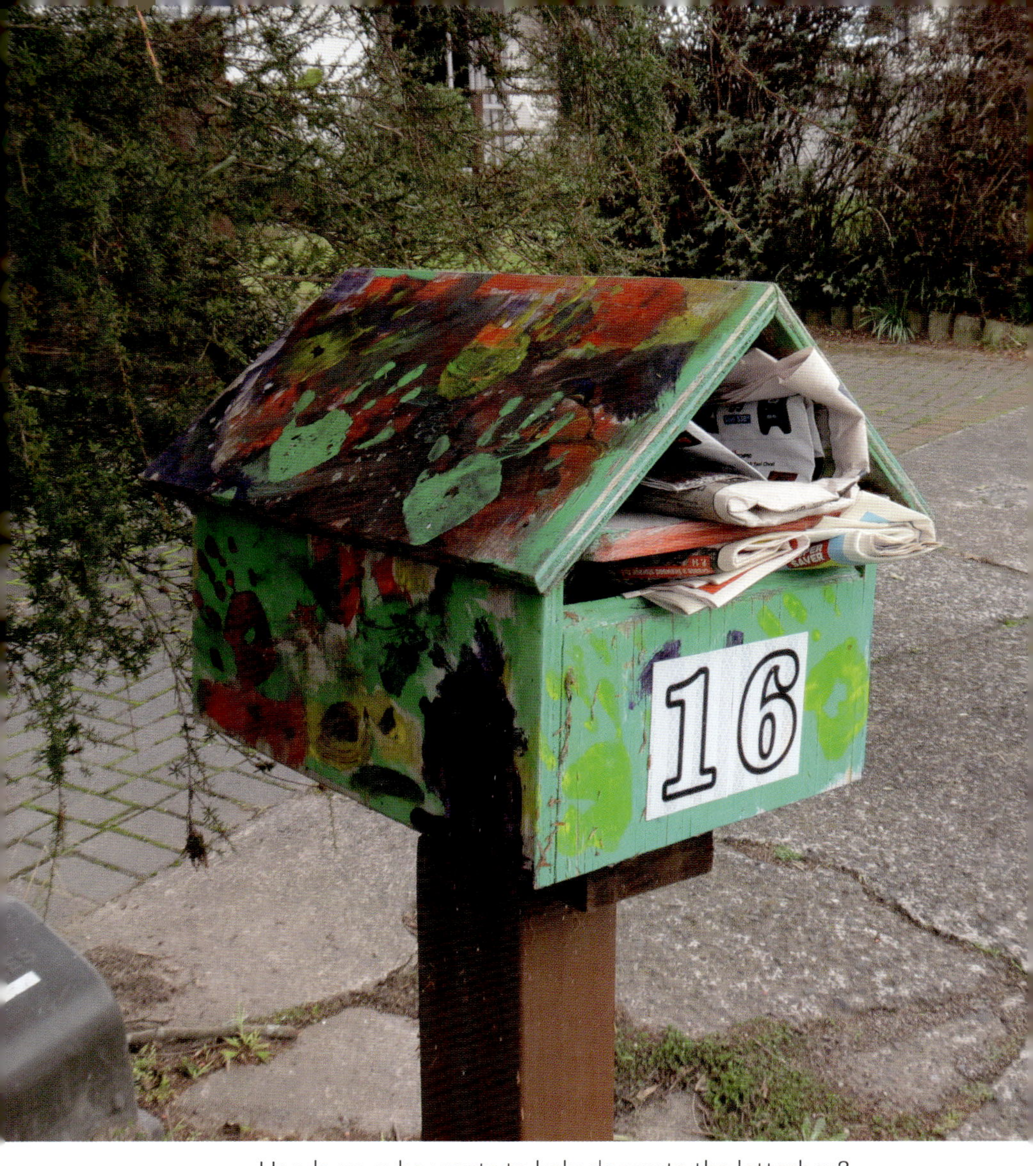

Hands up, who wants to help decorate the letterbox?

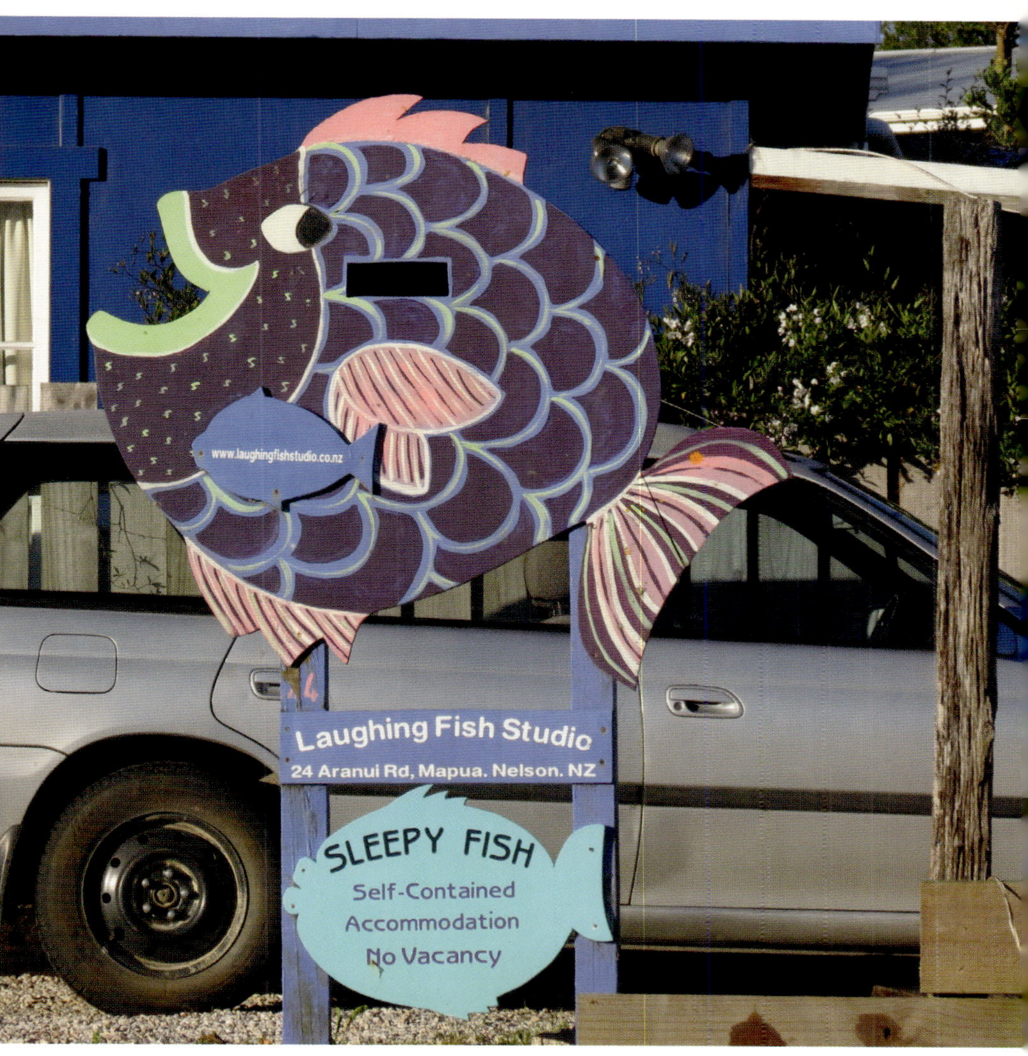

It's a fishy business.

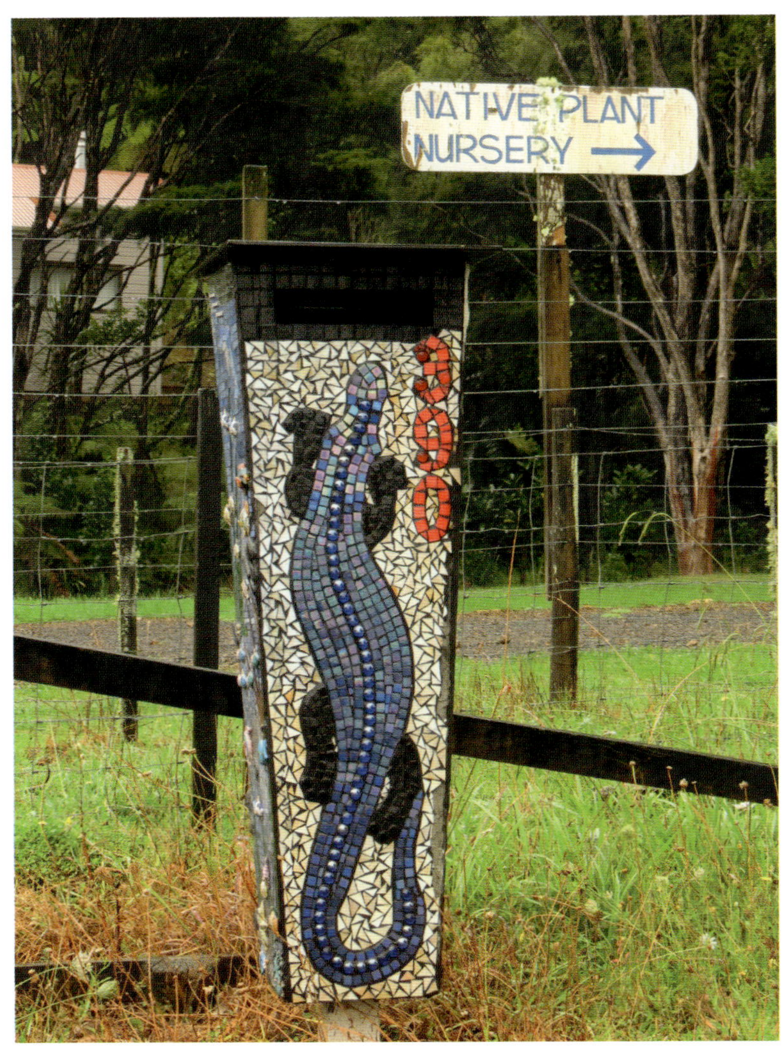

One of the locals — Coromandel striped gecko in mosaic.

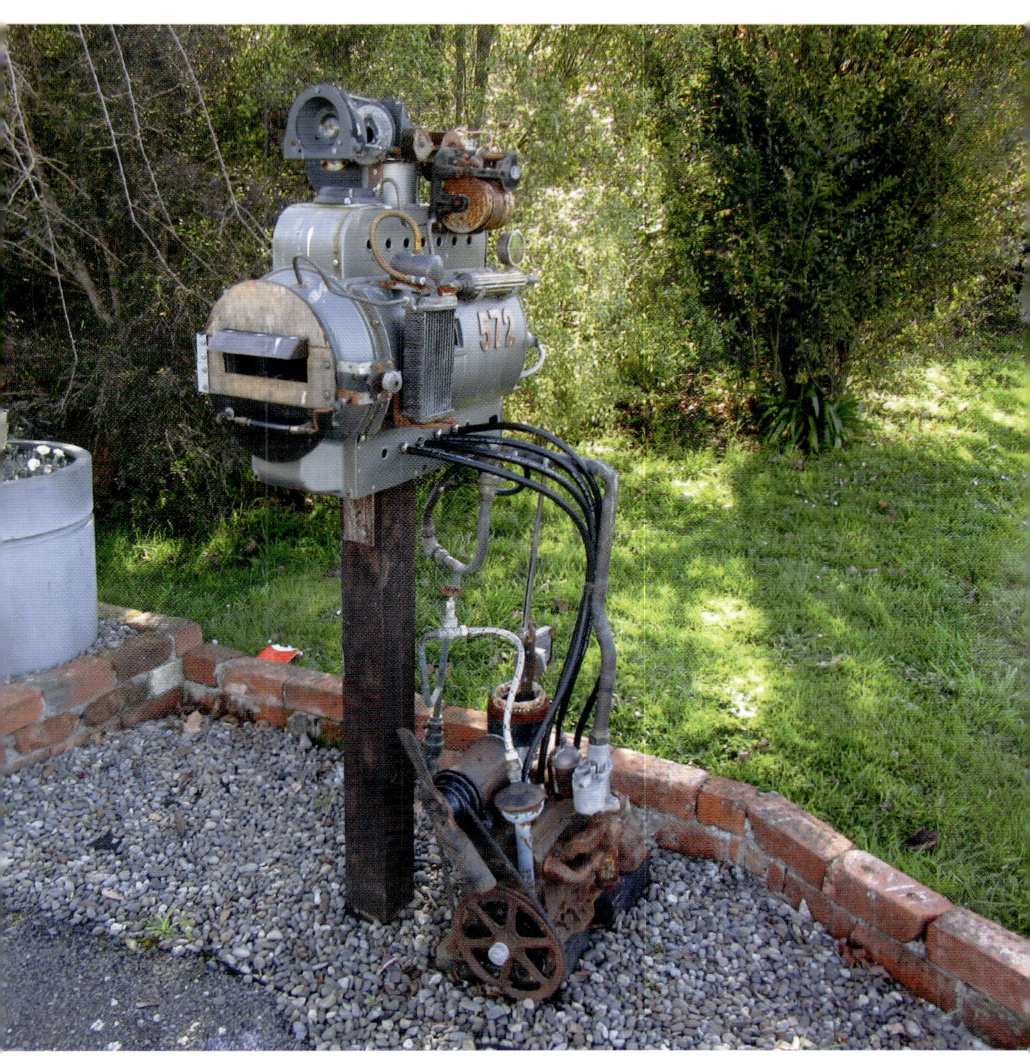

Steampunk post box.

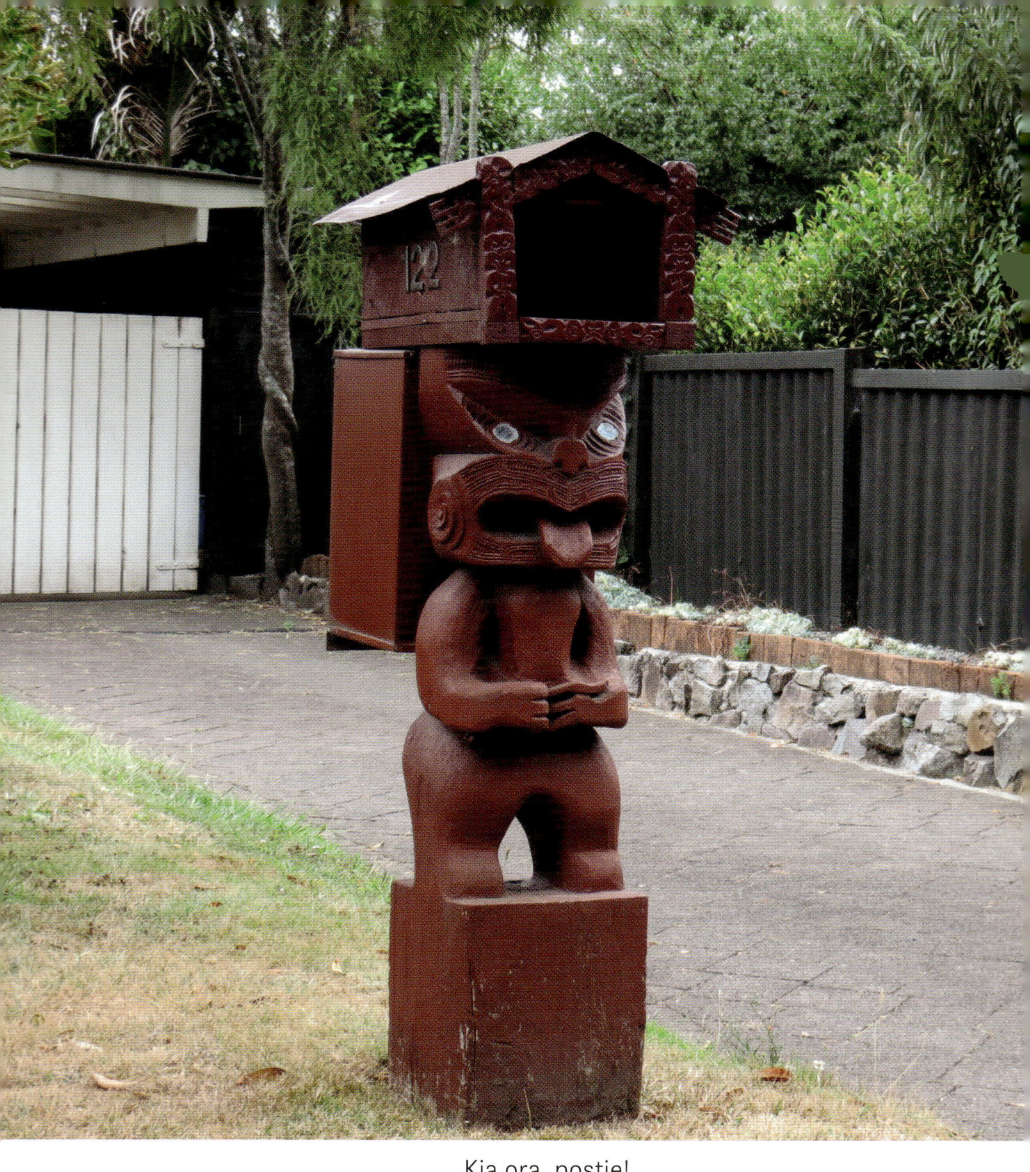

Kia ora, postie!

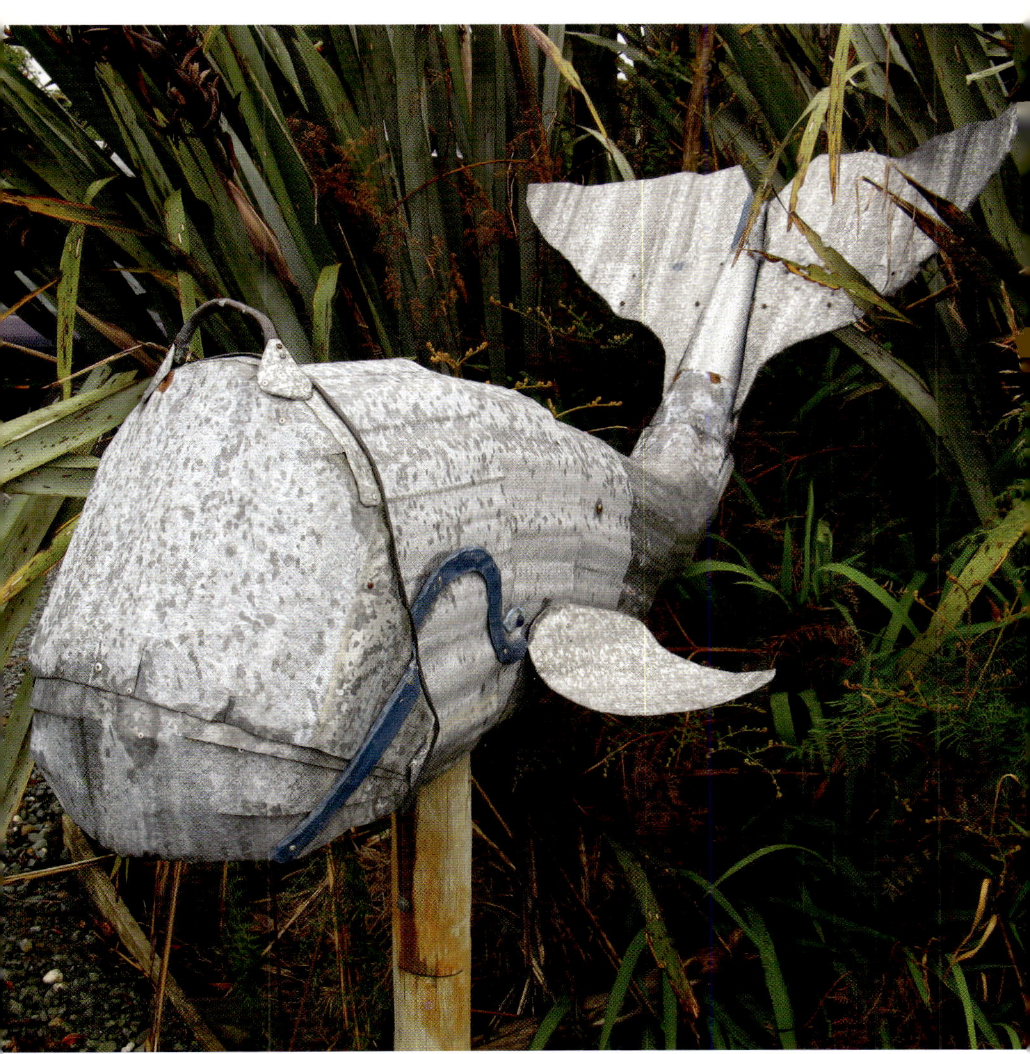

Mail whale.

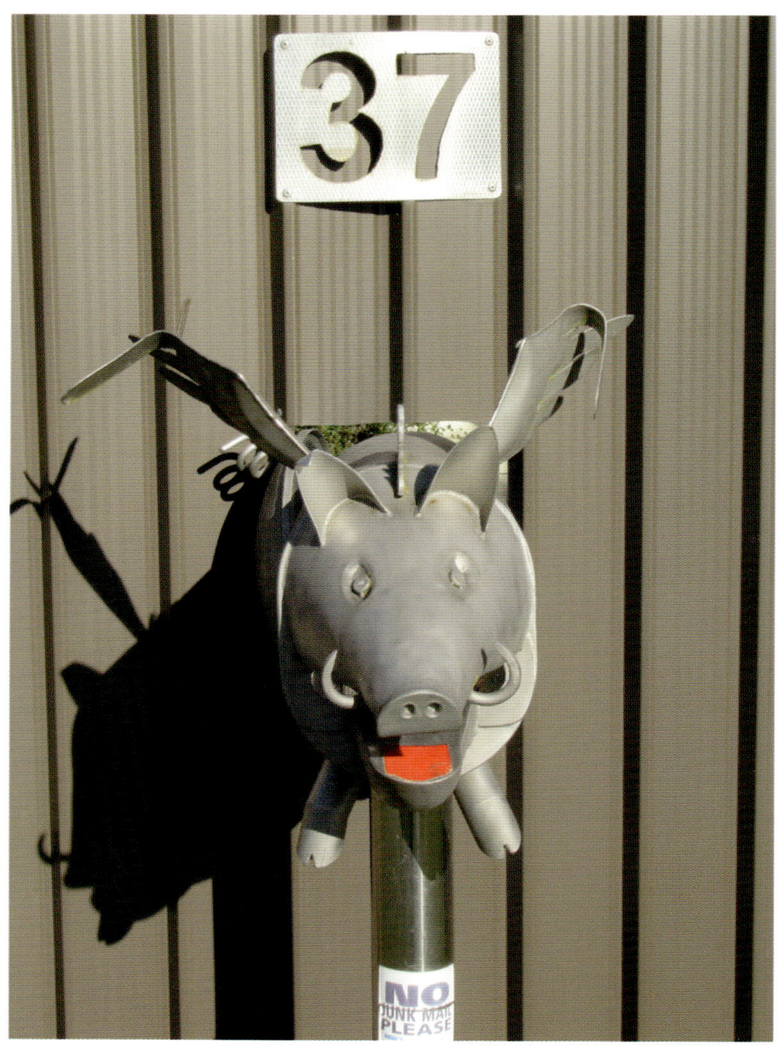

Pigasus waits for the post.

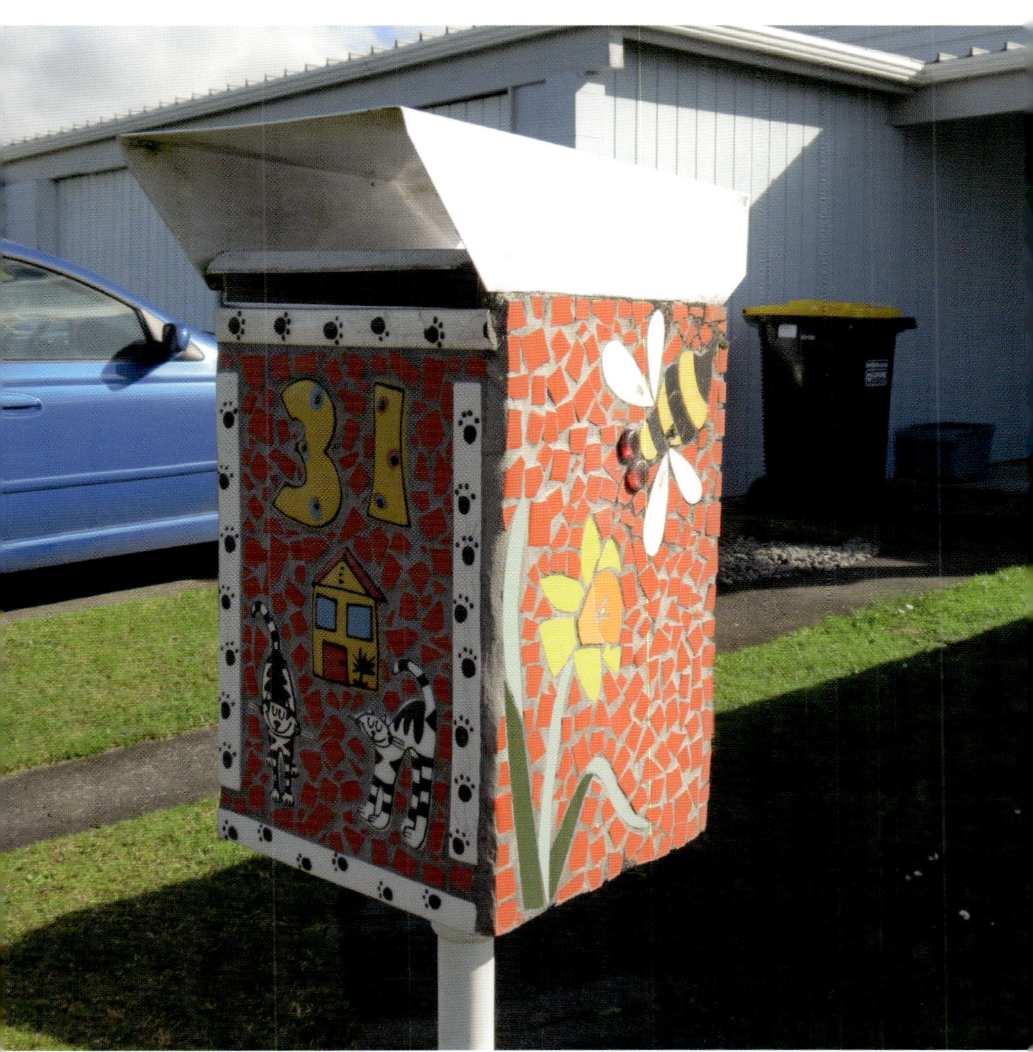

The cat's meow of mailboxes.

FROM SCREEN TO STREET SIDE

Movies like *Minions* and *SpongeBob SquarePants* have inspired some Kiwis to recreate their favourite screen characters and place them street side to delight not just the postie, but anyone who happens to pass by.

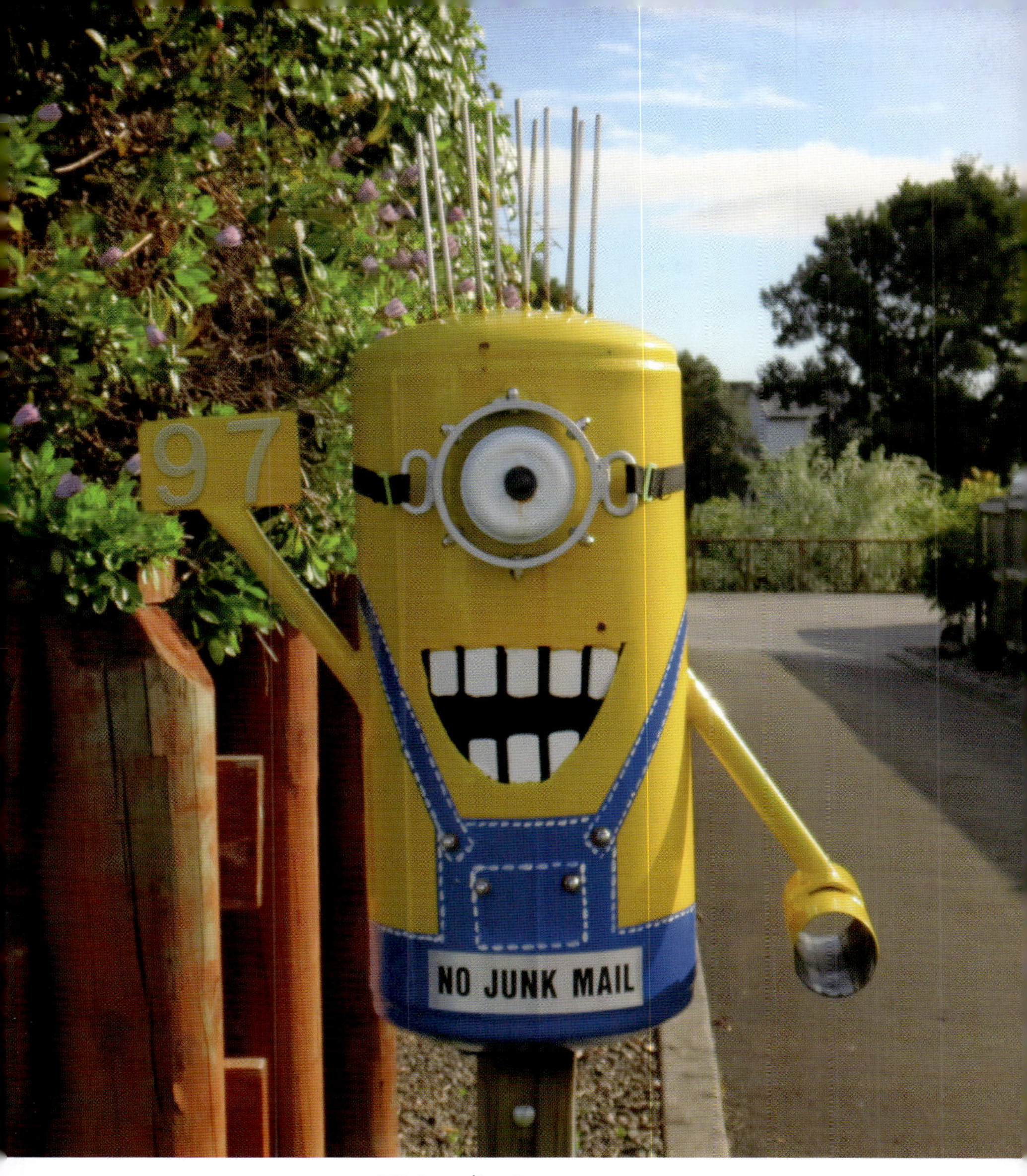

Minions live to serve.

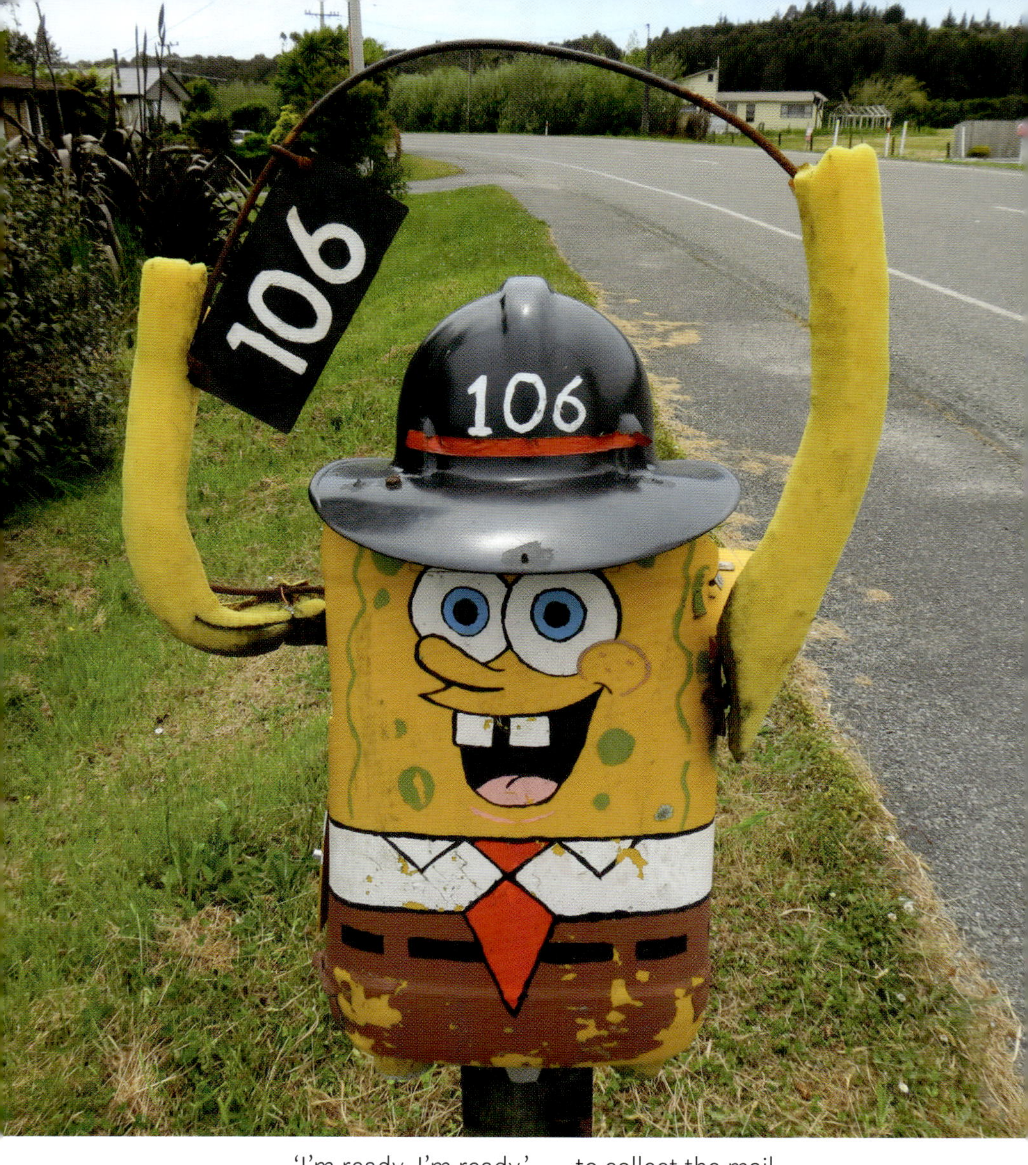

'I'm ready, I'm ready,' . . . to collect the mail.

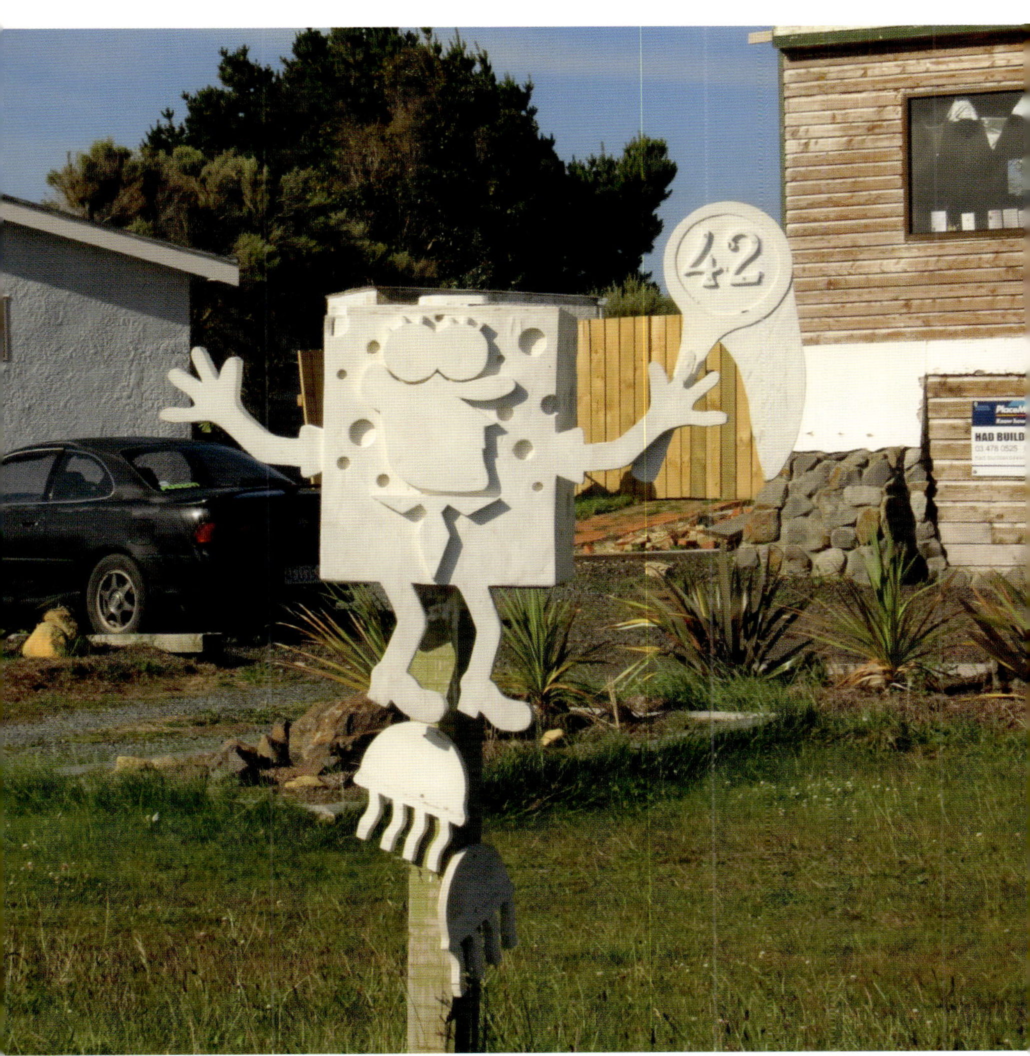

‘Hey, I may need a yellow paint job before I can be on TV again.’

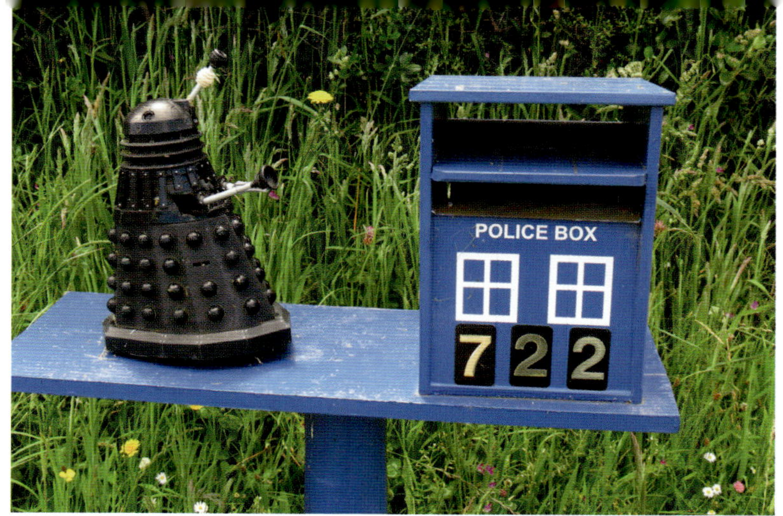

Dr Who's place.

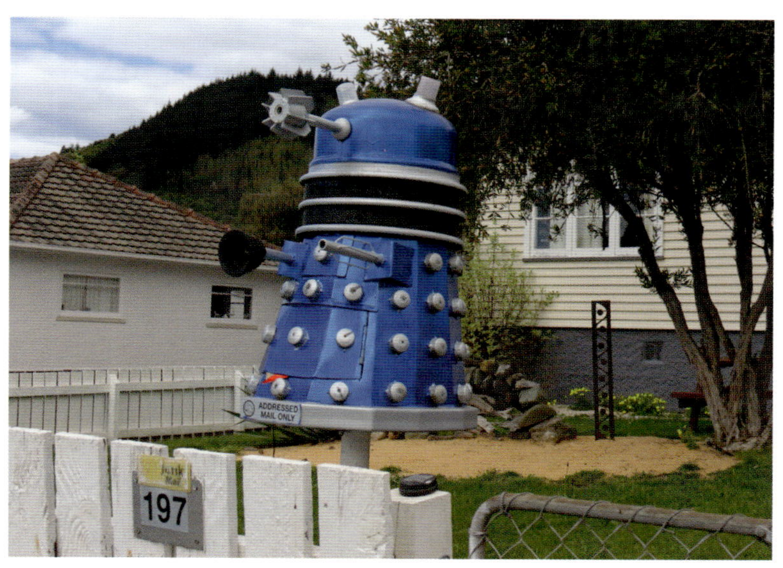

Exterminate, exterminate . . . the junk mail.

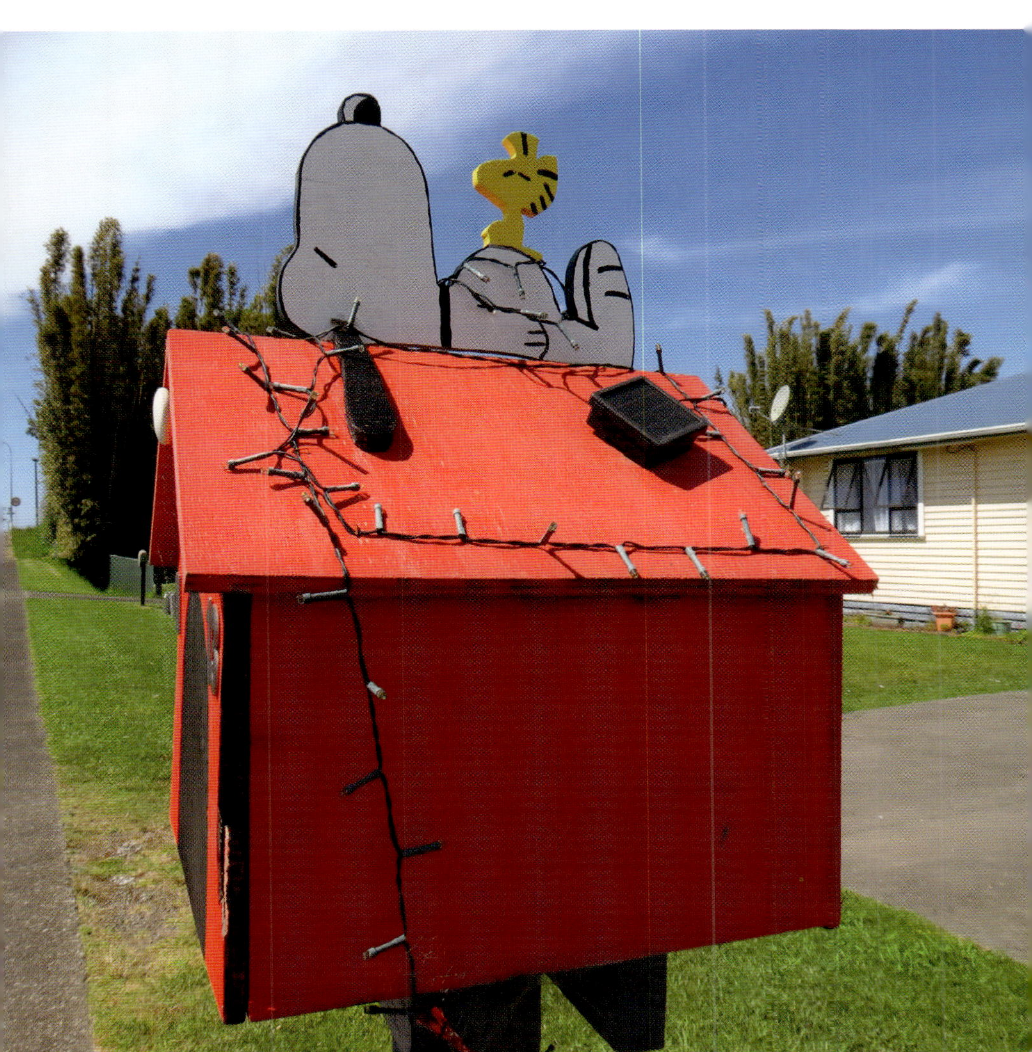

Snoopy daydreaming again.

OUT TO SEA

Wherever you are on land in New Zealand you are never more than 130 km from the sea. Auckland has one of the highest rates of boats per capita in the world, which is why it's known as the 'City of Sails'. Boating and fishing are popular pastimes for many Kiwis, we love our oceans and beaches!

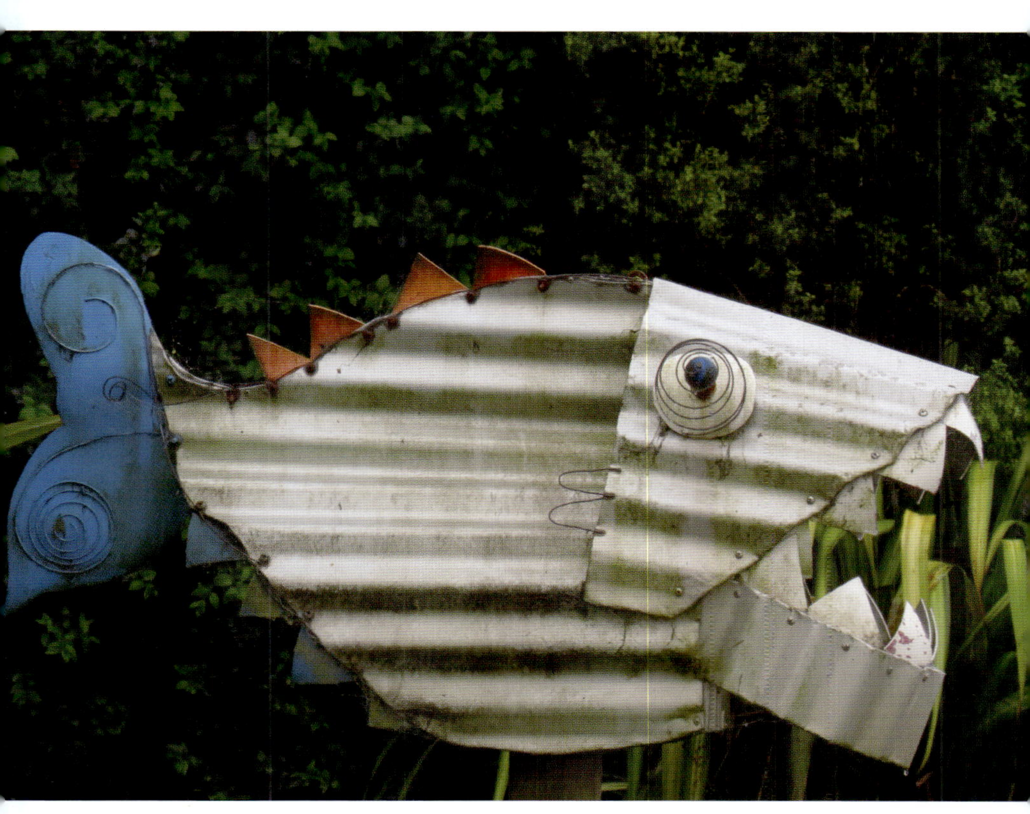

A nip from this guy might hurt a bit!

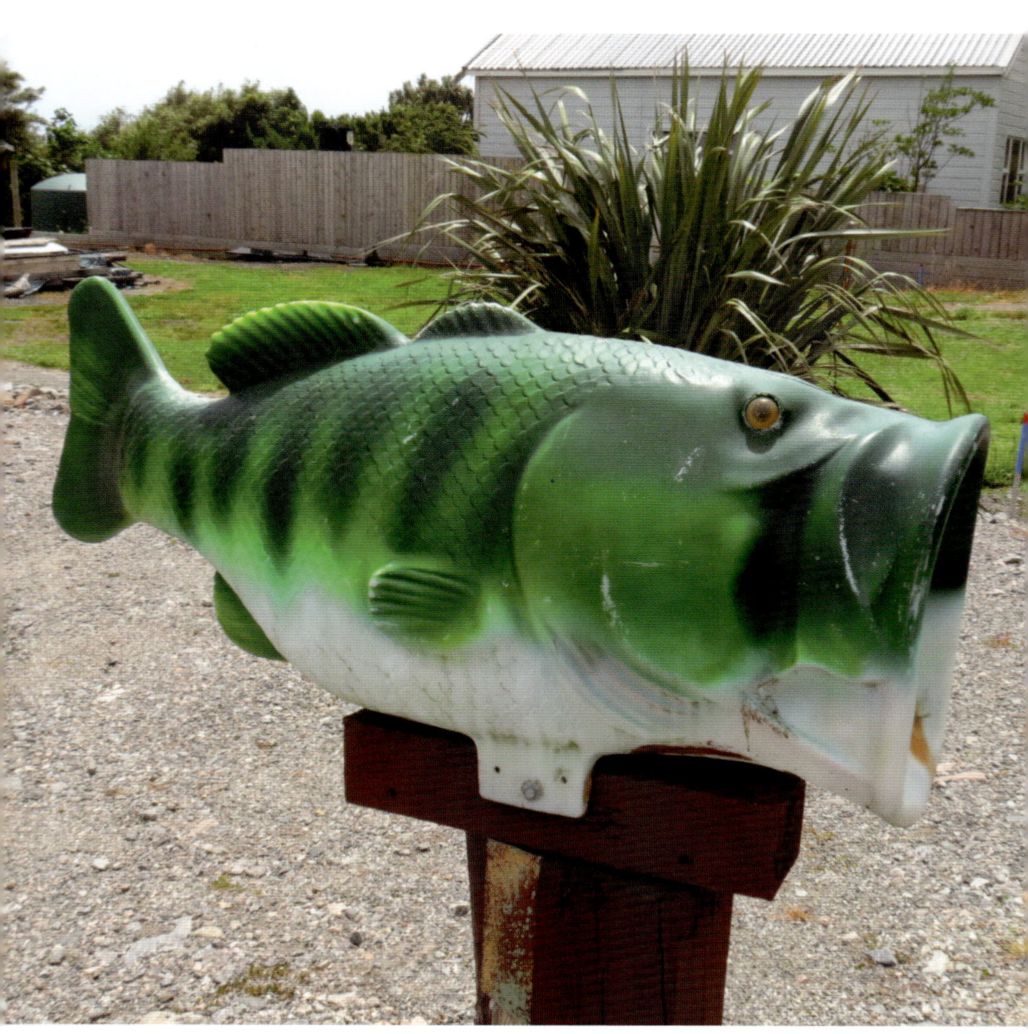

The one that didn't get away.

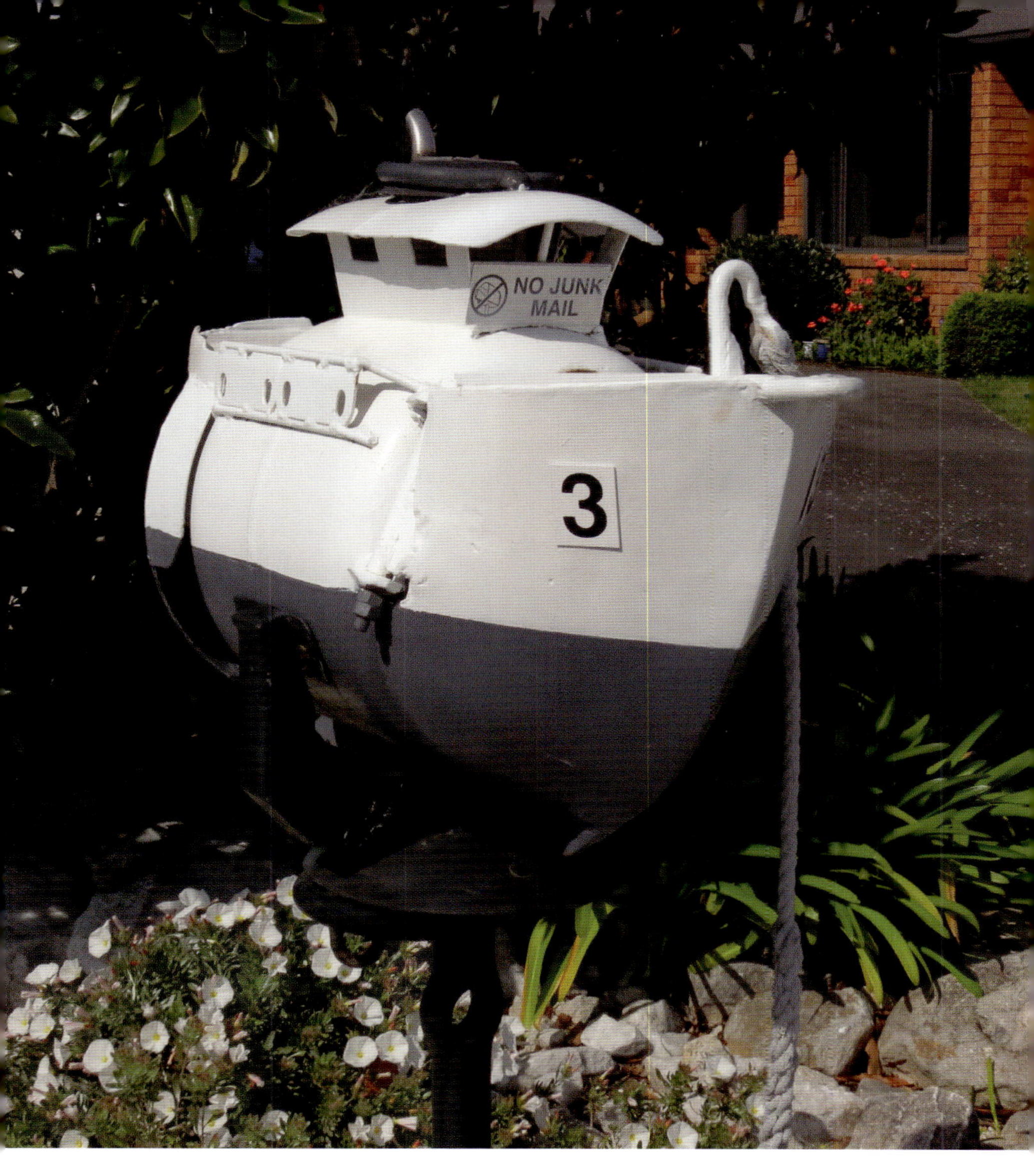

Land Ahoy!

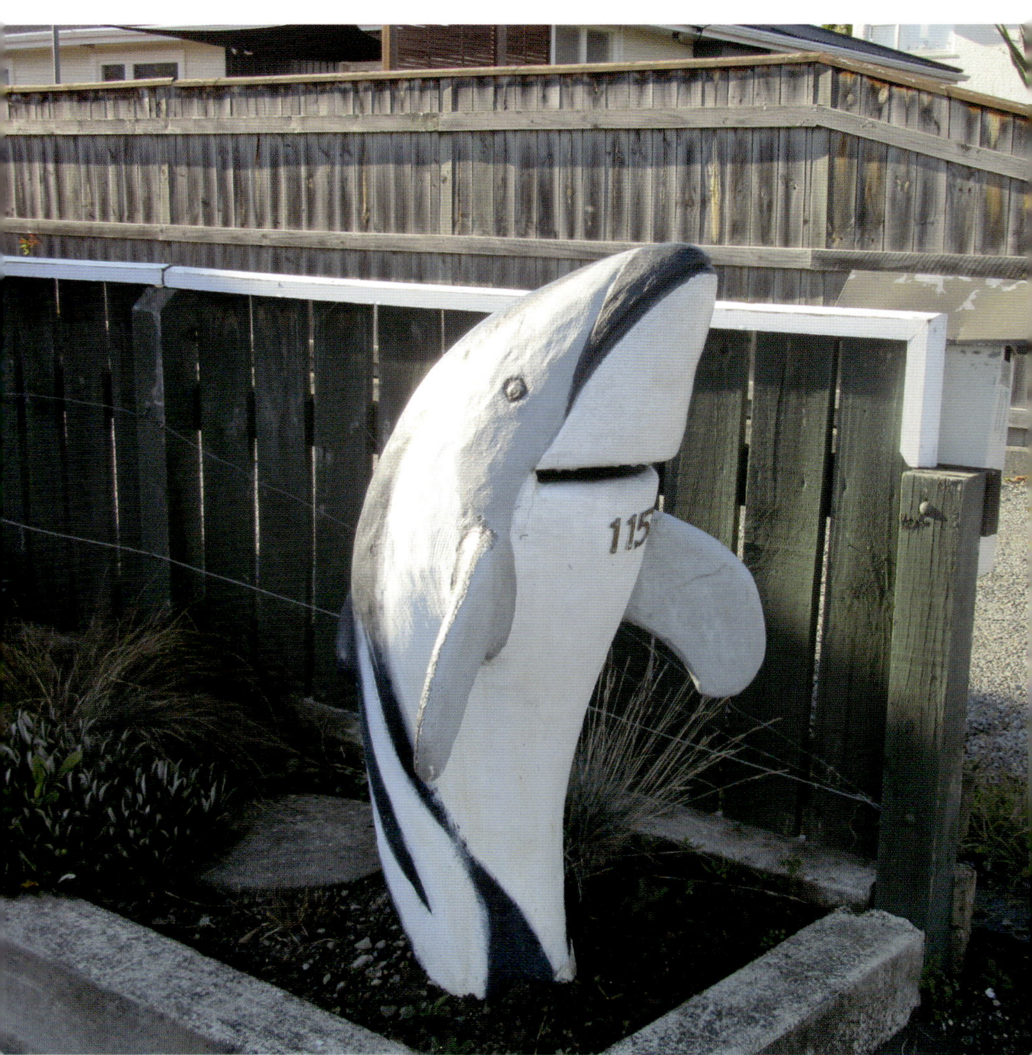

Marco the Mako.

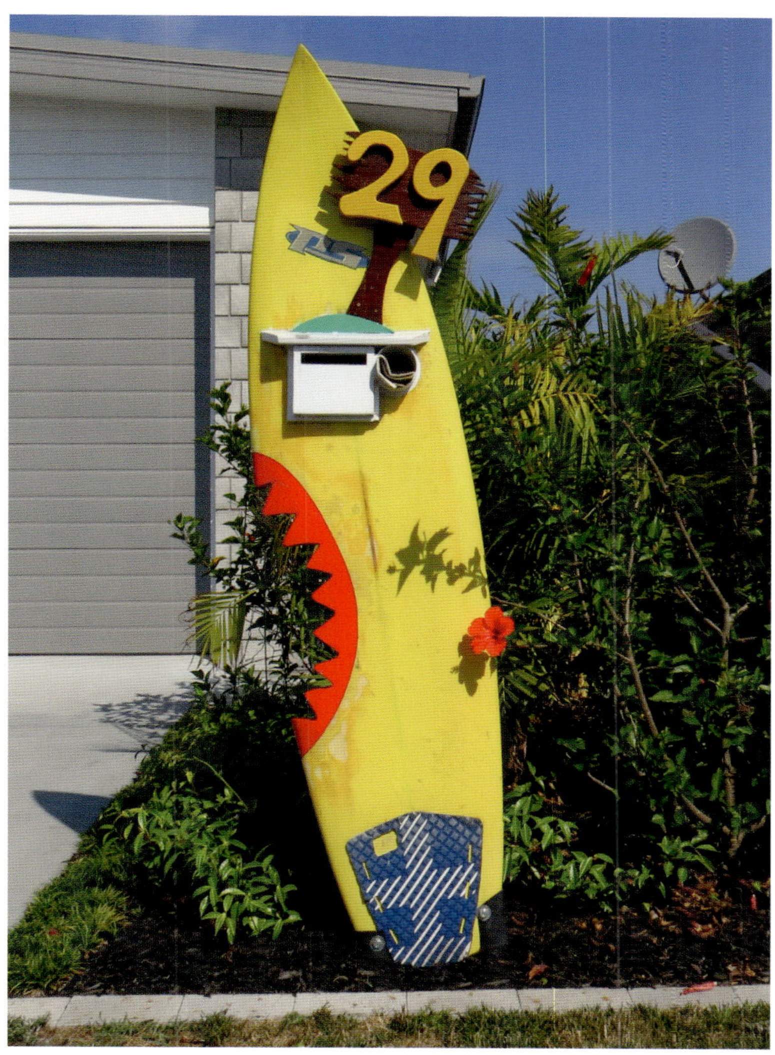

Bite me!

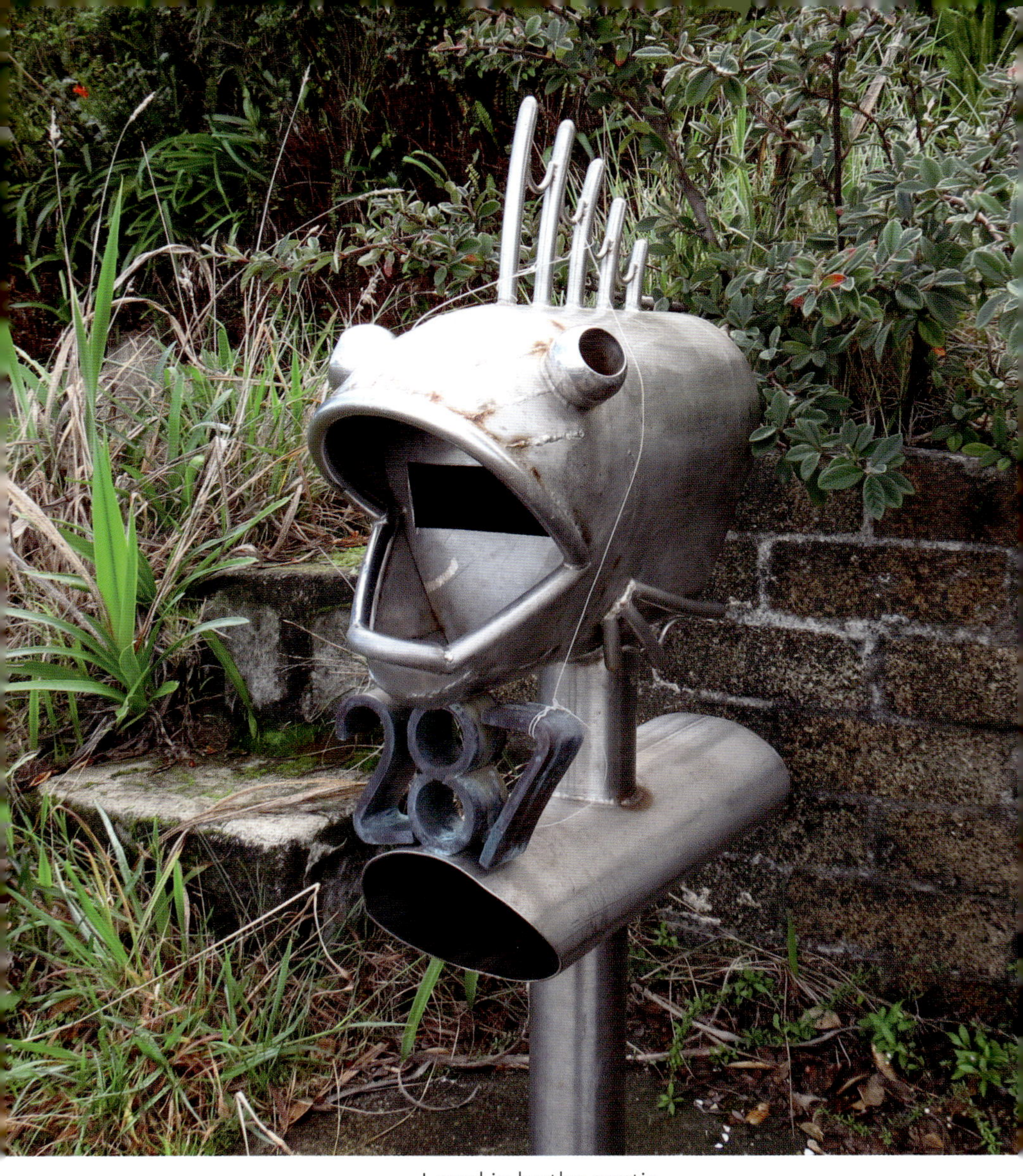

Lured in by the postie.

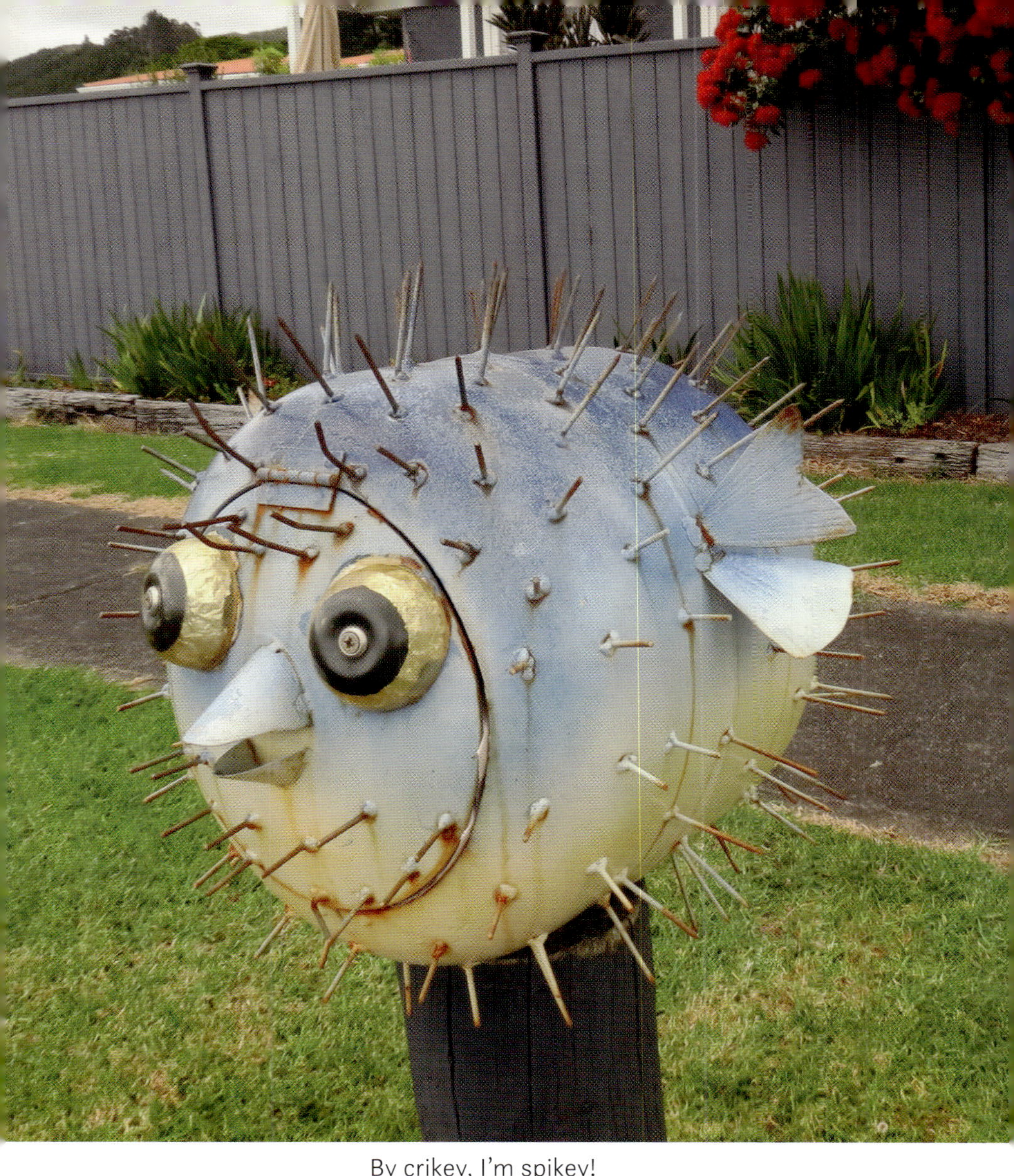

By crikey, I'm spikey!

KIWIS AT WORK

Letterboxes can be an eye-catching and inexpensive form of roadside marketing for Kiwi businesses. Need a hairdresser or a house mover? You might find them kerbside.

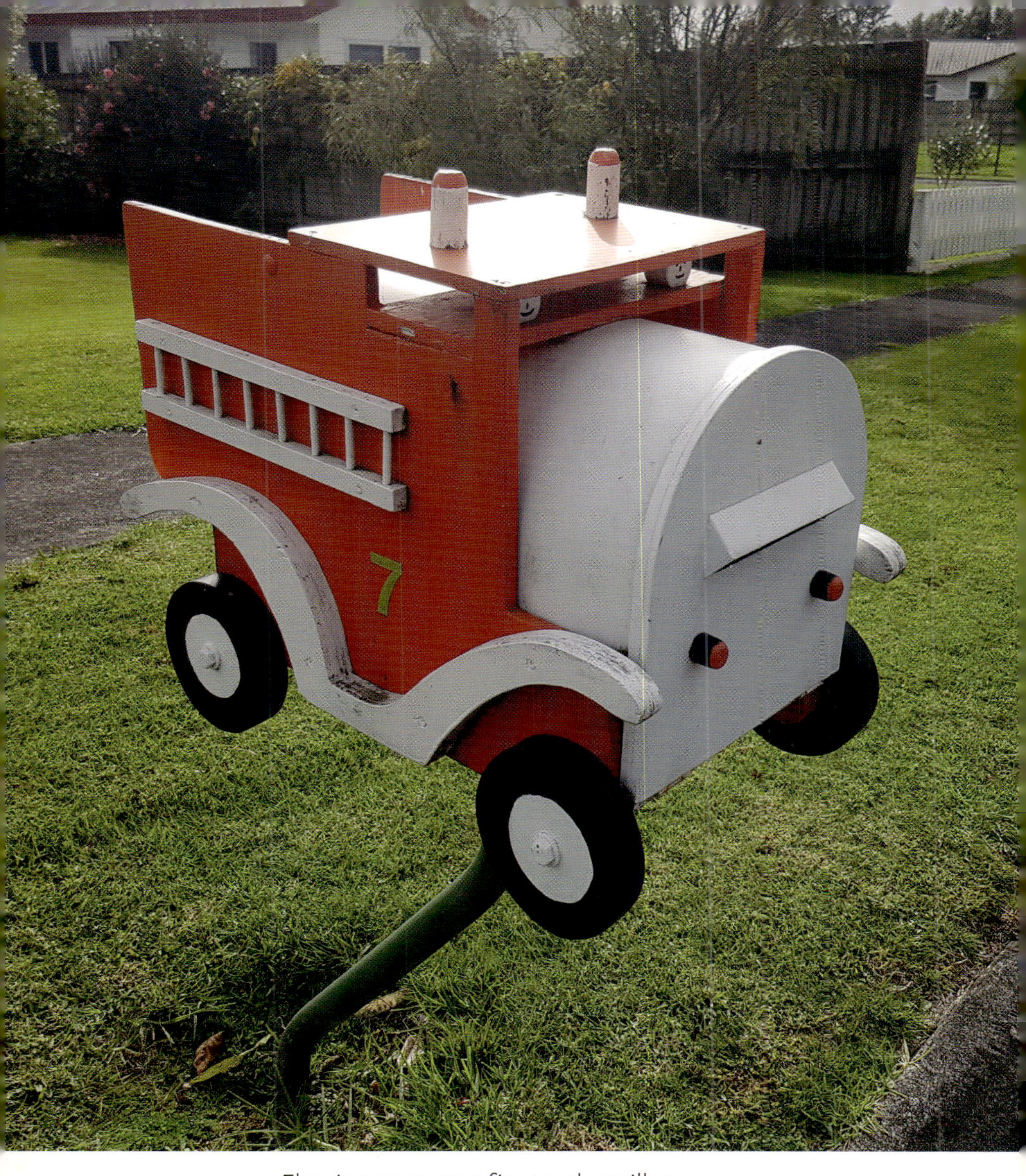

Flaming awesome fire truck mailbox.

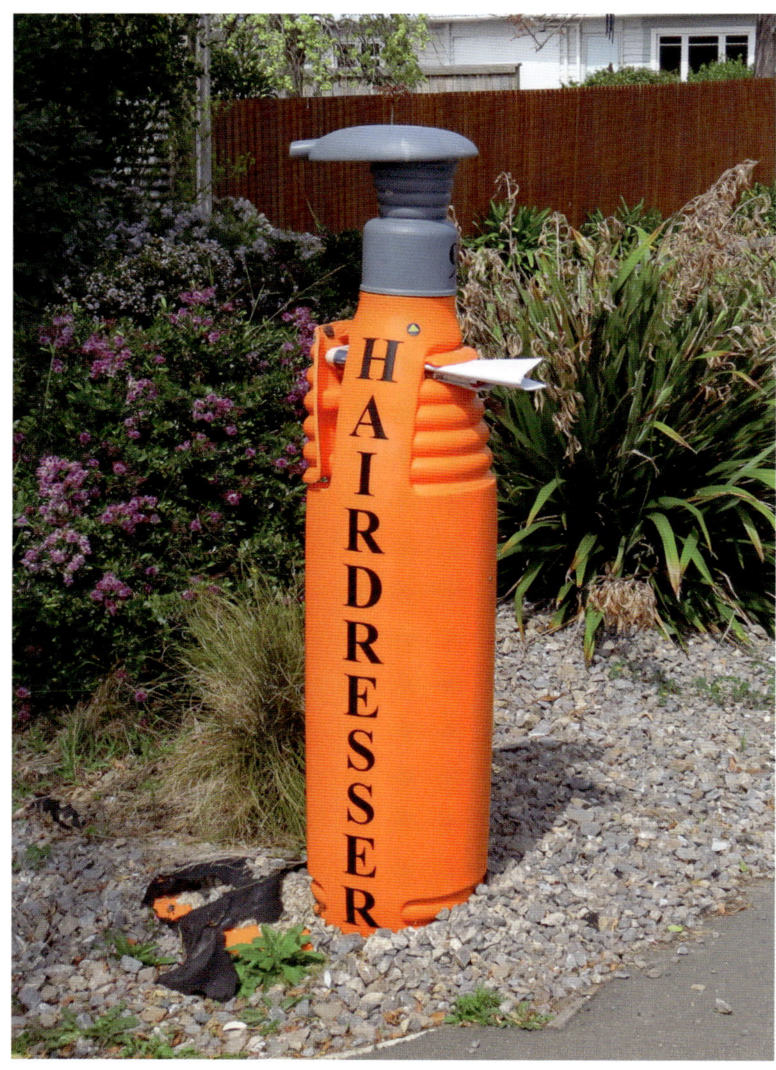

Cutting edge letterbox design.

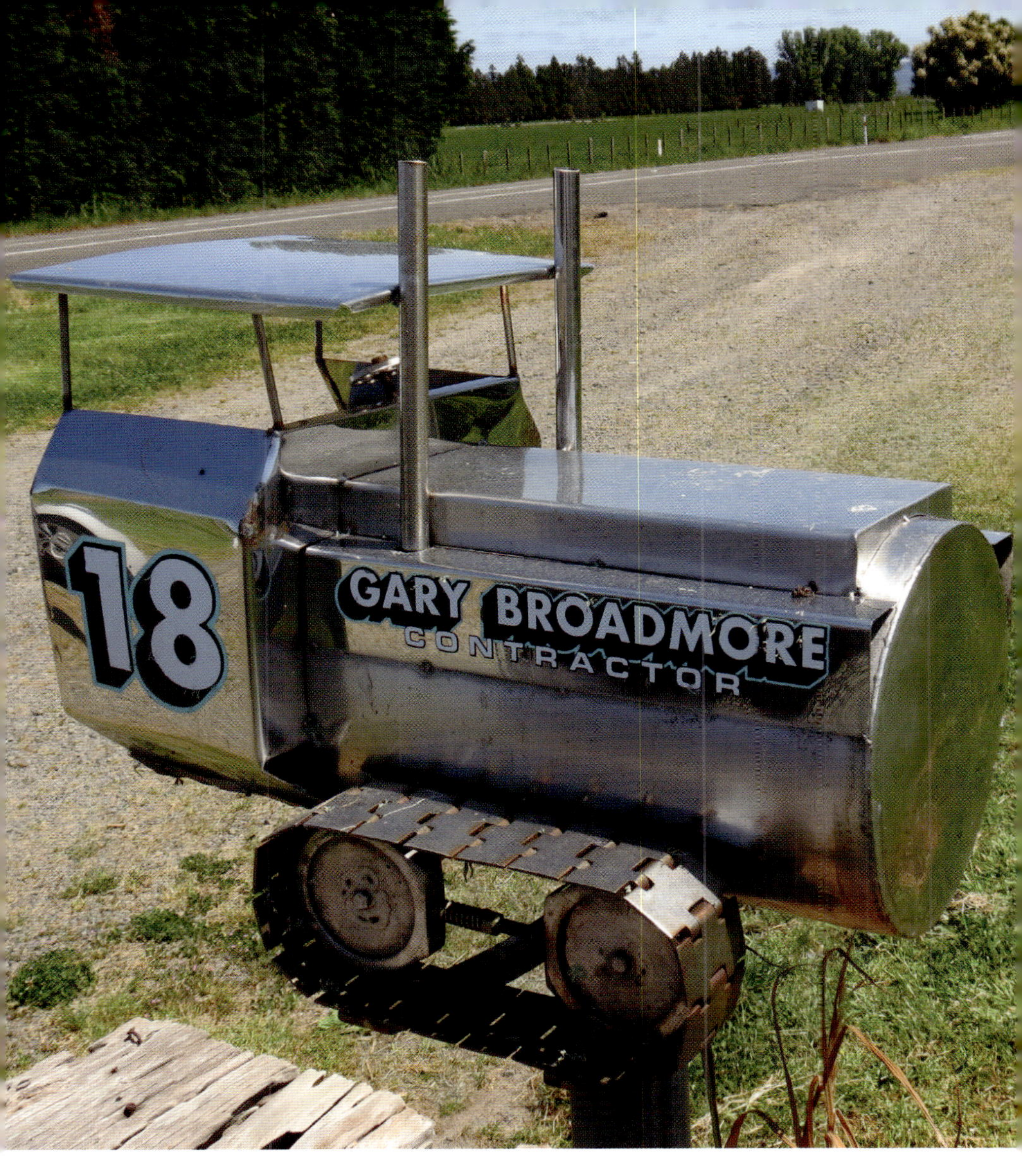

Clearing a path for the postie.

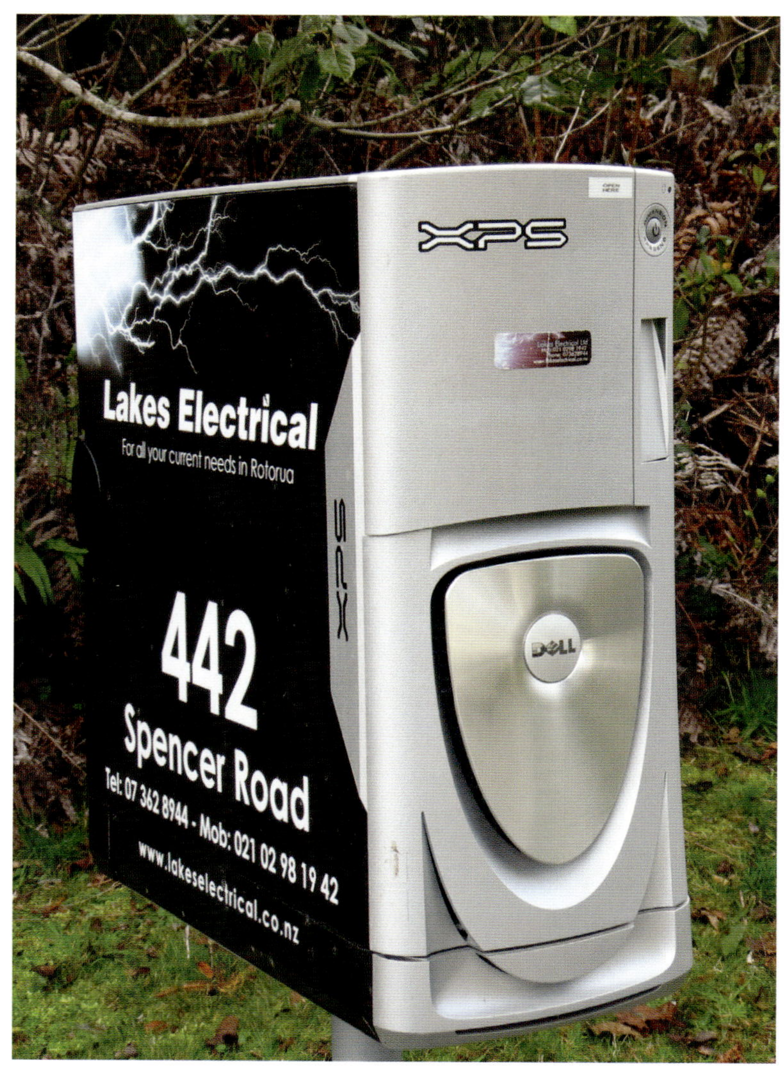

Searching for snail mail.

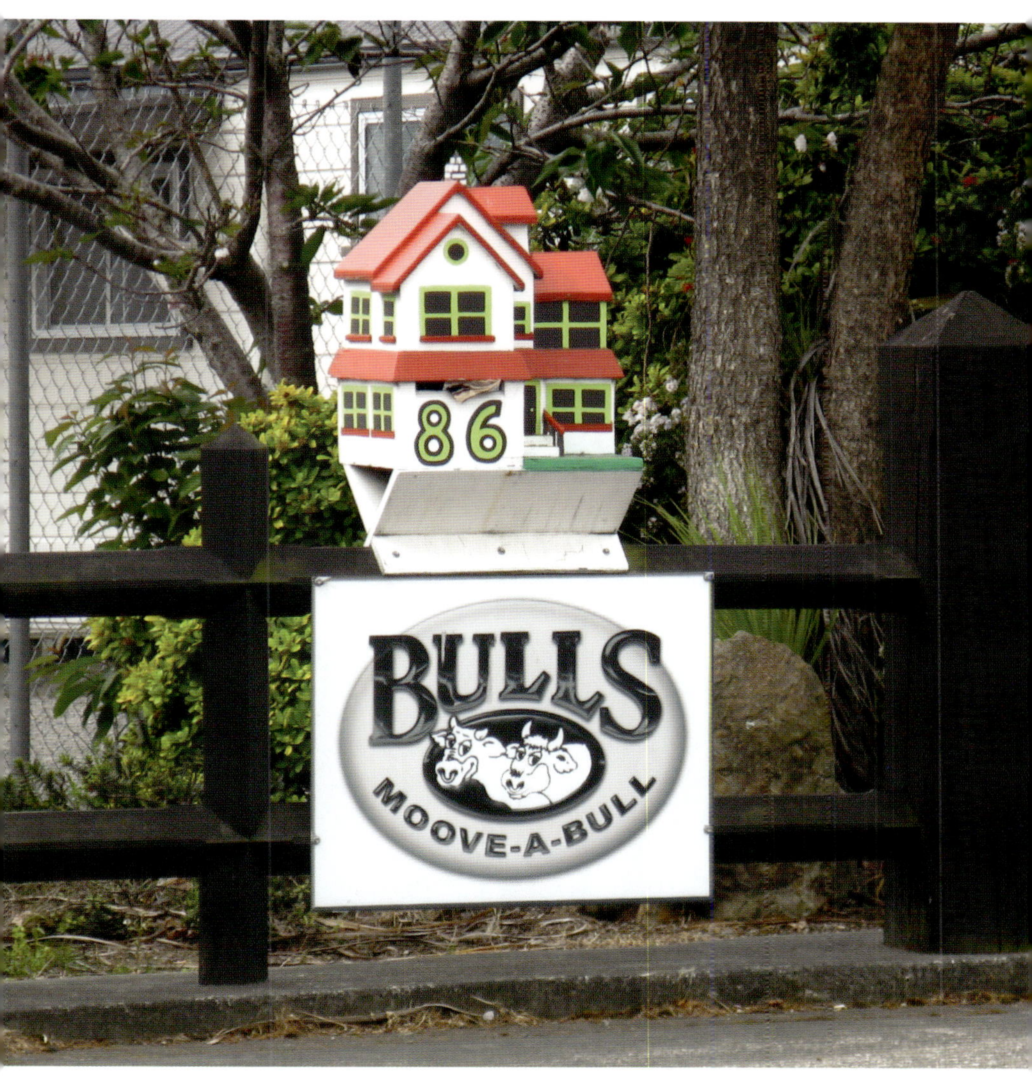

House moovers in Bulls.

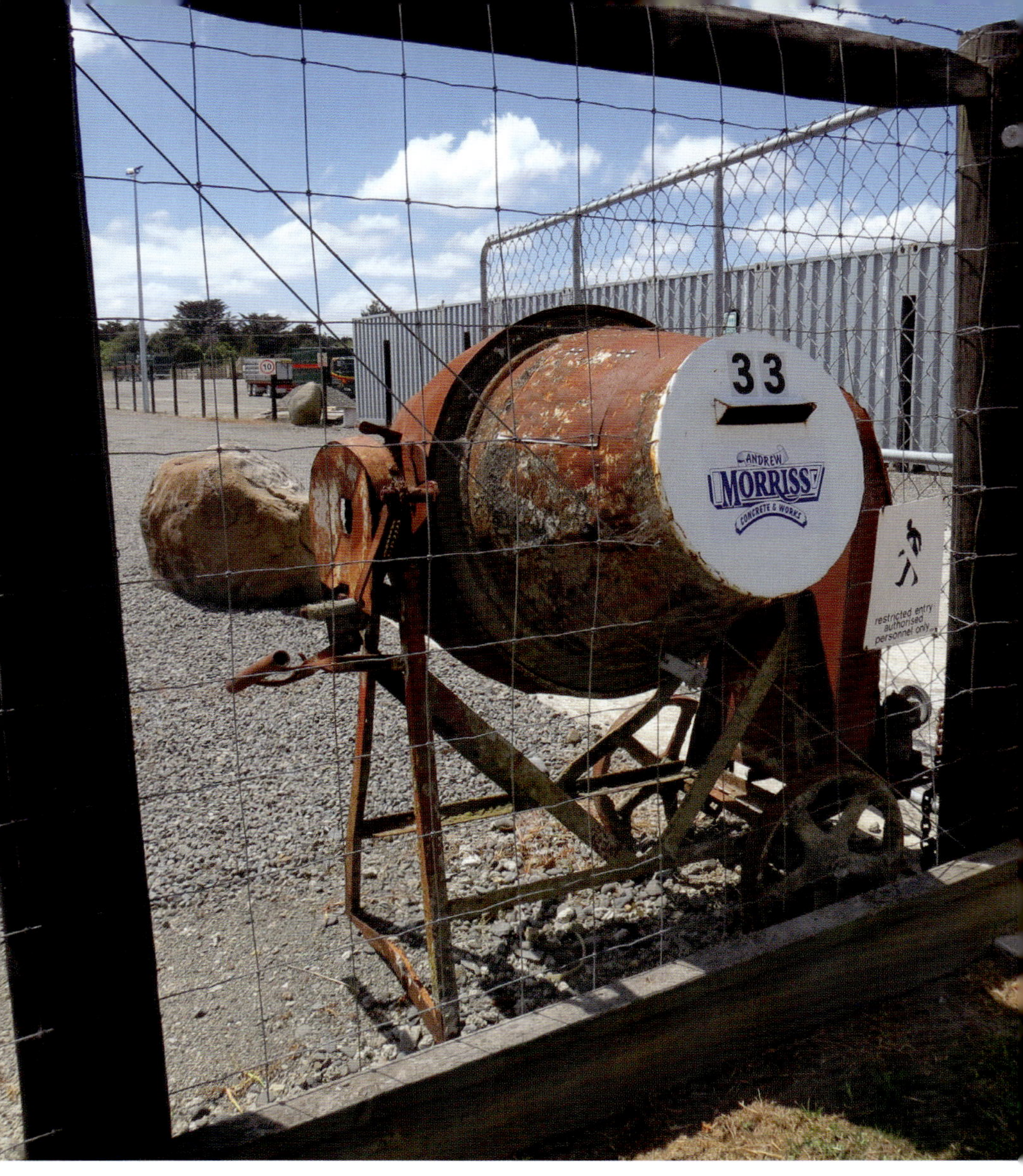

Mixing it up in Marton.

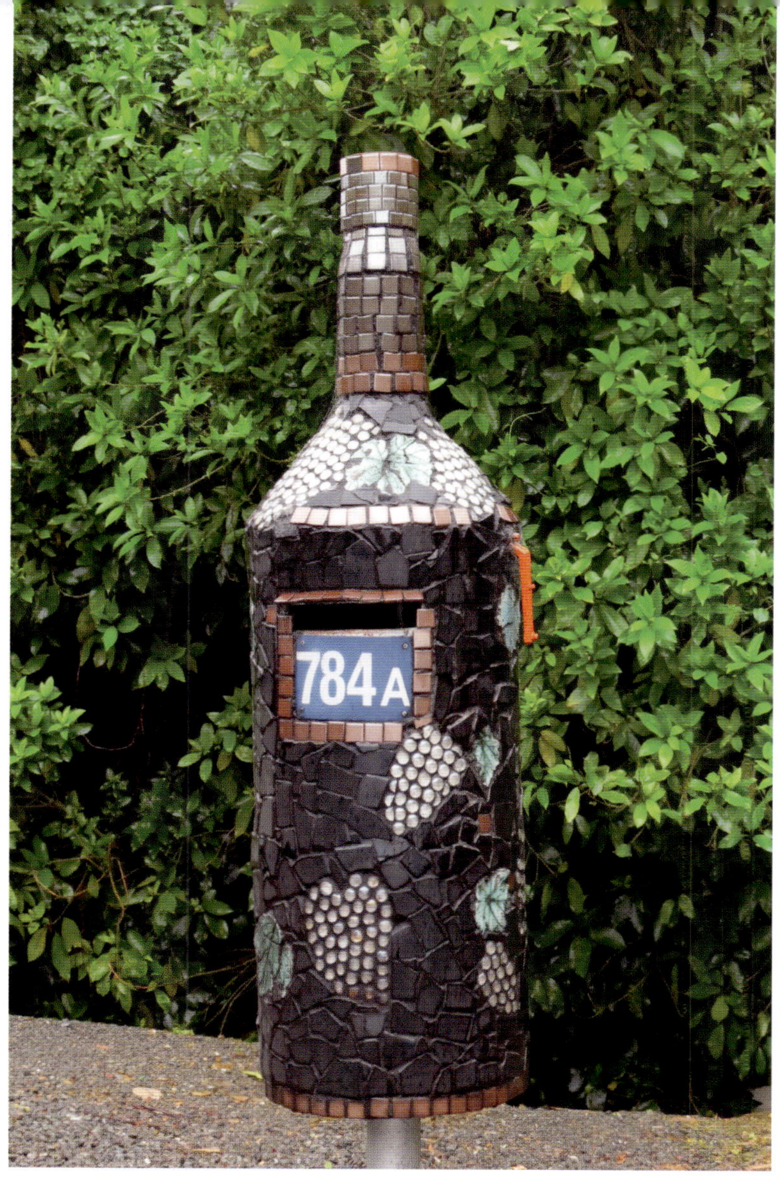

Multiple messages in the bottle.

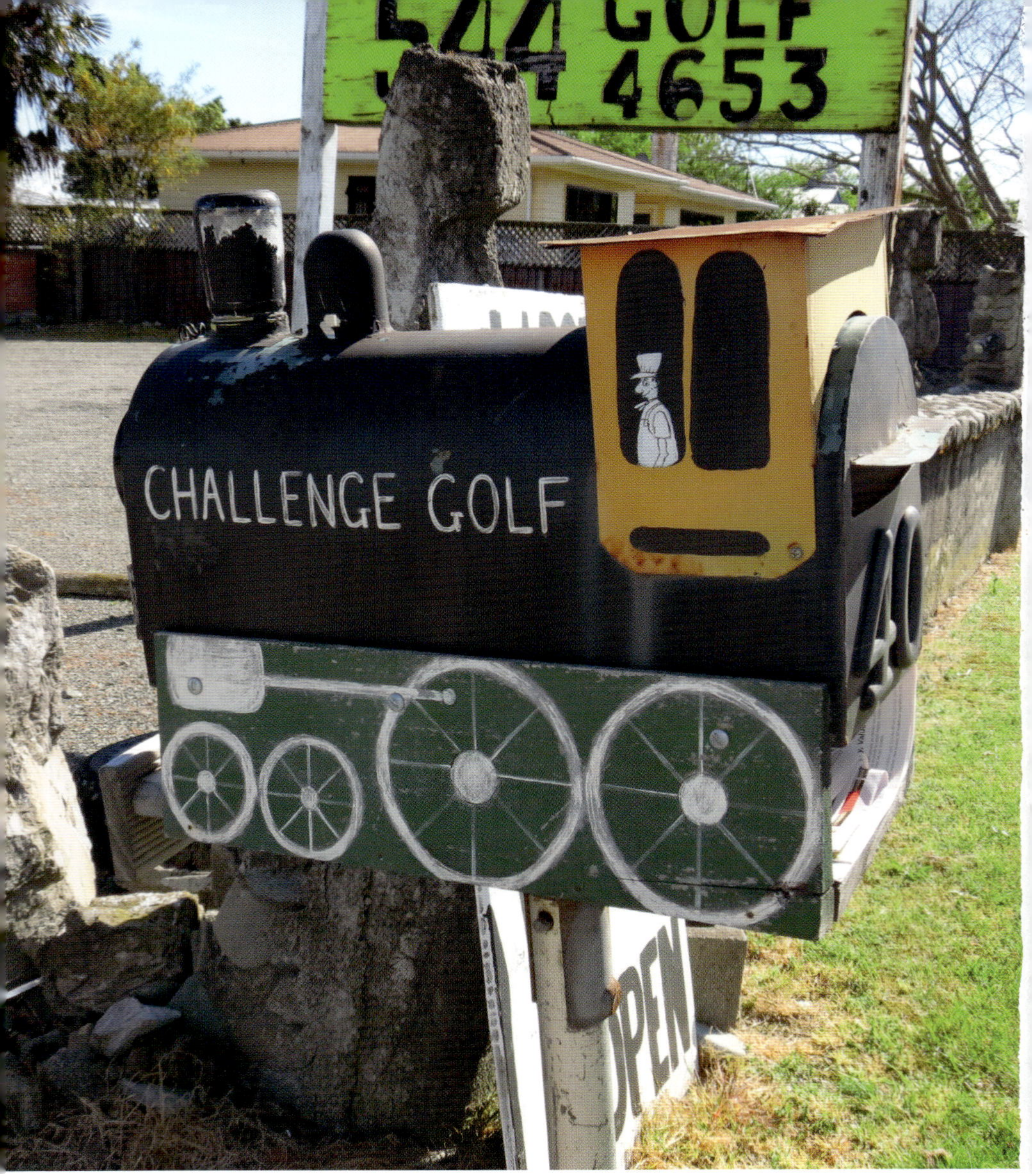

Steaming towards a hole in one.